The Analytic
Hospitality Executive

Wiley & SAS Business Series

The Wiley & SAS Business Series presents books that help senior-level managers with their critical management decisions.

Titles in the Wiley & SAS Business Series include:

Analytics in a Big Data World: The Essential Guide to Data Science and its Applications by Bart Baesens

Bank Fraud: Using Technology to Combat Losses by Revathi Subramanian

Big Data Analytics: Turning Big Data into Big Money by Frank Ohlhorst

Big Data, Big Innovation: Enabling Competitive Differentiation through Business Analytics by Evan Stubbs

Business Analytics for Customer Intelligence by Gert Laursen

Business Intelligence Applied: Implementing an Effective Information and Communications Technology Infrastructure by Michael Gendron

Business Intelligence and the Cloud: Strategic Implementation Guide by Michael S. Gendron

Business Transformation: A Roadmap for Maximizing Organizational Insights by Aiman Zeid

Connecting Organizational Silos: Taking Knowledge Flow Management to the Next Level with Social Media by Frank Leistner

Data-Driven Healthcare: How Analytics and BI are Transforming the Industry by Laura Madsen

Delivering Business Analytics: Practical Guidelines for Best Practice by Evan Stubbs

Demand-Driven Forecasting: A Structured Approach to Forecasting, Second Edition by Charles Chase

Demand-Driven Inventory Optimization and Replenishment: Creating a More Efficient Supply Chain by Robert A. Davis

Developing Human Capital: Using Analytics to Plan and Optimize Your Learning and Development Investments by Gene Pease, Barbara Beresford, and Lew Walker

The Executive's Guide to Enterprise Social Media Strategy: How Social Networks Are Radically Transforming Your Business by David Thomas and Mike Barlow

Economic and Business Forecasting: Analyzing and Interpreting Econometric Results by John Silvia, Azhar Iqbal, Kaylyn Swankoski, Sarah Watt, and Sam Bullard

Foreign Currency Financial Reporting from Euros to Yen to Yuan: A Guide to Fundamental Concepts and Practical Applications by Robert Rowan

Harness Oil and Gas Big Data with Analytics: Optimize Exploration and Production with Data Driven Models by Keith Holdaway

Health Analytics: Gaining the Insights to Transform Health Care by Jason Burke

Heuristics in Analytics: A Practical Perspective of What Influences Our Analytical World by Carlos Andre Reis Pinheiro and Fiona McNeill

Hotel Pricing in a Social World: Driving Value in the Digital Economy by Kelly A. McGuire

Human Capital Analytics: How to Harness the Potential of Your Organization's Greatest Asset by Gene Pease, Boyce Byerly, and Jac Fitz-enz

Implement, Improve and Expand Your Statewide Longitudinal Data System: Creating a Culture of Data in Education by Jamie McQuiggan and Armistead Sapp

Killer Analytics: Top 20 Metrics Missing from Your Balance Sheet by Mark Brown

Predictive Analytics for Human Resources by Jac Fitz-enz and John Mattox II

Predictive Business Analytics: Forward-Looking Capabilities to Improve Business Performance by Lawrence Maisel and Gary Cokins

Retail Analytics: The Secret Weapon by Emmett Cox

Social Network Analysis in Telecommunications by Carlos Andre Reis Pinheiro

Statistical Thinking: Improving Business Performance, second edition, by Roger W. Hoerl and Ronald D. Snee

Taming the Big Data Tidal Wave: Finding Opportunities in Huge Data Streams with Advanced Analytics by Bill Franks

Too Big to Ignore: The Business Case for Big Data by Phil Simon

The Value of Business Analytics: Identifying the Path to Profitability by Evan Stubbs

The Visual Organization: Data Visualization, Big Data, and the Quest for Better Decisions by Phil Simon

Using Big Data Analytics: Turning Big Data into Big Money by Jared Dean

Win with Advanced Business Analytics: Creating Business Value from Your Data by Jean Paul Isson and Jesse Harriott

For more information on any of the above titles, please visit www .wiley.com.

The Analytic Hospitality Executive

Implementing Data Analytics in Hotels and Casinos

Kelly A. McGuire, PhD

WILEY

Library of Congress Cataloging-in-Publication Data:

Names: McGuire, Kelly Ann, author.
Title: The analytic hospitality executive : implementing data analytics in
   hotels and casinos / Kelly A. McGuire, PhD.
Description: Hoboken, New Jersey : John Wiley & Sons, Inc., [2017] | Series:
   Wiley and SAS business series | Includes bibliographical references and
   index.
Identifiers: LCCN 2016024813 (print) | LCCN 2016026828 (ebook) |
   ISBN 978-1-119-12998-1 (hardback) | ISBN 978-1-119-22493-8 (ePDF) |
   ISBN 978-1-119-22492-1 (ePub) | ISBN 978-1-119-16230-8 (oBook)
Subjects: LCSH: Hospitality industry—Management—Decision making. |
   Hospitality industry—Statistical methods. | Big data. | BISAC: BUSINESS &
   ECONOMICS / Industries / Hospitality, Travel & Tourism.
Classification: LCC TX911.3.M27 M36 2017 (print) | LCC TX911.3.M27 (ebook) |
   DDC 647.94068—dc23
LC record available at https://lccn.loc.gov/2016024813

Printed in the United States of America

10 9 8 7 6 5 4 3 2 1

To my favorite analytic hospitality executives

Contents

Foreword

Data, it has often been claimed over the past several years, is the new oil. I'm not convinced this is entirely true, but there are some curious similarities. Just as oil slumbered as an unappreciated resource until the late nineteenth century and then awakened wholesale changes to the world economy, data in many ways has the potential to do the same. But in contrast to oil that sat beneath the earth for thousands of years relatively undetected, data is flooding all around us in seemingly unmanageable variety and volume. Data is everywhere, but perplexingly the more we have of it, the more it becomes increasingly difficult to harness and exploit.

This is particularly true in the hospitality industry where our culture has been historically high touch and low tech. Yet, every hour of every day hotels, restaurants, and casinos generate millions of data points as customers interact with reservation systems, loyalty programs, credit card exchanges, point of sale systems, and simply check in and out of hotels. Although the traditional success of most hospitality companies has largely been due to their ability to use customer service, facilities, and location as differentiators, this is no longer enough.

Today, our service-driven industry has become extremely competitive in almost every way conceivable. For small and large companies alike, there has never been a time with more focus on performance— financial performance, stock price, customer loyalty, market share, you name it. The competitive landscape has quickly transitioned to finding a way to best use data to drive strategy and performance.

As a hospitality industry executive and consultant for almost 30 years, I have witnessed this transition firsthand and I can appreciate what a challenging journey it has been and continues to be for many of us. Although I have enjoyed some success over the years helping to drive the adoption of data-driven decision making and performance enhancement during my time with Pricewaterhousecoopers, Host Hotels & Resorts, and now Hilton Worldwide, I really wish Kelly McGuire could have helped me out and published *The Analytic Hospitality*

Executive 25 years earlier. As you will soon realize when reading her book, Kelly serves up a brilliant recipe for understanding all of the key principals in a readable and business-faced format. If you are thinking about becoming a better analytic hospitality executive, then this is your guidebook.

I first met Kelly when I joined the advisory board for the Center for Hospitality Research at Cornell University's School of Hotel Administration. We are both alumni; she with a master's degree and a PhD, and I with an undergrad degree many years earlier. What impressed me about Kelly when we first met was that I immediately recognized her as an "hotelier." Not solely an academic mind, she had that rare combination of technical intelligence matched with a keen appreciation for the business of hospitality. It's actually easy to see how she came up with *The Analytic Hospitality Executive* because that is who she is. I know her to be an analytics evangelist who is passionate about helping the hospitality and travel industries realize the value of data-driven decision making.

In this book, Kelly McGuire masterfully articulates the keys for successfully building a strategic analytical culture in your hospitality organization. She will emphasize the absolute necessity for senior executive–level buy-in and support. Additionally, she will stress the need for an organizational commitment to fact-based decision making and the allocation of the right business resources. Not just dollars allocated to technology, but the dedication of the business to transition to an actionable data-driven decision-making process. The days of devoting 80 to 90 percent of resources to data collection and validation need to come to an end.

There is no message that resonates more strongly from Kelly's book than that it's all about the data. If you learn nothing else from this book and the real-life stories depicted within, please take one word of advice from those of us who have walked the path. Start with the data.

As Kelly explains in this book, data is often not the sexy part of analytics. The potentially rich data trapped in fragmented legacy systems like those prevalent in the hospitality industry are plagued with challenges. The possible solutions often lack clear ownership and funding as other priorities jump to the front of the line. In my view, this is always shortsighted as getting the data right is perhaps the most important building block for success.

Much like my golf game, it's always more appealing to find a short-cut. Hard work and practice are no fun for most of us. Every year there is new driver technology that promises to let us all hit it right down the middle and 50 yards further. Why take lessons and practice when you can just buy new technology? Of course that strategy continues to disappoint in lowering my handicap.

Similarly, many executives are often too eager to embrace the popular new technology and the vernacular of the day. Lately, big data seems to be the magic term that gets everyone excited. As Kelly will explain, today's big data is tomorrow's small data. It's not just science; there is a lot of art as well. Being too quick to buy a shortcut solution and rush to fancy dashboards without focusing on the underlying data and organizational alignment almost always lead to failure.

In my experience, and as Kelly describes in this book, data is the key to the successful creation of a strategic analytical culture. It's the business taking ownership and demanding a "single source of truth." It's the commitment to establishing a common business language and what Kelly describes as a sound and sustainable data management strategy.

In this amazing book, Kelly McGuire will provide a tool kit to help all of us navigate the path to a strategic analytical culture in our organizations. She understands the challenges hospitality companies are facing in these highly competitive times. Strategically leveraging data has never been more important. We all need to be better analytic hospitality executives. In that regard, this book is essential.

Dexter E. Wood, Jr.
SVP, Global Head, Business & Investment Analysis
Hilton Worldwide
#hotelieforlife

Acknowledgments

The experience of writing this book was very different from writing the first one. Of course, changing jobs and moving right in the middle of the process definitely influenced that. Having this project did add a little bit of stress, but it also helped me through the transition. It was a constant that reminded me of my passions and interests, as I was figuring out what to do with my extra furniture or trying to find a new dry cleaner. Of course, now that it's ready to be published, I suddenly have fewer excuses for not unpacking those last few boxes. . . . As with my first effort, the best thing about the process was that it gave me an excuse to reach out and reconnect with people who inspire me, and who I so very much enjoy speaking with. There is a fantastic community of dedicated analytic hospitality executives out there, and I am humbled and privileged to be a part of it.

I must start out by once again thanking the team at SAS that helped me through this book so soon after the first. My development editor, Brenna Leath, and my marketing support, Cindy Puryear, in particular, have made this process both easy and fun. Thanks for being responsive, even after I left the fold.

I also want to thank my previous boss, Tom Roehm, for pushing me to do this. One book wasn't going to be enough; I had to write two to prove, actually, I can't really remember what I was trying to prove . . . but I'm glad I felt I had to. I must thank my new boss, Jeremy TerBush, for being open to letting me see this through, for his genuine excitement about the project, and for how much fun we have had and will continue to have making a difference for the business, for our stakeholders, and for the careers of the individuals on our team. I have admired Jeremy's dedication, leadership, and achievements from afar for many years. It is an honor to be a part of his team.

A special thanks goes to Dexter Wood, for sharing his experience and his perspective through this process. Conversations with Dex inspired a lot of the thinking that went into the book. He pushed me to challenge the material and myself, and it is much appreciated. Thank you for authoring the foreword and the case study in Chapter 2, but more important for believing in the value of data analytics, for believing in this project, and for believing in me. And speaking of Big Red Analytic Hospitality Executives, I very much appreciate the genuine enthusiasm and passion that Dave Roberts has for analytics and for revenue management. He has been a great inspiration and a great advocate. Thank you, Dave, for your tireless pursuit of the importance of analytics in hospitality! I also appreciate the support and inspiration from Ted Teng, a consummate #hotelieforlife, whose dedication to advancing the industry and the people in it has been an inspiration to us all.

Many people generously gave their time to this project, and it is much appreciated. My partner in crime, Kristin Rohlfs; my other partner in crime, Natalie Osborn; and Alex Dietz, Anne Buff, and Analise Polsky lent me their expertise as technical editors, and the book is much better for it. Dave Roberts, Jeremy TerBush, David Koch, Bernard Ellis, David Turnbull, R. J. Friedlander, Natalie Osborn, Paul van Meerendonk, Kate Kiesling, Fanie Swanepoel, and Andy Swenson took time from their very busy schedules to lend their expertise to lengthy case studies. Michael Smith and Kate Keisling took a panicked phone call at short notice when I realized I was out of my depth. I also very much appreciate the inspiration provided by the analytic hospitality executives who let me quote them, learn from them, and be inspired by them.

Speaking of analytic hospitality executives, two more of my favorites should be personally recognized for their support of me and my efforts. Thank you, Mark Lomanno and Tom Buoy, for sharing your critical and thoughtful perspectives with me and letting me run with them, for your passion for the industry, and for the time you have spent making me and others better at what we do. I also appreciate the encouragement and advice from Gary Cokins, another prolific SAS author, and from Michele Sarkisian, whose passion for all things hospitality is both remarkable and contagious.

I highly value my relationship with the global team at HSMAI, who have been great advocates for education and the advancement of the hospitality industry, and great supporters of me as well. I must thank Juli Jones in particular, who works so hard and is so good at keeping the community together, and of course, Bob Gilbert, who is such a great advocate for our industry.

I am fortunate to have good friends and family who have been with me through this process: In particular, Alex Failmezger and Adam Sternberg, for providing moral support and feedback even through their job changes. My brother, Sean, who told me that my first book "was not a terrible read." And, of course, my parents, who have supported me through every crazy decision that got me to this point. If anyone is looking for a nontraditional hospitality analytics candidate, my mother is now quite well read and, I think, available—if you offer the right travel benefits.

I learned so much while I was at SAS. This book would not be what it is without that experience. I miss my colleagues and teammates very much. I thought of you often as I was finishing this book. I also want to thank my new team at Wyndham for being so welcoming, so much fun, and, well, so just plain excellent at what you do! Every analytic hospitality executive should be so lucky to have a team like you!

I was extremely humbled by the response to my first book. It is an honor to be a part of this community and to contribute to moving it forward. It has been such a pleasure to present the original research that Breffni Noone and I have worked on to the community and talk through those complicated issues with you. It has been a joy to hear your reactions to the blog that I coauthored with Natalie Osborn, and it has been just genuine fun to stand up in front of you to challenge our thinking and try to make us better. The biggest thank you goes to all of you who have read my work, shared it with your colleagues, assigned it to your students, and talked to me about it. Keep up the great work. We will get there, together.

About the Author

Kelly A. McGuire, PhD is senior vice president, revenue management and direct marketing for MGM Resorts International, where she is responsible for driving profitable room revenue for MGM Resorts International's Las Vegas resorts. Prior to this role, she was Vice President, Advanced Analytics for Wyndham Destination Network. She led a team of data scientists and developers who build custom analytic solutions for Wyndham Vacation Rental's companies and the RCI timeshare exchange. Prior to joining Wyndham, she led SAS's Hospitality and Travel Global Practice, setting the global analytics strategy for these industries, and supporting engagements around the world.

CHAPTER 1

Building a Strategic Analytic Culture in Hospitality and Gaming

I believe in intuitions and inspirations. . . . I sometimes feel that I am right. I do not know that I am.

—Albert Einstein

Hospitality executives struggle to find the balance between delivering a guest experience that fosters loyalty and repeat business, and delivering on their revenue and profit responsibilities to stakeholders, shareholders, or franchisees. If you invest too much in the guest experience, you could impact profits, but if you focus on too many cost-cutting measures to drive profits, you can negatively impact the guest experience.

Decisions made in one department of a hotel can have impacts across the organization. For example, without a good understanding of food cost, a marketing program providing restaurant discounts could affect profitability. Without understanding check-in and checkout patterns, a labor-savings initiative might create long lines at the front desk, impacting the guest experience. Today, your service mistakes are broadcast through social channels and review sites as they happen. The competition is no longer just the hotel next door, but it is also third-party distribution channels and alternative lodging providers like AirBnB, all waiting in the wings to win your guests from you. On top of all that, recent merger and acquisition activity is creating scale never before seen in this industry, and global economic conditions continue to be unstable.

When the stakes are this high, you need something to help shore up that balance between delivering an excellent guest experience and meeting profit obligations. Analytics can be that thing. Tarandeep Singh, Senior Director, Revenue Performance and Analytics, Asia, Middle East, and Africa says, "Analytics is like GPS—it helps you be on track, and even pings you when you go off." Fostering a culture of fact-based decision making ensures that the organization can find the right direction, understand the trade-offs, hedge against risk, know the next best action, and stand the best chance to be competitive in an increasingly crowded marketplace.

Einstein reminds us in his quote at the beginning of this chapter that there is still room for intuition and inspiration in this vision. Your intuition can be backed up by the data, getting you closer to "knowing" you are right. Inspiration for the right action can come from what the numbers tell you. Intuition and inspiration are even more powerful when paired with curiosity and questioning. David Schmitt, former director of Interactive Marketing Operations and Analytics for IHG, says in his blog, "The questions from the business are our North Star, the guidance and direction that provide clarity to analytics efforts."[1]

The goal is to cultivate a culture of asking good questions and letting the data provide the answers. There are so many examples today of companies who have successfully, and sometimes famously, derived insight from their data assets through analytics, which helped to create a huge competitive advantage or some remarkable innovation. This could be you. Let's talk about the characteristics of a strategic analytic culture first, and then I will tell you how this book can help you to build a strategic analytic culture in your own organization and set yourself up for success through analytics.

STRATEGIC ANALYTIC CULTURE

So, what does a strategic analytic culture (SAC) look like? Figure 1.1 outlines the interrelated components of a SAC.

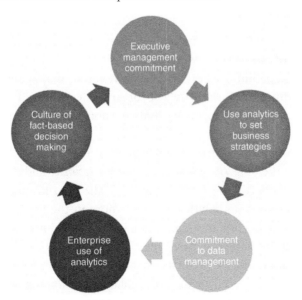

Figure 1.1 Strategic Analytic Culture Framework

A strategic analytic culture starts and ends with **executive management commitment.** This level of support is required to make the necessary investments in people, process, and technology, as well as to ensure the alignment among departments that is critical to enterprise-level thinking.

The executive management team uses **analytics to set business strategy.** Rather than being guided by individual intuition or aspiration, the data and analytics offer a fact-based pathway toward the strategy, which is based on market conditions, customer characteristics, and the company's operating circumstances.

The foundation of any analytics program is an organization-wide **commitment to data management.** Data management programs include:

- Data governance to provide data definitions and guidelines for storing and accessing information
- Data integration to ensure that data from disparate systems is matched and consolidated
- Data quality programs to ensure data is cleansed before being used in analytics
- Data storage infrastructure that facilitates access for analytics and reporting

An all-encompassing data management strategy facilitates **enterprise use of analytics.** Most organizations have isolated pockets of analytic capability, whether it be in revenue management, marketing, or finance. Enterprise use of analytics brings these siloed departments together, ensuring that decision making is not done in isolation.

Mark Lomanno, partner and senior advisor for Kalabri Labs, in an interview in the blog *The Analytic Hospitality Executive*, said that the role of analytics is becoming increasingly centralized in hospitality. "Traditionally the role of analytics has been more in the financial metrics measurement category, to some degree in the operations category, and in the marketing category; however, in the future all those will come together," Mark said. He predicted that over time, online hotel reviews and comments in social media will replace traditional guest satisfaction measures as the primary gauge of customer satisfaction, and that companies will be able to start predicting occupancy and rates by the quality and nature of the hotel's consumer comments and reviews. "This will force operations and marketing to work very closely together to react very quickly to what the consumer is saying," Mark said.

Mark's prediction points to the need to break down silos, improve communication, and synchronize decision making. When the entire enterprise is aligned around analytics, it creates a **culture of fact-based decision making**. You've probably heard the saying "In God we trust, all others must bring data."[2] Companies with a SAC back up all of their decisions with data and analytics, rather than instinct and internal influence. This doesn't mean that you stifle creativity. It means that creative thought is supported by an analysis to back up conclusions or reinforce decision making. In fact, strategic use of analytics can help organizations become more creative and more agile when it uncovers insights that were not apparent on the surface.

Ted Teng, President and CEO at The Leading Hotels of the World provided this perspective in a video interview for SAS and the Cornell Center for Hospitality Research: "We are an industry of emotional decisions. We badly need analytics and good data for us to make the right decisions." Ted explained that the hospitality market has completely changed and industry operators can no longer rely on how they did things 20 years ago. "There's a lot of talk about big data out there. I am happy with just small data—some data—that allows us to make better decisions that are based on facts rather than based on our emotions."

Where is your organization in this cycle? Are you getting stuck at executive commitment? Perhaps it's been too difficult to build a data management infrastructure? Is analytic competency still residing in pockets across the organization? This book is designed to help you achieve the SAC vision from the ground up, or from the top down if you are fortunate enough to have that kind of power and influence!

MOVING AHEAD AND STAYING AHEAD WITH PRESCRIPTIVE DECISION MAKING[3]

Most hospitality organizations today recognize the need for data-driven decision making, and they are making strides in that direction, or at least planning for it. In marketing, managers want to understand the customer better to improve targeting and value calculations. Opera- tions knows that demand forecasting can support better staffing and ordering decisions, and finance recognizes that performance analysis drives opportunities for efficiencies and strategic growth. As organi- zations embrace data, analytics, and visualizations, they evolve from "gut-feel" reactive decision makers to more proactive, forward-looking decision makers.

I believe that hotels and casinos are at a turning point in data and analytics. Most hospitality companies have implemented some level of data management and business intelligence, or at least are on the path. Many hotels and casinos have made investments in predictive analyt- ics solutions for revenue management or marketing. All organizations have at least some desire to provide access to the right information at the right time to the right resources to make the right decisions. If organizations successfully build out their data and analytic infrastruc- tures, they will be part of the way there. If they are able to successfully leverage the analytic results across their organizations, they will get ahead and stay ahead.

Analytic solutions are simply decision support tools. They must be used by managers who have the experience to interpret the results and take the appropriate actions. Revenue management systems, for ex- ample, drive revenue because the revenue manager can interpret the price and availability recommendations and implement them as part of a broader pricing strategy. The jobs of the revenue management system and the revenue manager are not the same. A hotel cannot simply hook up the revenue management recommendations to the selling system and walk away. At the same time, a revenue manager can't process the millions of pieces of information required to understand market oppor- tunity by hand. However, a great revenue management system man- aged by a business-savvy revenue manager is a winning combination.

An executive from a large hotel brand told me that one of the driving factors for their business analytics investments is to get better information into the hands of their senior executives faster. "Imagine how much more effective smart and charismatic leaders would be in an investment negotiation or even an internal meeting if they had instant access to performance metrics, to support whatever ques- tions they happen to get asked," he told me. "We have great, highly experienced leadership, they are doing a good job today, but I'm sure they could drive much more revenue with better information at their fingertips the moment they need it." It's not that the information doesn't exist, or that there aren't standard sets of reports available. The difference is in the flexibility of the data structure and speed of access to the information. To be able to access information in the right format at the speed of a business conversation, no matter what is needed at the time, is beyond the technical capabilities of most organizations today.

Once again, these systems are not supposed to replace the experience and ability of a top-performing executive, but rather, they should provide information to better interpret a situation, respond more quickly to a question, reinforce or demonstrate a point, convince an investor, or make a key business decision faster. This should be the goal not only at the senior leadership level, but also replicated throughout the organization. It will take the right decision support tools, backed by credible data and advanced analytics, and it will also take the right person in the role of interpreter and decision maker.

This is why I argue that we are at a turning point in hospitality and gaming. We are moving through the chain of analytic maturity, perhaps at different rates organization by organization or department by department within organizations. We are getting to the point where we will need a different type of business analyst and a different type of manager to move ahead and stay ahead. As the needs of the business change, the skill sets and competencies of analysts and managers in analytical roles will need to change, as will the organizational structures, incentive plans, and scope of responsibilities.

The evolution of the scope of decision making in hospitality can be thought of in three stages, based on the ability to access and analyze data. As I mentioned previously, different departments in the organization may be at different stages, but the goal is to evolve everyone to the final stage.[4]

1. **Descriptive.** At the first stage of analytic evolution, it is the best that organizations can do to develop and interpret historical reports. This is the descriptive phase. The organization could know that occupancy ran about 80% last month, or that

40% of reservations book in the week before arrival. Past revenue is tracked to identify historical trends. Decisions are based on this historical snapshot, which primarily involves reacting (i.e., putting out fires). Reports come from disparate systems, often are built in Excel, and pass through multiple hands before being finalized. Creating these reports is time consuming and prone to mistakes. Still, the business at least has some visibility into operating conditions and can report performance to executives—even if it takes a couple of days (or months) to pull together the information. As organizations evolve through this phase, they start to look at building out enterprise data warehouses and investing in business intelligence tools to improve the speed and accuracy of reporting. As more information gets into the hands of decision makers, they are able to react faster. For example, alerts are set up around key metrics so that managers can be made aware when they drop below, or rise above, certain critical levels.

2. **Predictive.** In the next state of analytical evolution, organizations begin to deploy advanced analytic techniques that allow them to anticipate trends and take advantage of opportunities. They start to apply forecasting, predictive modeling, and optimization algorithms to existing data, typically either in marketing with predictive modeling on patron data, or in revenue management using forecasting and optimization to set pricing. These models produce results like occupancy will be 80% next month, the marketing campaign will result in a 2% lift, or revenue is expected to trend down for the next several months. Organizations then prepare themselves to manage through these now expected events. They can be more proactive in their approaches, setting up the right staffing levels to meet expected demand, adjusting price to take advantage of peak periods, or deploying marketing campaigns at the right time to get the best forecasted responses.

3. **Prescriptive.** The final stage of analytic evolution is all about "what are we going to do about it?" In this phase, organizations are heavily supported by techniques like optimization,

which provides the best possible answer given all business constraints, or simulation, a "what-if" technique in which a complex scenario with multiple moving parts is modeled so that parameters and options can be tested to determine the impact on key outcomes. For example, marketing optimization might give you the best possible set of contact lists for all of your promotions that will provide the highest response rate, but still respect budgets and patron contact preferences. Simulation lets you test the impact of a particular pricing strategy on demand and revenue generation, or the lift associated with spending a little more on a marketing campaign.

Advanced analytic techniques like forecasting, predictive modeling, optimization, and simulation are valuable because they provide a vision into the future or a decision point to consider, but the true mark of a prescriptive organization is that analysts and managers have the business acumen to both ask and answer the question "what are we going to do about it?" It's fine to know that occupancy was 80% and it will be 90% next month. However, the true prescriptive manager can use that information, with their knowledge of the market and the operations, to build a plan to get to 95%. The skill set associated with this manager is different than the skills required in the descriptive or predictive phase, but clearly it is one that can move the organization forward—replicating the instincts, charisma, and acumen of the executive I described previously across all functional areas.

MAKING IT HAPPEN

For many organizations, this evolution in decision making will happen first in individual departments. The goal is to move the entire organization toward prescriptive decision making, supported by data and analytics. Success in a small area can become the inspiration that facilitates broad growth of analytical capabilities.

The point is that knowing what happened and what will happen is no longer enough. We need to build a culture of "what are we going to do about it?" in which the whole team uses the organization's data and analytics to make fact-based decisions that move the organization forward.

Focus Areas for a Strategic Analytic Culture[5]

Moving your organization toward a strategic analytic culture requires more than just investments in analytic technology. Building a SAC starts with people, process, organization, and technology, in three focus areas within your organization.

1. Business analytics skills and resources
2. Data environment and infrastructure
3. Internal analytic processes

Focus Area 1: Business Analytics Skills and Resources

Find the right balance of resources. Building a strategic analytic culture is not simply hiring a bunch of analytic modelers and letting them play with your data, but rather striking the balance between analytic rigor and business application. Your best revenue managers understand their markets and their business, sometimes even better than they understand the forecasting and optimization algorithms underlying the revenue management system. And that's okay. It is their ability to interpret the analytic results and apply them to their markets that makes them successful. Think about how to achieve this business acumen supported by analytic rigor across the organization.

To accomplish this, organizations may need to move to a structure where the advanced, predictive analytic models are created and managed by a central team of trained and experienced analysts, who work closely with counterparts in the business. The analyst's role is to build the model with the guidance of and questions from the business, and then the business interprets the results through their experience and business acumen. When there is a shortage of analytical talent, this structure ensures analytic rigor is maintained, but also puts power in the hands of decision makers to access the right information when they need it to move the business forward. It releases the requirement that managers be highly analytical, but requires them to be analytical enough to interpret the numbers and savvy enough to read market conditions. In other words, it allows them to become prescriptive managers. I provide more detail about organizing an analytics department in Chapter 11.

Make analytics more approachable. Analytical skills are in short supply. In fact, in the United States it is estimated that demand for deep analytical resources will be 50% higher than supply by 2018.[6] Organizations will need to figure out a way to make analytics more approachable. Highly visual, wizard-driven tools enable nontechnical users to explore and share "aha moments" without having to be PhD statisticians. They say a picture is worth a thousand words, and that's true in analytics as well. Graphics are accessible and easy for executives to consume quickly. This ease of access will help to foster the commitment to fact-based decision making. Enabling business users to create and share insights will further the mission of enterprise use of analytics, while simultaneously freeing the limited supply of analytical resources to focus on the more rigorous analysis. In Chapter 3, I talk about visual analytics applications that can help move the organization to approachable analytics and self-service data visualization.

Focus Area 2: Information Environment and Infrastructure

Without a strong foundation of reliable and accurate data, analytic results will be suspect, and buy-in becomes impossible. You can spend all meeting, every meeting arguing about whether revenue per available room should include the out-of-service rooms, or instead spend the time making strategic decisions about price position relative to the competitive set. A sound data management strategy gets you on the road to analytic success, and away from the need to confirm and reconfirm the data. Here's how to establish the foundation for a commitment to data management:

1. **Establish a data governance discipline.** As data and analytics become centralized, data governance ensures consistency in data definitions, data integration guidelines, and data access rules. This is crucial to establishing a "single version of the truth" in results and reporting, as well as to building a sustainable process for continuing to advance organizational data acquisition.

2. **Upgrade your data architecture.** In order to effectively leverage the insights trapped in today's fast moving, diverse volumes of data, you need a modern data infrastructure that can support enterprise-class analytics and dynamic visualizations.

3. **Bridge the gap between IT and the business.** A strong partnership between IT and the business must be built to ensure that the infrastructure described previously facilitates exploration and fact-based decision making. A key new resource to add to the organization could be the "translator" between IT and the business—someone who understands how to interpret the business requirements into an IT context, and vice versa.

4. **Capitalize on advanced analytics, not reporting.** Any SAC relies on forward-looking analysis to stay ahead of trends and proactively identify opportunities. This requires moving from descriptive analytics that simply illustrate where you are today, to the use of predictive analytics like forecasting and optimization, which can identify what could happen and help you determine the best possible response in advance.

Chapter 2 of this book will demystify data management so that you can work with your peers and IT to establish a strong, credible data platform as the foundation of your analytics efforts.

Focus Area 3: Internal Processes

Enterprise use of analytics is not as simple as "everyone log in and go." With limited personnel and technology resources, organizations will need processes in place to ensure access to critical analytical or IT resources. Then, the organization can better identify, prioritize, and address analytical requirements—whether it be deploying a new retention model or investing in a new analytical tool.

Manage analytics as an ongoing process, not a one-off project. Internal processes must be designed around sustainable, long-term analytic performance throughout the analytics life cycle. You will need to think not just about developing models, but deploying them, embedding them into a business process, and monitoring and improving them over time.

Facilitate collaboration. Traditionally, hospitality, like so many other industries, has operated with siloed departments. To facilitate collaboration, the silos that prevent collaboration must be removed. Technology may be the glue that binds departments together, but true collaboration will require realigning incentives, changing organizational structures, and breaking down barriers. Resources across the organization should be empowered and given incentives to act in the best interests of the enterprise, not just their departments.

This is not an insignificant effort in most organizations. Collaboration across the enterprise is not possible without at least one active and influential ally at the top of the organization who is able to drive change. Frequently, a grassroots effort from one department stalls out when that department is unable to gain momentum and get executives' attention. Chapter 11 describes in further detail how analytic hospitality executives can turn their grassroots efforts into an enterprise-wide initiative.

> *You can talk all you want about the analytics cycle, the importance of integrating data, the value of advanced analytics, but I think the most important element in any analytics program is intent. What does the business want to get out of the analysis? What do they think is the measure of success? It is easy to make assumptions during an analysis and end up delivering something that the business didn't expect, doesn't want, or can't use. Take time to clearly define the intent with the business before starting any analytics project, and you will be set up for success.*
>
> —Vivienne Tan, Vice President, Information Technology,
> Resorts World Sentosa

GETTING STARTED

So, how do you get started? Read the rest of this book, obviously! In all seriousness though, building a strategic analytic culture is a journey that should be accomplished in phases. I talk again, and in more detail, about this phased approach in Chapter 11, but here is a summary to set some context (also see Figure 1.2).

1. **Establish.** The first phase is where you implement the enabling analytic technologies, create processes, and place people within key departments. Here it is most important to ensure that you have solid processes to build on, well-trained people, and

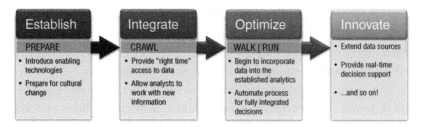

Figure 1.2 A Phased Approach

the right technology to support current operations as well as future growth.

2. **Integrate.** Next, you begin to integrate data and analytics across a few key departments. Get a cross-functional team together to define metrics and identify opportunities, then start providing analysts with manual access to new data sources. Let them get comfortable with the data, so they fully understand how it will impact results and decisions.

3. **Optimize.** As analysts become comfortable, it's time to automate. Data can be incorporated into models and results operationalized. Since the analysts are already familiar with the data, they'll be more likely to understand and accept new results and new decisions.

4. **Innovate.** When your automated processes become ingrained in organizational decision making, you've built a platform for innovation. Sometimes, innovation is simply adding a new data source or a new analytic technique. Other times, it may require starting from the beginning with the establish phase. Either way, you've got a process in place for ensuring success.

You'll need organizational buy-in to embark on this journey, and that isn't always easy to achieve. Find a project that is easy to complete and highly visible. Perhaps you start with one small initiative that is a pet project of a visible executive. It can also be helpful to find a project that bridges the gaps between two siloed pockets of analytic capability, since those departments are already comfortable with their own data. Leverage the entire cycle from data governance to automating analytics so that you can set up repeatable processes. Start small, and win big, but don't lose site of the ultimate goal—developing a high performance organization built on a solid foundation of data management and advanced analytics.

The most immediate and important executive action is to start asking for proof. Force your teams to defend any recommendations with data. Find out if there are additional data sources or analytical tools that would help them to make better decisions, and make that happen. Encourage collaboration across departmental boundaries. As your success grows, you'll find your peers recognizing the momentum and wanting to get on board themselves!

HOW THIS BOOK CAN HELP

In the rest of this book, I provide you with information and strategies to help you identify opportunities within your organization to start on the path to a strategic analytic culture—or to help you cross the finish line if you are nearly there already! This book is intended to provide hospitality executives with the information they need to make the right decisions about analytics strategy, people, and technology, to survive and thrive in today's highly competitive market.

The foundation of a strategic analytic culture is data. Chapter 2 helps to demystify big data and describes the tools and processes available to manage it. I talk about the importance of establishing a common business language and how to set a data governance process in place that will make and keep you successful. I give you strategies for identifying data sources that could provide value to the organization, and talk about how to access, integrate, cleanse, and store that data.

Chapter 3 describes why visualizations are "worth a thousand words." Everyone wants to be able to communicate more effectively, particularly to leadership and stakeholders. In this chapter, I discuss how to create powerful visualizations that get your point across without complicating the message. I describe the technology enablers, provide tips for creating powerful visualizations, and give examples of visualizations.

Everyone seems to be talking about analytics these days, and many companies throw that term around to describe practically any use of data. In Chapter 4, I discuss the difference between descriptive and predictive analytics, provide a high level definition of common types of analytics (like forecasting and data mining), and explain how these analytics are typically used. I also describe considerations for executing analytics. I won't make you into a PhD statistician, but I will make sure that you can understand what a statistician is talking about (at a high level) so that you can make the case for analytic investment, and hopefully make one or two folks on the team think you know your stuff!

Chapters 5 through 10 describe how analytics can add value to the individual functional areas in hospitality and gaming (operations, marketing, sales, revenue management, performance analysis, and gaming analytics). I highlight the kinds of data that are available, or that should be gathered, and provide examples of where advanced analytics can be used. I talk about the technology investments that make sense and the resources that could support your efforts. If you run one of these functions, I'll hopefully inspire some thinking about where you can get started within your group. If you work with one of these functions, I'll help you to understand how they are thinking about analytics so that you can prepare to work with them to take advantage of joint opportunities. If you run the whole show, I'll help you understand what your functional areas should be working on, and maybe give you some inspiration about how to prioritize analytics projects.

The final chapter provides strategies for you to set up your organization so that analytics support decision making across the enterprise. I describe how to get started with analytics in your organization, as well as options for organizing analytical resources. This chapter also has a few case studies from analytic hospitality executives who have been able to advocate for the value of analytics in their organizations.

Data and analytics, and the technology that supports them, are very complicated and getting more so every day. It is easy to be distracted, confused, or intimidated. It's easy to make mistakes. I am merely scratching the surface in all of these areas in this book. My hope is to arm hospitality executives with enough information to work with peers across their organizations to set up programs that will improve organizational decision making, and to initiate, participate in, and understand conversations with IT or analysts. You should never be afraid to ask follow up questions, and persist until you get an answer that makes sense to you. Keep in mind that a great analyst or technologist should be able to explain complex topics in plain language. You will be doing them a favor by forcing them to practice this skill.

NOTES

1. David Schmitt, "First Comes Clarity, Then Come the Tools & Data," All Analytics, February 6, 2013, www.allanalytics.com/author.asp?section_id=2092&doc_id=258158.
2. Quote from William Edward Denning, the father of statistics—okay, maybe that's overstating things a bit, but he was a really important, really influential American statistician, and this is a cool quote.
3. Portions of this section were taken from the fall 2015 issue of *Gaming and Leisure* magazine, "Moving Ahead and Staying Ahead with Prescriptive Decision Making," http://gamingandleisuremagazine.com/gl_articles/moving-ahead-and-staying-ahead-with-prescriptive-decision-making/.
4. The author would like to gratefully acknowledge Tom Buoy, one of her favorite analytic hospitality executives, for inspiring this description of the evolution of analytical decision making.
5. Portions of this section were adapted from the SAS white paper "Building an Analytics Culture: A Best Practices Guide," 2012.
6. U.S. Bureau of Labor Statistics, U.S. Census Bureau, Dun & Bradstreet company interviews, McKinsey Global Institute analysis.

CHAPTER **2**

Data Management for Hospitality and Gaming

Before we can get big data, we need small data, and before small data, we need clean data.

—Tarandeep Singh, Senior Director, Revenue Performance & Analytics, Asia, Middle East & Africa, IHG

Y ou can't have analytics without good data. We all know this. So, I will start with the data. I will be honest, I used to think that data management was about as unsexy as you could get. It was always the boring stuff you had to address before you could get to the good stuff, the analysis. My opinion has dramatically changed over the past few years. In fact, I've come to realize that an organization's data is probably the second most important asset it has, after people, and, yes, I mean more important than the properties you own, or the brands in your portfolio. Therefore, your data management strategy is crucial to your long-term success. And, it turns out, data management is actually a pretty interesting strategic problem. The decisions you make about how to define, access, store, and surface your data are as important as the analytic techniques you deploy and the reports you create from them. In fact, these decisions determine whether your analytic programs will ultimately be a success or a failure.

In this chapter I talk about data management for hospitality and gaming. Many organizations are so eager to get to the analytics that they forget about establishing a sound and sustainable data management strategy. My goal is to help non-IT personas understand the issues related to data management at enough level of detail that they can participate in discussions with IT to provide the requirements that will support their organizations' data management strategies. I don't want to turn you into a database architect, but I do want you to understand the implications of decisions that are made about the data that supports your analysis and reporting efforts.

I start by establishing why a data management strategy is so important, and I then define the data challenges that organizations are facing today, as data comes at us in greater volume, velocity, and variety than ever before. I cover the key definitions and considerations across the components of data management including acquisition, storage, integration, cleansing, access, and governance. In these sections I explain the emerging technology enablers that facilitate a holistic data management strategy. Finally, I provide tips about how you can get started building a data management strategy, even if you don't have the resources or budget to invest in technology just yet.

DATA MANAGEMENT CHALLENGE AND OPPORTUNITY

If you were to ask any analyst how they allocate their time during an analytics project, they will likely tell you that they spend a disproportionate amount of time on data preparation (access, integration, and cleansing), and consequently have little time left to analyze, let alone make decisions. In fact, many believe that analysts can spend up to 80% of their time manipulating data, leaving only 20% to actually solve problems. Some say that the value of a data management program is to reduce the data preparation to 20%, preserving 80% for problem solving. I would advocate for a slightly different approach. If you've got the extra time, why not save 30% for innovation (Figure 2.1)? After all, isn't innovation where competitive advantage comes from?

Most data management initiatives are designed to facilitate access to the information that analysts and managers need to make the decisions that will move the business forward. This information needs to be clean and credible to ensure accuracy and executive buy-in. Many

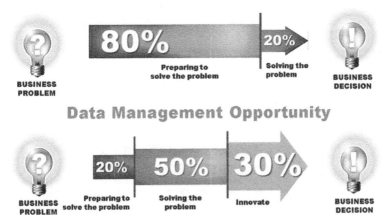

Figure 2.1 Data Management Challenge and Opportunity
Source: Image courtesy of SAS Institute, Inc.

organizations get bogged down in these two elements; when data isn't clean and credible, they end up arguing about sources and definitions rather than devising solutions or making decisions. To do data management right, you need to build an organizational structure around the data management program, with sound data governance rules in place. Figure 2.2 outlines the components of a comprehensive data management strategy.

Across the top of the figure are listed some *corporate drivers* of data management programs. These are typical and high level. Your organization might have others in mind. The important point here is that there are defined goals and objectives of the program, which will dictate the specific formats, sources, strategies, and accesses that will be required. For example, the executive that I interviewed for one of the case studies in this chapter had a goal for his data program that the "up and out" reports, as he called them, which went to the executive team and the company stakeholders, be consistent, accurate, based on a single source of the truth, and easy to access. After this first data management project was successful, they moved on to incorporating other data that met different goals. You may not tackle all drivers at once, but it is probably a good idea to define what they are so that you do not make decisions that will restrict you later.

Data governance, shown on the left side of Figure 2.2, is the process of defining the rules, processes, and principles that govern the

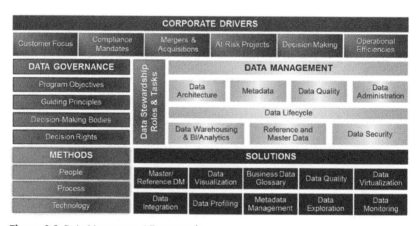

Figure 2.2 Data Management Framework
Source: Image courtesy of SAS Institute, Inc.

data program, which involves making decisions about what the definition of key metrics are, where the data sources come from, who has access, how updates or new sources will be handled, and what security will be required. This should be executed by a cross-functional team representing the major lines of business plus IT. This step is crucial to a successful data management program. Part of the role of data governance is to define the people, process, and technology components of the program (see them listed in the Methods section in the figure).

The corporate drivers, data governance, and methods are the wrappers around the processes and technology that comprise the data management program. From a day-to-day perspective, the data stewards manage the program according to the rules and processes set up by the data governance board.

I am not going to cover every element in Figure 2.2 in detail, but I include the figure here to demonstrate that data management is much more than just buying a warehouse. In the next few sections, I plan to give you enough information to get you started on the journey, to have conversations with your counterparts in IT and across the organization, and to think through what is required to be successful.

I will start out by talking about expectations and goals for data governance. Then I will cover the remaining key components of data management.

Data Governance

The data governance process can start even before a single piece of technology is purchased, and in fact, it absolutely should start before any major technology investments. In this section, I present a case study example of a data governance project that justified investment in some visualization technology. They started with the data, however, and this made the technology investment more impactful because the requirements became clearer during the process of establishing the data governance framework.

In "The DGI Data Governance Framework," prepared by Gwen Thomas from the Data Governance Institute, data governance is described as "A system of decision rights and accountabilities for information-related processes, executed according to agreed-upon models, which describe who can take what actions with what information, and when, under what circumstances, using what methods."[1] The outcome of governance may be different depending on what corporate driver is being addressed, but in general, the expectations of data governance are:

- Establishes guiding principles for data sharing
- Clarifies accountability for data definitions, rules, and quality
- Aligns data policies with business strategies and priorities
- Formalizes data stewardship, minimizing the "data dilettante" syndrome
- Formalizes monitoring and measurement of data critical projects

A successful data governance initiative will:

- Position enterprise data issues as cross-functional
- Foster improved alignment between business and IT
- Eliminate data ownership arguments and turf wars
- Establish business stakeholders as information owners
- Remove IT from business decision making
- Ensure data is managed separately from applications
- Align data quality with business measures and acceptance
- Invite new rigor around monitoring and measurement

You can see the benefits of a good data governance program, including ensuring that the business takes ownership of its data, while working in partnership with IT to deliver that data to the organization. I talk a bit more about how to evaluate data sources through this lens of data governance later in the chapter. I have also listed several resources in the references at the end of this chapter that you can access for more information about issues around data governance, including links to some of the great work done by my former colleagues in the SAS Best Practices Group.

CASE STUDY: DATA GOVERNANCE, DEXTER E. WOOD JR., HILTON WORLDWIDE

CASE STUDY

Like most large hospitality companies, Hilton Worldwide has grown both organically and through major mergers and acquisitions. When growth happens in this way, the organization ends up in a situation where performance information is captured and stored in a variety of legacy systems scattered throughout the enterprise and around the globe. Typically, one of the biggest challenges with such a complex and siloed data infrastructure is that key performance indicators from reports created by different groups around the world are not always consistent. This could be because of how different functions calculate the metrics, which systems the numbers are sourced from, or, in a fast-moving global company, because the numbers changed between yesterday's analysis and today's meeting. As a result of these inconsistencies, analysts and executives spend valuable time tracking down the source of the disparity, as opposed to interpreting and taking action on the results.

When Dexter Wood took on the role of senior vice president and global head of business and investment analysis, he was at the center of the pressure to support increased performance analysis and reporting requirements as Hilton continued to fully integrate the company and pursue a market-leading growth strategy. He saw a huge opportunity to create a single source of the truth for these critical activities to keep the organization from continuing to waste time validating data definitions. There was a budget for technology to streamline performance analysis and reporting, but before making any major investments, he pulled together a cross-functional team that represented the major functional areas to tackle the issue of inconsistencies in key performance indicators. "We thought it was important to do the business side first, to define the business rules and metrics. Only after that, would we work on the data to support them and invest in the technology to surface them," said Dexter.

The other issue that the team needed to address early on was the scope of the project. "Right from the beginning, we knew we weren't going to be able to fix the data across the entire enterprise all at once, so we focused on identifying the key business metrics that could best provide insight for the executive team and help drive performance," he continued.

(continued)

(*continued*)

Dexter and the team successfully launched the first phase of this data governance program in time to support the lead-in and follow-up to Hilton Worldwide's 2013 initial public offering. The streamlined access to consistent and well-defined metrics helped Dexter's team be responsive to the wide variety of requests for information and kept senior leaders focused on understanding and driving performance.

The team made a few key decisions that ensured the success of this initiative:

- **Clearly defined, relatively small scope for the project.** The team decided to limit the initial phases to what Dexter refers to as the "up and out" reports. They wanted to improve consistency and timeliness for the analysis and reporting that provided the most insight to the senior leadership team and that supported communication outside the company to the analysts and investor community.

- **Cross-functional team of decision makers.** Dexter worked with a cross-functional team of his peers to define the single source of the data and the business rules and definitions of key metrics. This team was made up of leaders from commercial functions, the brands, operations, and finance and development. It was very important that the members of this team had the power to speak for their functional area, as well as to support and enforce decisions that were made.

- **Focus on data governance.** The team realized the importance of focusing on the data from a business stakeholder perspective and prioritized establishing alignment on key data metrics where consensus was lacking. They wanted a comprehensive process that addressed almost every aspect of the data, from understanding exactly what data was required, through mapping out source systems and determining which would be used for each data metric, to establishing and agreeing on definitions for key metrics. They also sought to assign specific ownership of each metric to one of the team members as part of the overall data governance structure.

Dexter refers to the data definitions developed by the team as a *common business language*. This set of common metrics, derived from defined source systems, ensures that every executive sees the same set of information, and every functional area understands and can explain how these metrics are defined. "Developing the common business language was more difficult than any of us anticipated. It was very surprising how differently each of us thought about some of these common industry metrics depending on our context and point of view. It was an eye-opening exercise for us," said Dexter.

Dexter cautioned that you need to set aside plenty of time, more than you may think, for any data governance initiative. Be sure to set the right expectations with executives and stakeholders from the beginning and keep reinforcing the value of getting the data right. "It is tempting to rush to the technology solution, to building visualizations and analytics, without considering the data. However, if you don't take the time to do the data governance and metric definition work first, you end up with misalignment between business functions, validation issues, and other problems that will impact the credibility of the solution. Then you have to go back and do it anyway, which takes even more time," he said.

Now that you have some exposure to the responsibilities and benefits of data governance, let's talk about the components of a data management program. Remember, data governance is the process, whereas when we start talking about data management, we begin to address the technology. I start out by describing the phenomenon formerly known as big data, which got us into this mess to begin with. Then I will talk about issues around data storage and data integration.

The Data Formerly Known as "Big Data"?

Big data is what happened when the cost of storing information became less than the cost of making the decision to throw it away.

—George Dyson, The Long Now Foundation, March 19, 2013

The data resulting from the evolution of the Internet, e-commerce and the social web, along with rapid innovation in data gathering and processing technology, generated a phenomenon that became known as *big data*. While the market seems to be moving away from this term, the concept behind it is still relevant. We are still being impacted by the data deluge, and many organizations have yet to get their arms around what it is and how to deal with it.

Which is why Dan Ariely, a behavioral economics researcher and professor from Duke University, a few years ago famously compared big data to teenage sex, because:

Everyone talks about it.

Nobody really knows how to do it.

Everyone thinks everyone else is doing it.

So everyone claims they are doing it too.

This is probably true for the hotel industry as a whole even today, although progress has been made in some areas like revenue management and reputation management.

The reality is that data will always get bigger, as one of my favorite analytic hospitality executives has been explaining to me for years (while trying to get me to stop using the term). Today's big data is going to be small in five years. So, either we keep coming up with larger and larger adjectives, or find another way to talk about the same thing. In fact, SAS has already started to refer to big data as *complex data*. This is probably a more accurate way of describing the problem. It's the complexity that is creating the challenge, not just the size or scope.

To set up the discussion in the rest of this chapter, it's worth discussing the big data phenomenon and why it became such a big deal. Then, I'll start referring to it as complex data. I promise. Well, I'll try, anyway.

Gartner says organizations have a big data challenge "when the volume, variety, and velocity of data exceeds an organization's storage or compute capacity for accurate and timely decision making."[2] While *big data* certainly became a big buzzword, the phenomenon was driven by some very real evolutions in technology that have made it possible to access and unlock insights from larger and more complex data sets than ever before. This big data phenomenon was not simply caused by the data itself, but more so by the fact that we finally have the technological capacity to capture, analyze, and derive insights from it.

Two key components of Gartner's definition of big data are particularly relevant for hospitality:

1. The "three Vs"—volume, variety, and velocity. The important point here is that it isn't just the amount of data that challenges organizations. The social world is creating a variety of new data sources, many in nontraditional formats like text, video, audio,

location data, or click streams from websites. Organizations are not used to storing or analyzing this variety of formats. In fact, experts, including analysts like Gartner and IDC, estimate that 70 to 90% of the data generated today is *unstructured*, or in less traditional formats. This puts tremendous pressure on a traditional IT infrastructure that was not set up to handle this kind of data. I will explain this more later in this chapter. Data is coming at us fast, too. A tweet is stale almost at the moment it is created, and a guest is only in "that" location at that moment before they move on.

2. This brings me to the second important point in the definition: "exceeds an organization's storage or compute capacity for accurate and timely decision making." If the data is such that you can't derive value from it at the speed of business, you have big data, no matter how large it actually is. It's a twofold problem. Most legacy technology infrastructures are not set up to manage even the volume of structured transactional data that is being generated today, let alone to accommodate these new formats. Additionally, these environments were optimized for quickly and efficiently extracting, transforming, and loading transactional data, not for performing complex analytics across a massive data set.

Recent technology innovations have made it possible to capture, comprehend, and act on all of this complex data. These technology platforms are evolving quickly, and there is plenty of very detailed information available through a variety of sources, some of which I've listed at the end of this chapter. In the next few sections, I outline some things you should consider in the areas of data storage, data integration, and data cleansing.

DATA STORAGE

As the variety and velocity of data increases (adding to volume), data storage needs to be:

- Cheaper (because you need a lot of it)
- More flexible (to handle nontraditional data formats)
- Faster (at the speed of data creation)
- Scalable (because you will continue to collect more and more data)

Technology innovation happening today is addressing these four key needs. To put the issue of databases designed to handle complex data in context, let's first look at why unstructured data sources are causing technology problems by contrasting them with more traditional, structured data.

Structured data is any data that has relationships such that it can be sorted into rows and columns. Think about sales data, which can be associated with a store, a date, or an item. Or, think about customer profile information, which can be associated with a customer or customer ID (Figure 2.3).

Contrast this with *unstructured data*, which does not have any predefined relationships within or among similar data (Figure 2.4). This is all of this "new data" like reviews, emails, call logs, surveillance clips, or web data. Imposing structure on this data requires some effort, and depends greatly on what you plan to do with it. For example, reviews

125	94	62	32	116	41	−25	0	0	0	0	12,012.00	12,012.00
125	81	27	54	118	10	−58	0	0	0	0	3,094.00	3,094.00
125	54	27	27	87	20	−20	0	0	0	0	2,995.40	2,995.40
125	71	31	40	87	16	−7	0	0	0	0	5,444.40	5,444.40
125	101	28	73	87	10	−13	0	0	0	0	7,981.00	7,981.00
125	84	20	64	72	22	−21	0	0	0	0	6,287.00	6,287.00
125	111	26	85	93	39	−20	0	0	0	0	9,508.75	9,508.75
125	96	30	66	87	30	−8	0	0	0	0	8,255.35	8,255.35
125	40	14	26	81	6	−62	0	0	0	0	3,192.00	3,192.00
125	46	17	29	42	18	−18	0	0	0	0	2,900.00	2,900.00
125	51	18	33	42	24	−7	0	0	0	0	4,372.50	4,372.50
125	61	36	25	42	25	−15	0	0	0	0	5,228.50	5,228.50
125	25	10	15	42	4	−40	0	0	0	0	1,687.00	1,687.00
125	68	40	28	42	32	−8	0	0	0	0	6,272.50	6,272.50
125	92	48	44	42	41	−11	0	0	0	0	8,022.50	8,022.50
125	52	29	23	42	19	−50	0	0	0	0	3,279.00	3,279.00
125	60	29	31	42	15	−15	0	0	0	0	3,478.00	3,478.00
125	62	36	26	42	16	−12	0	0	0	0	4,125.00	4,125.00
125	39	23	16	42	3	−16	0	0	0	0	2,474.00	2,474.00
125	36	20	16	42	10	−13	0	0	0	0	2,541.00	2,541.00
125	65	32	33	42	30	−5	0	0	0	0	5,146.00	5,146.00
125	80	35	45	42	23	−17	0	0	0	0	8,496.40	8,496.40

Figure 2.3 Structured Data

Figure 2.4 Text Reviews—How Do You Structure These?

could be used to identify important conversation topics, understand consumer sentiment, profile guests for targeted marketing, or identify value drivers. Depending on who wants to access the data and what they will do with it, the imposed structure could be very different. Unstructured data can get large very fast (think about the size of a daily security video file compared to the size of an outlet's daily sales files).

At the root of the challenge with these two different data types is the storage and access methodologies required to take full advantage of the insights contained in the data. Structured data is typically stored in a *relational database*, which stores the data points according to their relationships with other data points in the database. Relational databases are set up with a predefined data schema that the data is then fit into as it is loaded into the database. New data is added according to its relationship to the data already contained in the data set. Most of today's technology infrastructures are set up to handle this kind of data, which is then generally made available through static reports.

I like to think about relational databases like a silverware drawer you may have in your kitchen. The silverware drawer sorts your place settings—forks, knives, and spoons—in separate, but related, slots. A row across the drawer makes a place setting. Before you put the silverware in the drawer, you probably had to buy an insert. This insert is the predefined schema for the drawer. Now, every time you empty the dishwasher, you sort forks, knives, and spoons into the appropriate slots. If you buy new utensils, you add them to the predefined slots.

But what happens if you decide you need iced tea spoons or a new set of serving utensils? If you didn't plan for these utensils ahead of time, they won't fit neatly into your silverware schema. What if you got rid of that predefined schema (the drawer insert), and just put all the silverware together in one drawer? When you needed to add new utensils, any utensils, you would not need to know ahead of time what their relationship was to the rest of the silverware in the drawer, you could just place them in there. Further, if the drawer filled up, you could start using another drawer, or put the silverware in a shoebox or Tupperware storage bin. It is easy to get more storage space without needing to buy any specialized equipment (more inserts).

New databases are moving toward this more flexible structure, which does not require a predefined schema. This is why some have been talking about Hadoop as an emerging platform for storing and accessing complex, unstructured data. Hadoop is a database that is designed to handle large volumes of unstructured data through a methodology similar to my no-insert utensil drawer. Hadoop works because it is cheap and scalable, flexible, and fast.

- **Cheap and scalable.** Hadoop is built on commodity hardware, which is exactly what it sounds like—really cheap, "generic" hardware. It is designed as a "cluster," tying together groups of inexpensive servers. This means it's relatively inexpensive to get started, and easy to add more storage space as your data, inevitably, expands. It also has built-in redundancy—data is stored in multiple places, so if any of the servers happen to go down, you don't lose all the data (there are forks in every drawer, so you always have access to forks, even if one drawer jams).

- **Flexible.** The Hadoop data storage platform does not require a predefined data structure, or data schema (like the utensils drawer insert). You can just "throw the data in there" and figure out the relationships later.

- **Fast.** Hadoop is fast in two ways. First, it uses massive parallel processing to comb through the databases to extract the information. Data is stored in a series of smaller containers, and there are many "helpers" available to reach in and pull out what you are looking for (extending the drawer metaphor: picture four drawers of utensils with each family member retrieving one place setting from each drawer at the same time). The work is split up, as opposed to being done in sequence. The second way that Hadoop is fast is that because the database is not constrained by a predefined schema, the process of loading the data into the database is much faster (picture the time it takes to sort the utensils from the dishwasher rack into the insert, as opposed to dumping the rack contents straight into the drawer).

Many companies have put a lot of effort into organizing structured data over the years, and there are some data sets that make sense to be stored according to traditional methods (like the utensils you use every day, which have a specific, defined, and routine purpose). These databases are not only optimized for efficient extraction, transformation, and loading (ETL), but they also make it really easy to render and build standard reports, because the schema has been optimized specifically for this purpose. Because of this, most companies see Hadoop as an addition to their existing technology infrastructure rather than a replacement for their relational, structured, database.

Because of the flexibility of the data stored in Hadoop, it is not best suited for operational analyses or production models. It is really designed to facilitate reporting, exploratory analysis, or model development. Hadoop is not as good at any real-time, or near real-time, applications as relational databases are. For this reason, Hadoop will likely not be the basis for a production solution such as, for example, the revenue management system, but rather, will support revenue management's ad hoc analyses for innovation and strategy development.

The other important factor to consider is that Hadoop is an *open source* database. Open source is basically software for which the original source code is made freely available and may be redistributed and modified by anyone. This is part of what makes Hadoop cheap, and why there has been so much innovation on Hadoop. The downside is that it requires a specialized skill set and a pretty large amount of coding to make it work in your environment. For example, right now Hadoop does not come with any pre-built security, so your Hadoop coders will need to build that in themselves. This is no small undertaking.

DATA INTEGRATION

Regardless of the size or structure of the data, one of the biggest challenges in hospitality has always been that disparate systems collect and manage all of the wide variety of data that we need to gain insights about our business. These systems speak different languages and collect data in different ways and in different formats. In order to effectively analyze data from disparate systems, the data needs to be integrated (meaning combined to form one unified view). This involves extracting data from source systems, transforming that data (transposing columns, standardizing values), and loading it into a data storage area. This ETL process involves detailed knowledge of where all the data is and, as I mentioned in the discussion on Hadoop, an extensive amount of coding. This code needs to be adjusted every time the data changes (you add a new menu item or room type), an upgrade to a system is made, or a system is added or replaced.

Many companies invest in a data warehouse to integrate and store data from disparate operational systems. The benefits of data warehouses are:

- **All of your data is in one place.** The data warehouse integrates data from the disparate systems into one location according to a predefined schema.

- **Speed.** Data warehouses are very good at quick ETL of data from the transactional system and can quickly render reports on historical data.

- **Reduces the processing burden on operating systems.** Instead of hitting the transaction system directly when you need data, you make the request from the enterprise data warehouse (EDW). The data is pulled from the transaction system at some scheduled interval, so that the selling system can focus its processing power on executing transactions instead of delivering data.

However, data warehouses also have their drawbacks.

- Relatively inflexible:
  - They have a **fixed data schema**, so any new data or changes to data collection in source systems needs to be recoded.

▪ They are **optimized for reporting but not necessarily for analytics**. Analytics typically require wide tables (a lot of different information about one entity for predictive purposes). Reporting requires long, dimension-based tables (many instances of total sales by period). Analytical resources need to write code to restructure data in formats that are appropriate for analytics and to find a place to store that restructured data before they can run any analytical models on it.

▪ **Batch processing.** The ETL process for a data warehouse typically operates in batch (all data transferred at once with less frequency, say once a day or once an hour). This means that data in the data warehouse is only updated periodically.

▪ **Processing intensive.** The ETL processes can also be very processing intensive. Large amounts of data are moved around, and transformations can be extensive depending on how diverse data formats are and how "dirty" the data is.

This inflexibility means that adding data or creating new views, tables, or analyses requires a lot of coding, which breaks every time something new is added to the source systems (and we never add new technology or new data to the hospitality infrastructure, right?). This is time and resource intensive. Processing takes time, slowing down access, increasing time to results, and consuming computing resources that could be used for analytics or reporting.

Enter *data federation*. Data federation is a data management mechanism that treats autonomous data stores as one large data store. The rules for how the data relate to each other are kept in the federation layer, and data integration is done "on the fly." This means that data is stored in its original format in the individual systems and then only integrated when the user wants to access it. It can also mean that the data is available in "real time" —whatever the source system is holding currently is available, rather than waiting for the batch to run.

The benefit of data federation is that with reduced movement of data there are fewer chances for data errors. There is a significant reduction in the workload associated with moving data around, especially if some of it is not ever going to be used. This frees up computing resources. Data federation also increases the speed of access to the data for the users, as data is available closer to "real time."

Typically, data virtualization goes hand in hand with data federation, so you might have heard this term as well. Data virtualization is defined as any approach to data management that allows an application to retrieve and manipulate data without requiring technical details about the data, like how it is formatted or where it is physically located. Virtualization facilitates data access, because the user doesn't need to know where the data is stored, or what format it is in to access and use it. The virtualization layer takes care of that. It can also provide some data management capabilities. (Note that you can have federation without virtualization, or virtualization without federation, but they most typically operate together for maximum benefit. You really don't want me to get into the details on this, although some of it is quite logical, but only some of it).

The biggest benefit of data virtualization is that it provides much easier data access for business users. The location and characteristics of the data are transparent to the business user who wants to access the data for reporting, exploration, or analytics. They don't have to understand technology architecture or write complex code to find and use the data. The second benefit is a dramatic reduction of coding burden on IT. IT does not have to write special code every time the user has a unique need, and, for some technical reasons that are not important to us, the ETL coding burden is lesser as well.

There are a few things to consider with both data federation and data virtualization:

- **Impact on transactional systems.** Data federation applications can still burden transactional systems with too many requests for data, so you may still need a data warehouse to store data from certain transactional systems.
- **Data governance**. A unified approach to data management like this will require different, and stricter, data governance rules. IT will need help from the business to understand who uses the information and how, so you need to be prepared to establish strong data governance (which is a good idea anyway, as I described earlier).

▪ **Historical information.** With a data federation method, you can only access the data that is in the source systems at the moment you ask for it. This means that if the source systems aren't keeping historical data or if they write over history, you need to store that information elsewhere (like in a data warehouse).

We may never get away from the need for EDWs, but we may be able to get away with smaller versions in an environment that still facilitates access to data by business users. Implementing data management technology like I described will require investment and business process change, but it should dramatically streamline the data management process, helping business users get to the data when and how they need to.

CASE STUDY: BUILDING AN EDW, ANDY SWENSON, PINNACLE ENTERTAINMENT

CASE STUDY

Andy Swenson is Vice President, Database Marketing & Revenue Management for Pinnacle Entertainment, which is a U.S.-based gaming, leisure, and hospitality company that operates 15 gaming entertainment properties across the United States. Andy's team was just finishing a two-year data warehouse project as I was writing this book, so the topic of this chapter, data management, was fresh on his mind. He had a lot of advice for others who are planning to embark on such an endeavor. As he says, "None of the analytics vision is possible unless you get the data right."

The first and most important thing that he emphasized was that these projects always take longer than anyone initially expects. He and his team had the benefit of having gone through projects like this before, so this time they estimated up front that it would take two years, hoped it would be 18 months, and ended up finishing in two years. I asked Andy to talk to me about the elements of the project, how long they take, and why that duration is so important for the project success.

Andy told me that before any coding even happens, the first step in the process—mapping out the data model—will take several months, and in their case it took six months. This step is so crucial to the success of the entire project that it definitely should not be short cut in any way.

(continued)

(*continued*)

"It's easy to underestimate this step because we deal with data very differently without a data warehouse," he reminded me. Before you work with a data warehouse, your only exposure is to data sets held on a local machine, or stored and accessed as files on a server. The data sets are generally viewed in isolation, or potentially a few might be joined on the fly for an analysis, so you do not have to consider their relationship to one another. In a data warehouse where the data will be integrated, these relationships must be defined carefully. If this is not set up properly from the beginning, the promised results will not be realized. As he says, "If you don't do it at the beginning, or take the time to do it right, you'll end up redoing it later, when the project is already late and over budget."

Andy also pointed out that different constituents likely have different methods for defining fields and source systems. The business likely has some legacy methodology that they don't even really think about that also impacts data definitions. He said that during this process it would not be uncommon for the team to decide on a path, run the plan by a stakeholder a second or third time, and then hear something like "Oh no, wait, but if the change comes in less than three days before arrival, we cancel and rebook because by then we have a change fee and the system won't let us charge unless we totally rebook, so these cancellations are not actually cancellations" (this was actually my example, but you get the idea), or potentially something even more convoluted than that. Because some of these business processes and data definitions are so embedded in the organization and so second nature, it takes a lot of time, and a lot of communication, to unravel them.

After the data model is designed, the next step is to build the data warehouse. Andy says that while this takes time, if you have the right resources, ones who are experienced in database design and execution, this is the easiest and most efficient step. He says this step can take another six months depending on how rich your data is and how deep into big data you want to go, but with the right team in place, it is easily estimated and rarely slips.

The final phase is validation. This is another component that can take much longer than planned but is crucially important to the success of the project. In the validation phase, you test the database. Everything from ETL (extraction, transformation, loading—how the data gets into the database) to the accuracy of the data needs to be thoroughly tested before the data is made available to the teams for use. Any problems need to be fixed, which will likely require interaction with and between the technical resources and the business. There will be problems, no matter how diligent you were during the data modeling phase, or how good your technical resources are. It is much better to uncover those issues, troubleshoot them, and fix them during the validation phase than when the database goes live, or you risk losing credibility.

Remember, the data has to be credible, and the users have to believe that it is within a high tolerance, in order for the database project to be successful. This is why the data model and the validation phases are so important. The team needs to ensure that the data is set up and working correctly so that the users will be confident. The last thing you want is for the users to uncover mistakes, especially lots of mistakes. This will diminish their faith in the data and undermine the success of the project.

As is typical with most data warehouse projects, Andy said that the scope of this project included only a portion of the company data. The executive team prioritized hotel and marketing data for this round and intend to kick off another phase to include the other ancillary outlets and some more nontraditional data next. They intend to bring in the next data sets soon, and it will very likely involve a similar timeline.

I've heard time and time again that it can be difficult to justify long timelines to executives, particularly for what seems to be a "just the data" phase. I asked Andy about this. He said that the idea of faster access to information was very compelling to the executive team. They really responded to the idea of quick data manipulation that would allow them to get answers to their questions faster, so they were ready to invest what it took to get that done. The team set realistic expectations of the project duration and delivered on time. The combination of selling the value, and then setting the right expectations ahead of time helped to ensure executive buy-in.

I asked Andy what piece of advice he'd give to others who are planning a similar project. He said the most important success factor is communication. "Involve as many stakeholders as possible as early as possible. There's always a balance between the meeting getting too big and including all of the right people, but really, you can't start regular status meetings and communication channels too early, and you need to keep all potential stakeholders involved," he said.

DATA QUALITY

The next topic under data management is data quality, or data cleansing and enrichment. All of the data in the world, stored in the best database formats, is of no use if it is not clean and credible data. Data quality can be thought of as the state of completeness, validity, consistency, timeliness, and accuracy that makes data appropriate for a specific use. As you can tell from that definition, data quality is a fairly complex subject. Data quality techniques are generally categorized as follows[3]:

- **Profiling.** Data profiling refers to the analysis of data to capture statistics (metadata) that provide insight into the quality of the data and aid in the identification of data quality issues, and is generally the first step in a data quality initiative. For example, an analyst could run general descriptive statistics on the number of guests per room, like mean, median, minimum, maximum, and the distribution of values. Any values outside of the normal range (say, 1–4) might be incorrect entries and candidates for evaluation. Profiling can identify the length and type of data fields, missing values, or common patterns in the data. This analysis helps to speed up the identification and resolution of data quality issues.

- **Generalized "cleansing."** This refers to the modification of data values to meet domain restrictions, integrity constraints, or other business rules that define sufficient data quality for the organization. A good deal of data in hospitality is generated by user entry. Additionally, source systems may collect data in very different formats. Generalized cleansing can help to reconcile incorrect entries, inconsistencies in data collection, or different data formats. For example, say a field for gender should be either M or F. Data cleansing algorithms would scan through the data to identify any values that don't conform to M or F, which could include a missing field, lowercase letters, a different value, or the full words "male" and "female." The algorithm would replace the incorrect values with the corrected values, or flag them for manual adjustment.

Sometimes, general cleansing can become quite complex. For example, point of sale data from a table service restaurant might contain a large number of zero customer (cover) transactions. On the surface, this doesn't make sense, so you might categorize it as user error. However, with further investigation, there could be business processes that require a zero cover count such as an adjustment to the check or takeout orders (I'm not saying it's a good business process, I'm just saying there might be one). The data quality rules would need to distinguish between a mistaken entry and a regular business process. If it's a mistake, you might have the algorithm count the number of entrees and use that as a proxy for the correct cover count. As you can see, cleansing usually requires a good understanding of business processes.

- **Parsing and standardization.** This technique refers to breaking text fields down into component parts and formatting values into consistent layouts based on industry standards, local standards (for example, postal authority standards for address data), user-defined business rules, and knowledge bases of values and patterns. For example, if first and last names came through in one text field, parsing Kelly McGuire would break it into two separate text fields—First Name: Kelly, Last Name: McGuire. Standardization helps to apply a common format to all data. For example, do you want to store names of states as abbreviations (NC) or with full values (North Carolina)? Different systems collect and store data like this in different formats, so standardization ensures that all values are consistent.

- **Matching.** Matching refers to identification, linking, or merging related entries within or across sets of data. This process is most commonly used for customer records, so obviously it has a good deal of value for hospitality. This process merges and removes duplicate records for a consolidated, accurate guest database. When exact matches aren't found, *fuzzy matching* can be applied. This is a method that finds approximate matches that, while not exact, are likely matches. For example, Bob and Robert with the same last name and address are likely the same person. Two people with different last names but the same address could be a household. Kelli and Kelly with the same last name, address, and phone number are probably the same person. Algorithms can be tuned to certain probabilities of being a match (for example, do two out of five key fields match? Three out of five?).

■ **Enrichment.** This refers to enhancing the value of internally held data by appending related attributes from external sources. For example, consumer demographic attributes or geographic descriptors acquired from third-party sources added to the guest profile can provide additional insight about each guest and the guest database as a whole. Data can also be enriched with analytic results, like scores, which we will discuss in subsequent chapters.

Once the data goes through an initial cleansing, data quality solutions automate the processes listed previously, so that they can be applied to new data as it is added to the database. Exceptions are flagged, so the database administrators can make corrections and additions as they surface. As I started to learn about data quality, I was interested to find that data quality methods actually leverage analytics quite a bit. For example, matching algorithms provide a probability that the two entries should be combined and profiling tracks patterns in the data so that deviations from those patterns identify quality improvement opportunities.

MEASURING THE BENEFITS OF DATA MANAGEMENT

Getting data management right clearly takes time, which most executives who have never dealt with data have a hard time understanding. I constantly get asked for advice about how to justify investment in data management, or how to quantify the benefits. I wish I had a silver bullet answer to these questions. I don't. But I do know that organizations who charge ahead into an analytics project without taking the time to prepare their data end up having to go back and do it anyway, adding unplanned time and cost to the project.

Figure 2.5 Benefits of Data Management
Source: Image courtesy of SAS Best Practices.

Most of the benefits in data management can be expressed instead as risks or costs of not taking the time to implement data governance and data quality initiatives. That said, the four elements in Figure 2.5 are generally accepted as key benefits of data governance and data quality initiatives. Productivity and efficiency are increased when data management is handled at the enterprise level because analysts no longer have to manipulate data or argue about definitions. They can go straight to the analysis and interpretation. Costs are reduced over time through automation and time savings. Many industries, such as casinos, are highly regulated. Data management can help to ensure compliance, so that the right data is collected and reported on, thereby reducing risk. The trick is to find the burning issue in the minds of the key stakeholders, whether it might be a productivity increase or a risk mitigation, and emphasize how your data management initiatives will support that goal.

RESPONSIBLE USE OF DATA

So, now that I've gotten you excited about big data opportunities, you are probably ready to run out and grab every piece of data you can get your hands on. That is certainly the message coming from third-party data resellers, big data vendors, and technology experts. It all sounds so compelling; it's tempting to think that you can just shove all of that new data into a database and you're good to go.

Regardless of how inexpensive storage space is getting and how fast processing is becoming, capturing, storing, and analyzing data still takes resources, both technology and human capital. Administrative overhead is required to ensure that the data is updated regularly and integrated properly into the data infrastructure. If the data will be used in analytics, it will need to be stored differently than if it is used for reporting or ad hoc analysis. Unstructured databases built on an open-source code platform require investment in specialized skills and extensive coding for configuration. You may have to pay for some data sources, so they need to have a return associated with them.

"The first thought when approaching a new data source is often 'How can I get this data in the system?' Really, our first thought should be 'What different decisions can I enable with this data?' We should be more creative and thoughtful about how we approach new data sources. We make many types of decisions, and such data may well have significant value outside tactical day-to-day decisions, where the data may or may not add value," says Alex Dietz, advisory product manager, IDeaS, a SAS Company.

Perhaps more important, sometimes adding more data to an analysis simply does not result in a better answer. In this case, I am talking about additional data sources, as opposed to more of the same kind of data. More of the same kind of data can add confidence and statistical rigor to an analysis.

Additional data might not result in a better analytical answer if:

- The data does not have a significant causal relationship with what you are trying to predict (it simply does not influence these factors, so it won't make a difference in the answer).
- The data does not change significantly over time, so adding it to an algorithm would not result in a different answer. Think about weather data, for example. Weather data might do a good job of explaining what happened to hotel demand in the past (identifying a storm in the past as a special event so the forecast would treat those dates differently in the future), but how do you incorporate weather into a forecast for future dates? If it's March now, and I'm setting prices for November, I only have

the "average" forecast for that time period (temperature). Is this really useful?

- The data is extremely volatile or "dirty," so it is too unreliable for the algorithms. In other words, it would just add to the uncertainty of the forecast. Regrets and denial data fall into this category for revenue management. Theoretically, this information could help in demand unconstraining, but this type of data is very unstable. Collected by a call center agent, it is subject to user error. Collected via a website, it is subject to noise from shopping, an inability to identify unique visitors, or an inability to identify exactly what the user was focused on in a page with multiple products. Not being collected across all demand sources would bias the response toward one channel's characteristics, when others may have very different demand patterns.

These are all important considerations when it comes to what data "belongs" in an algorithm, versus what data is used for strategic analysis outside of the routine or production models. Regrets and denials, for example, could help in a marketing analysis or website performance analysis, even if they add too much noise to an unconstraining algorithm.

There are lots of detailed technical and analytical methodologies for assessing and transforming data to make it useful for reporting and analysis, which I won't go into here. Rather, I provide some business-oriented suggestions for how to think about a new data source, and discuss potential problems that could arise from throwing too much data at a problem. Regardless of whether you are collecting this data for yourself, or evaluating a vendor's data strategy, you should think through the benefits and drawbacks, which I describe next.

Define the Business Problem

I always advocate starting with the business problem you are trying to solve (increase forecast accuracy, understand price sensitivity, track market activity, etc.), and then determining what data is necessary to solve that problem. In reality, you are likely to be offered or come across data sources that seem like they might be useful, but it's not clear how. Having the goals of your function or organization clearly in mind will help you understand how to place that data. Will it meet a tactical (day-to-day pricing) need or fit into a more strategic analysis (market position, future opportunity)? Are there ongoing projects that might benefit from this new data?

For example, one recently available data source is forward-looking demand data from Travel Click.[4] This data source provides future demand for the hotel and its competitive set across channels and segments, so it is a natural source for revenue management to evaluate. First, revenue management determines some basic information about the data set, like how often it is updated, what level of detail is provided, and what fields are included. Then it is time to determine how the data would be used in their business processes. There is the possibility that the forward-looking demand data could improve forecast accuracy in the revenue management system, by providing a directional input about market performance. However, the level of detail and included fields need to match with the forecasting and optimization algorithms, and the data needs to add some explanatory power that is not already picked up by the booking pace or market demand patterns.

More strategically, outside of the system, the forward-looking demand data could help revenue management assess their competitive value in the market. The hotel's pace by segment over time as compared to the competitive set will provide some intelligence about the hotel books relative to the competition, and can help reinforce who the primary competitors are and which market segments are most attracted to the hotel's offering. As the hotel tests out distribution strategies, it can validate the success against the benchmark for the market. All of this activity can be done proactively, so that adjustments can be made in advance of the stay date.

Revenue management can find a lot of potential uses for the data set, but the final step in the analysis is to think through whether other departments might make use of the data. For example, marketing could evaluate the success of targeted promotions to certain segments, time periods, or channels by benchmarking against the competitive set. Again, this can be done proactively, so adjustments can be made in advance of the stay date. Sales might have a similar use for the data, ensuring the hotel is getting its fair share of group business.

Evaluate the Data

As I just described, the first important step in evaluating a potential new data source is to determine what business value you will gain from accessing that data. You should clearly and specifically define not just the insight you expect to be able to gain from that data source, but also who will benefit from that insight and what actions will be taken as a result. Knowing the "fit" at the level of business value will help you justify the investment in acquisition.

I spoke with a head of analytics for a major hotel company who said he constantly pushes this important point with his team, whether they come to him with a new data source or a new analysis result. He says, "I always ask them 'So what?' What would I do differently now that I know this? If I find out that my gender split for one brand is 55 percent women whereas another is only 45 percent, what does that change? What could I realistically do with that information, and so, do I really care?" Thinking of the "so what" is a crucial first step to ensure that your analysis stays focused and you aren't wasting time on data with no real value.

Once you understand the potential business value, you need to be sure the data can actually deliver. The second step is to understand the characteristics of the data source. This is an important part of data governance, so when working with your data governance group, ask the following five sets of questions:

1. **What is this data?** Where does it come from, how is it collected, and what does it look like? You should start by understanding who is collecting the data, how it will be collected, and what the characteristics of the data are. Does it come from a reliable source that will provide the data at regular intervals? How does it get transmitted to you? How big is it? What fields are included? Are there many missing values? How are the fields calculated? Is it closely related to any data you are already collecting? Understanding where the data comes from will give you a sense of how reliable it is. If it is heavily driven by user entry, then you need to assess the business process around the data collection. User-driven data is notoriously unreliable unless it has a tight business process around it. The more familiar you become with the data itself, the better you will be able to answer the rest of these questions.

2. **How will the data fit within your database structure?**
   Next, evaluate how the data will fit within your existing structure. Will you need to integrate it with other data? If so, you
   need to ensure that the data are at similar levels of detail,
   and have common fields to match. Will you need to link it to
   other data tables somehow? Will it need special permissions to
   access? For example, a property-level manager should only
   be able to see their property's data, but the regional manager
   must see multiple levels of data. Do you need to do any summary or drill down on the fields?

3. **How often is the data updated and how?** Your systems
   will need to be set up to receive and store the data in a timely
   fashion. If the data comes too fast, and the ETL process takes
   too long, it might be useless by the time you are able to access
   it. For example, tweets or location data are stale almost as they
   are created, so if you aren't able to process them in time to use
   them, it's not worth the trouble. Further, if the data delivery
   process is unreliable (as in, it frequently doesn't show up, or
   shows up with missing values, etc.), and you are counting on it
   for a critical piece of insight, you may want to look elsewhere.

4. **What tools/algorithms will you need to analyze the
   data or report on the data?** Determine whether you will
   need to bring on any specialized technology to analyze the
   data at the level that you can unlock the insights. For example, unstructured text data requires different analysis tools
   than forward-looking demand data. Reporting on the data
   may require a different type of technology. If the data source
   will require new technology investment, you need to be able
   to justify the investment with the value that you will unlock
   from the data.

5. **Who will want access and what will they need to do
   with the data?** This is a crucial final question to ask, once you
   understand the data structure. If, after careful evaluation, no
   one will want access to the data (or analytical results), it is not
   worth spending the time and resources to collect, store, and
   manage that data. On the other hand, if multiple groups want

access, and would take different actions on that data, all of the stakeholder's needs must be considered so that you do not make any decisions in the collection, storage, or access process that restricts usage.

These questions are very high level, but can quickly become very complex. You should have a partner in your IT organization who can take this to a more technical level. If you have already made as much of this assessment as possible yourself, however, you will save everyone time and energy—and probably make some new friends in IT while you are at it!

If you are collecting this data yourself, as Dexter described previously, I would suggest forming a cross-functional team within the organization that can help to assess data needs and brainstorm opportunities. You will likely find that other departments could benefit from access to a new data source, but they might require expanded information or additional parameters. Knowing this up front saves work later. This group could also be responsible for broader data governance or data stewardship, instead of just this one-off analysis.

If your system provider is collecting this data on your behalf, challenge them in the same way you would challenge yourselves internally. Make sure you understand all of the data inputs and their influence on the outputs. After all, you need to be able to trust the output and explain where any recommendations or decisions come from!

The Problem with Big Data in Analytics

If you are just interested in using a new data source for reporting, or for descriptive statistics, the previously outlined steps will keep you out of trouble. Incorporating more data into a predictive model or forecasting analysis is trickier. In this section I am going to introduce some statistical concepts that you should be aware of as you plan to add data to an advanced analytic application, or evaluate an analytics system provider that is talking about new or additional data sources.

The principle known as *Occam's razor* comes into play in analytical applications. It is a principle of mathematics developed in the fourteenth century, which basically states that simpler explanations are, other things being equal, generally better than more complex ones.

Occam's razor cautions us that simply throwing more data at a statistical problem might not necessarily generate a better answer. Many statisticians follow this guidance, believing that you should always select the simplest hypothesis, or simplest formulation of the problem, until simplicity can be traded for predictive power.

Note that when I talk about "more data" in the next few paragraphs, I am talking about more "predictor variables," not more observations within the same data set. Generally speaking, more observations will help to increase the reliability of results, because they will help to detect patterns in the data with greater confidence.

Two different statistical phenomena can occur in predictive analysis with the addition of predictor variables to a model, multicollinearity (Ott and Longnecker 2001) and overfitting (Burnham and Anderson 2002). In both cases, the addition of variables decreases the reliability or predictability of the model (I'm only going to define them at a very high level here, so that you can verify with your analysts whether there's a concern).

1. **Multicollinearity** happens in a multiple regression analysis when two or more predictor variables are highly correlated, and thus do not provide any unique or independent information to the model. Examples of things that tend to be highly correlated could be height and weight, years of education and income, or time spent at work and time spent with family. The real danger in multicollinearity is that it makes the estimates of the individual predictor variables less reliable. So, if all you care about is the model as a whole, it's not that big of a deal. However, if you care about things like what variable has the biggest impact on overall guest value or on likelihood to respond to an offer, then you do have to watch out for multicollinearity.

2. **Overfitting** happens when there are too many parameters relative to the number of observations. When this happens, the model ends up describing random error, not the real underlying relationships. Every data sample has some noise, so if you try to drive out too much error, you become very good at modeling the past, but bad at predicting the future. This is the

biggest danger of overfitting a model. This is particularly problematic in machine-learning algorithms, or really any models that learn over time, like segmentation or revenue management forecasting.

3. **Bias-variance trade-off** (Talluri and van Rysin 2005). Revenue management researchers say, "It is natural to suppose that a model that fits historical data well . . . [and] has low estimation errors, will also generalize well and give low forecast errors. This, however, is *not* the case." In the forecasting world, this is known as the *bias-variance trade-off*. For forecasts, there are two kinds of errors that can be reduced. Variance error can be improved by adding more data that fits the model. The second kind, bias, is adversely affected by more data. So there is a trade-off between minimizing variance and minimizing bias. Adding more data to historical data may reduce the variance, but it creates the "overfitting" problem as described earlier, which increases the bias.

Again, it is more important to know that these problems exist, and to use this information to determine whether a vendor you might be evaluating knows and has dealt with them, or your analysts have accounted for them, than it is for you to understand the statistical underpinnings and the methods for accounting for them. There is plenty of very technical information in statistics and forecasting research if you want more details.

CONCLUSION

In this chapter, I have defined advances in technology that are enabling organizations to capture the volume, variety, and velocity of today's data This will help you identify opportunities to capture and gain insight from existing and emerging data sources. I hope I have also convinced you of the importance of taking the time to define a data management strategy utilizing a cross-functional team. The team should have the goal of not only establishing the rules for consolidating, defining, and integrating current data, but also ensuring a sustainable process to continue to maintain and improve the quality and completeness of the data. This foundation is crucial in supporting the reporting and analytics initiatives I discuss in subsequent chapters.

Good analytics start and end with good data. Good data comes from a good data management strategy. There are a lot of options for how to approach developing a data management strategy. The right one depends on the organization's goals and business strategy, as well as the scope and condition of your data. My aim in this chapter was to give you enough information to be an active and productive participant in developing the data management strategy.

Of course, it doesn't stop with the data. Once you have it, and it's clean, credible, and integrated, it's time to derive some insight from it. In the next chapter, I talk about data visualization. The chapter that follows discusses advanced analytics.

ADDITIONAL RESOURCES

- ▦ The Data Governance Institute, a vendor-neutral organization dedicated to best practices in data governance, www.datagovernance.com.
- ▦ Smart Data Collective Blog, a good resource for blogs about all things data, www.smartdatacollective.com/node?ref=navbar.
- ▦ Webinar Series, "The Mavens of Big Data," www.sas.com/en_ca/events/2015/mavens-big-data/episode-guide.html.

NOTES

1. The DGI Data Governance Framework, prepared by Gwen Thomas of the Data Governance Institute, www.datagovernance.com/wp-content/uploads/2014/11/dgi_framework.pdf.
2. Doug Laney, Gartner 3-D Data Management, 2001.
3. These categories were taken from Gartner's IT Glossary for data quality tools: www.gartner.com/it-glossary/data-quality-tools.
4. Travel Click, Demand 360°, "Capitalize on Opportunities to Increase Revenue with Complete Insights into Future and Historical Demand for Your Hotel and Competitive Set," www.travelclick.com/en/product-services/business-intelligence-solutions/demand360.

CHAPTER **3**

Data
Visualization[1]

In my crystal ball, and I have several, if you look forward 5 or 10 years to 2020 or 2025 . . . there are significantly more visuals and visual cues and fewer Excel spreadsheets. Today everybody has spreadsheets, and we're kind of attached, but I think we need to be more visually data oriented because that will allow us to see more possibilities.

—Kathy Maher, Senior Vice President,
Global Sales and Revenue, Wyndham Hotel Group[2]

They say a picture is worth a thousand words. For data-obsessed analysts, it is easy to forget this simple statement. For managers attached to their spreadsheet reports, it's even easier. Analysts love a good data set, and are extremely comfortable deriving relationships from rows and columns of performance data. Managers become so accustomed to scanning through their reports for their key performance indicators, they forget that there could be a better way. For most people, it's difficult to see the forest for the trees in a complex chart full of numbers, particularly when they are looking at it for the first time. Using visualizations reduces complexity and allows you to tell more compelling stories with your data. If you really want to inspire others to take your recommended action, you aren't going to do it with rows and columns full of numbers—you need to tell a highly visual, simple, and compelling story with that data.

Figure 3.1 Simple, But Compelling, Visualizations
Source: Mike Hlas, "The Most Accurate Pie Chart You'll Ever See," Gazette, *March 31, 2014, http://thegazette.com/2011/05/25/the-most-accurate-pie-chart-youll-ever-see.*

The picture in Figure 3.1 is one of my favorite examples of a compelling visualization. It tells the exact story, no more and no less than the viewer needs to understand what the chart represents, and the action that should be taken (which is eat more pie!).

The same advances in technology that enable capturing, storing, and analyzing complex data are changing what is possible in terms of visualizations, but they are also introducing a new set of challenges. In this chapter, I describe some of the emerging trends in visualization, tell you what to look for in a visualization tool, and explain how to create compelling visualizations that inspire action.

WHY ARE VISUALIZATIONS SO IMPORTANT?

Seventy percent of all sensory receptors are in the eyes, and the brain devotes roughly 30% of its power to vision (Grady 1993; Merieb and Hoehn 2007). Visual displays are powerful because sight is one of the most important ways we learn about the world around us. They support cognition by providing aids to memory. Displays act as visual cues to trigger thought and analysis responses in our brains.

When data is in a table, we are only able to process the data one value at a time. When the same data is put in a graph, we can benefit from the eye's ability to recognize patterns and relationships, interpret them, and register the values as a whole. At first, producing and interpreting graphs may be uncomfortable for analysts who are used to viewing and interpreting spreadsheets. However, as you are called upon to present information to other departments, the general manager, asset manager, or owners, graphs will be much easier for them to interpret as you tell your story.

The following list outlines the benefits of using data visualization over spreadsheets:

Spreadsheets	Data Visualization
End-user focus on isolated figures or values	Allows end-user to visually register values as a whole
Less emphasis on interrelationships between results	Represents interrelationships in an interactive manner

(continued)

(*continued*)

Spreadsheets	Data Visualization
Higher-level expertise needed for analysis and interpretation	Facilitates collaboration and communication through singular representation of the data
Limited data sources	Ability to analyze and incorporate data from numerous sources
Relatively static view	Ability to interact through animation, drill down, and flexible autocharting formats

As data sets become larger, visualizations offer the ability to interpret thousands or even millions of data points. They facilitate collaboration by allowing everyone to start with the same information (such
as a graph of RevPAR for the last month), and interpret it from there.

VISUALIZATION TECHNOLOGY

*At its heart, my work is about how to think clearly and
deeply, using evidence, and all that has to pass through
some presentation state.*

—Edward Tufte, statistician

As data volume, velocity, and variety have increased, so have the tools
to visualize data. Reporting tools have become faster, more flexible,
and more accessible to a wide variety of users. Tools like Tableau, Mi-
croStrategy, and SAS® Visual Analytics provide users the flexibility of
self-service reporting, removing reliance on IT to create reports, and
putting the power into the hands of the end user. Big data reporting
tools can render reports from billions of rows of data in seconds. Users
no longer have to pre-determine what type of graph they want to
create. The visualization tools will render the visual in the format that
makes sense for the data, and let the user tweak it as they'd like.

Furthermore, visualizations are now available on a variety of mobile
devices, so the information can be where the viewer is, instead of the
viewer having to wait until they are in front of a computer. It's becoming
easier for anyone to build mobile apps, deploy information via email,
or create a visualization on the fly during a meeting. This easy access
to information is helping executives make decisions proactively, rather

than waiting for the report to show up on their desks hours or even days after the information is created.

> *One of the analysts in my team happens to be really good at creating reports in our visualization tool. The tool makes it really fast and efficient. One morning, just before lunch, she and I were discussing the challenges we had with this daily email report that went to everyone right up to the CEO. The report frequently was automatically emailed out blank or with data problems before we could correct it, and our CEO would always notice and have to ask about it. It made more sense to turn it into an app, so the C-Level would always have the "latest" info available. I asked my analyst to build the app, and by the time I was back from my lunch meeting, the app was done. If I had to go to IT to build the app, my request would have been put in a queue, and it would have taken months!*
>
> —Executive from a large global hotel company discussing the advantages of self-service reporting

These technological advances are of great benefit to hospitality organizations because they no longer have to be dependent on IT or a vendor to create reports and visualizations. Every system vendor will tell you (if you can get them to admit it) that reports are the most requested enhancement, but they can never create enough reports in the right formats to satisfy the user base. Every company wants to see their data in a slightly different way, and every company wants to see more data than just what is in any given system. Every IT department will also tell you that they have difficulty keeping up with report requests, particularly for ad hoc (onetime) analyses. Now, with these flexible reporting tools, users can create their own visualizations exactly how they want them, both for regular reporting needs and also for ad hoc analyses and special projects.

In the next few sections I describe what you should look for in a visualization tool. I lay out the advances in technology that are available to facilitate ease of access and use, and provide tips for what to look for when you are evaluating a visualization tool.

DATA HANDLING

The technology advances that I described in Chapter 2 are facilitating better access to more data for visualizations as well. Leveraging advances in big data storage, data virtualization, and in-memory processing, visualization tools can now process more data much faster, even creating graphs from billions of rows of data in seconds. As data needs grow and become more complex when you are evaluating a visualization tool, think about the following factors:

- **Speed.** Your analysts and business users need to be able to render complex reports quickly. Many new visualization tools are leveraging in-memory processing (more about this in Chapter 4) to render reports from billions of rows of data in milliseconds. Ask how fast the visualization tool processes data, and ask to see a demonstration on a large and complex data set.

- **Capacity.** Similar to my first point, as data sets get larger, the visualization tool needs to be able to grow with the data set. You do not want to "hit the limit" of your visualization tool just as your users become comfortable using it.

- **Variety.** As your data variety increases, you need to be sure that the data visualization tool can easily handle data in different formats. Can you visualize text data? Click stream data? Location data? Find out what it takes to incorporate your entire breadth of data.

- **Flexibility.** The main reason why reports are so cumbersome for most organizations is the amount of data configuration that is required every time the users want a different view or to drill down at a different level. In the past, IT has had to create OLAP cubes (online analytical processing cubes), which are multidimensional datasets (e.g., sales by region and date) that define the relationship of any data point to others in the set. Any time a user wanted a different relationship defined (sales by region, store, and date), a new OLAP cube would have to be built. Today, this is no longer required. This dramatically increases the flexibility of the tool, and reduces the burden on IT. Further, it is not necessarily even important that the data all be stored in the same database in order to use the same visualization tool (data virtualization, as I discussed in Chapter 2, helps with this).

Functionality

Visualization tools should facilitate the creative and effective dissemination of information. There are many very cool functions available in today's visualization tools that can help you see your organization's data in a very different way. For example, mapping allows you to see data in a geographical layout—making location relationships clearer. Some solutions even allow you to import CAD drawings so you can visualize, for example, sales or usage of the function space, or data about specific machines mapped on the casino floor layout. It is amazing what seeing this data laid out according to location relationships can reveal.

Some solutions will also allow you to create animated visualizations. These show how relationships of data change over time. I have seen two really interesting examples of how this works. One was a graph demonstrating the path, speed, and intensity of hurricanes from the last three decades. The graph was a map of the United States, and a bubble represented the hurricane with the size and color indicating intensity. When the graph initiated, you could watch hurricanes track up the East Coast of the United States, gaining and losing intensity as time passed. You could visually understand the impact of a major hurricane as you saw a much larger bubble track farther, or hover over an area for longer than previous bubbles. The other animated graph was a map of the results of the 2008 Democratic Party primaries. It showed Hillary Clinton and Barack Obama's popularity ratings in the months of the primary elections. The size of the bubbles represented the polling results (what percentage of Americans would vote for that candidate if the election were that day), the x-axis was time, and the y-axis was the number of delegates each had won. It was really interesting to watch the bubbles go neck and neck, trading places as time went on, and then finally Obama's bubble gaining in size and position as he secured the nomination. Obviously, both of these examples were built more to demonstrate the animation than to gain insight, but it was very compelling how they were able to clearly show the relationships more so than a static graph would.

Most visualization tools provide purely business intelligence capability. You can create charts and graphs that facilitate drill down, splitting, or historical trends. They help you detect historical patterns in the data and uncover relationships. However, they are limited to understanding the past, not predicting the future. I speak more about the difference between descriptive and predictive analytics in Chapter 4. Some visualization tools do provide basic predictive analytics, which puts even more power in the hands of the analysts and business users. Business users can uncover basic statistical relationships or build a high level forecast without needing to call on the analysts. If they discover relationships that require a more in-depth analysis, they can then take the project to an analyst for further investigation.

Usability

Users need data visualization for a variety of business intelligence and analytics activities, including reporting, scorecards, operational alerting, data discovery, and analysis. Rather than just giving users "new toys" to play with, organizations should examine how they can match visualization technologies and practices to user requirements. Across the board, however, a key element in the success of visualization is data interaction; users need broad capabilities for manipulating data, including the ability to drill down, cross cut, slice, and dice data directly from graphical interfaces.

For many organizations, dashboards take the center stage for data visualizations, especially those created for the executive team. The most effective dashboards display only the key metrics that matter most to the information consumer, they are not crowded with lots of dials and figures. They display the metrics in such a way as to facilitate comparison against each other or to a threshold. This allows the viewer to quickly and easily determine which metrics need to be managed immediately, and which are operating within expected parameters. The dashboards should also allow for drill down, should the user want a more detailed view.

Clearly, dashboards and preconfigured reports are very useful for keeping a finger on the pulse of the business. However, visualizations are also useful to explore unknown data sets to uncover trends or patterns in the data. A good visualization tool also facilitates this activity, which can be a crucial first step in a deeper analysis. Visualizing reservation data over time can quickly illustrate an increasing or declining trend, and running a visual correlation matrix, where the strength of the correlation is indicated by color, makes it very easy to identify significant relationships. Exploratory data visualization can decrease the amount of time it takes to construct an analysis, because the business user has already detected patterns and identified key variables. The analyst can pick it up from there, without having to define the problem and also do the preliminary data investigation.

The other important benefit of a visualization tool is that it facilitates access to data and analytics for a wide variety of resources across the organization, putting power in the hands of the end user. Analytics is no longer the domain of highly specialized resources or the IT organization. Wizard-driven interfaces, graphical displays, and automated analysis mean that one no longer needs to know how to code, and one does not have to have an advanced degree in analytics to conduct some light analysis. This democratization of analytics changes the organization from supporting an isolated, specialized function to building a widespread analytics culture.

Some would argue that moving an organization toward fully self-service analytics, where everyone in the organization who might need or want it has access to data and analytics, could end up being counterproductive. Users without a basic understanding of numerical relationships and statistical techniques could very easily draw incorrect conclusions from comparing mismatched data. This is certainly a danger. As organizations move toward more access to data and analytics through data visualization, a good deal of care needs to be taken to ensure that the data is prepared properly, and that users are restricted only to data and techniques that will "keep them out of trouble," so to speak. In fact, IT may need to put more work into creating these environments than they did when only the specialists had access to the information. Alternatively, the organization may decide to narrow the group that has freeform access to the data and restrict other users to certain types of data or only preconfigured reports. The time spent preparing the data, regardless of how widespread access is, will be well worth it, however, as it will speed up organizational decision making and allow the specialized resources, including IT, to focus on their particular tasks.

VISUALIZATION TYPES

Many visualization tools provide *autographing* or *autocharting* capabilities. This means that the system will recommend a graph based on what it knows about the data and its relationships, rather than the user having to define those relationships. Even with this automation, I still think it is important to define a few visualizations (both popular and new), and give suggestions of when they are best used. Some of this may appear basic, but you would be surprised how often mistakes are made even with the most common graph types.

Bar charts. Generally used to present and compare data, bar charts are most useful when it is important to show changes in *magnitude*, the size of certain elements relative to others. They can be horizontal or vertical. For a horizontal bar graph, the *x*-axis contains a category, so it doesn't have a scale, and the *y*-axis is the measurement, so it does have a scale (this relationship is reversed for vertical bar graphs). You can compare several elements at once—for example, sales by category by year across multiple years—but bar charts can get complex if you add too many elements. Grouped charts (Figure 3.2) present individual elements separately on the *x*-axis. They are useful when you want to compare each element in the category and also compare across categories. The grouping makes it harder to tell the difference in the total of each group. In a stacked bar chart, the elements are stacked on top of each other for each category, facilitating easier comparison of the total,

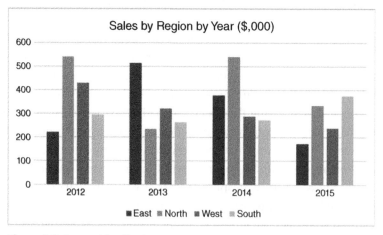

Figure 3.2 Grouped Bar Chart

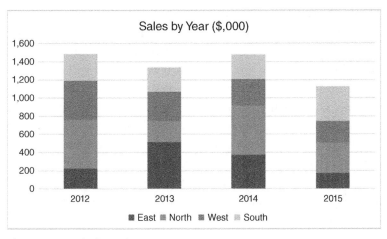

Figure 3.3 Stacked Bar Chart

although the individual elements become harder to compare to each other. Figure 3.3 shows a stacked bar chart.

Histograms. Histograms are a specialized form of bar chart where the data represent continuous rather than discrete categories. They show frequency or the percentage of time that the category shows up in your data. Because the continuous category may have a large number of possible values for the data, the values are typically grouped. For example, you could graph the number of loyalty guests by age range (20–29, 30–39, 40–49, etc.). Unlike the bar charts I just described, both the *x*-axis and the *y*-axis of histograms have scales. The histogram represents the *distribution* of the values in your data set. Figure 3.4 shows a histogram.

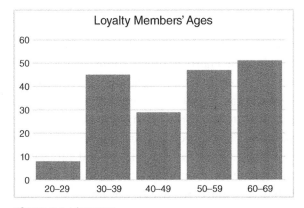

Figure 3.4 Histogram

Line charts. Line charts are also used to present and compare data. However, these charts are most useful when changes in the direction of data are the most important relationship to display. Line graphs typically display a comparison between two variables plotted on the horizontal (*x*) and vertical (*y*) axes. Generally, the *x*-axis measures time, whereas the *y*-axis usually represents the quantity. Therefore, line graphs are most typically used to display time-series information, where the *x*-axis represents the continuous variable (like time), and the *y*-axis represents the measurement (scale). As with bar charts, multiple lines representing different categories to compare across quantity and time can be used, but too many categories can become difficult to view. Figure 3.5 shows a line chart.

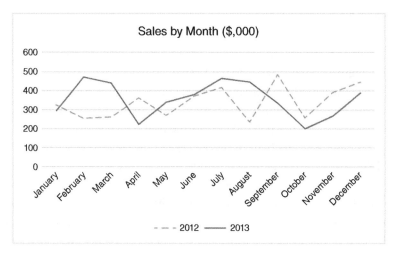

Figure 3.5 Line Chart

Pie charts. Pie charts are used to represent categorical data that represent parts of a whole. The values of the categories are a percentage of the entire value. Pie charts frequently replace a simple table where a grand total is broken out into categories. Pie charts are very easy for the "nonnumerical" person to understand, but they can get overly complex or difficult to interpret when there are too many categories (see my visualization tips section later in this chapter). The percentages must always add up to 100%. That may sound silly to mention, but trust me, look at enough infographics and sooner or later you'll notice some bad behavior. Figure 3.6, while not my favorite pie chart (my favorite is at the beginning of this chapter), is a good example of one.

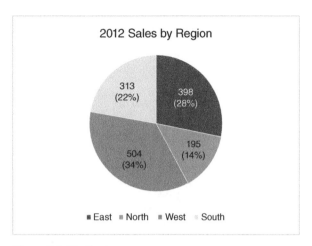

Figure 3.6 Pie Chart

Many in the data visualization community argue vehemently against pie charts. They point out that pie charts can very easily mask important relationships. Depending on how you size and format these charts, they can make misleading representations. I suggest reading the white paper I reference at the end of this chapter, "Save the Pie for Dessert" by Stephen Few, who is the founder of Perceptual Edge and a visualization expert. This will give you a good perspective on the problems with pie charts.

Scatter plots. Scatter plots are used to show the relationship between two different quantitative measures taken on the same type of object or individual. Each dot represents a single observation or individual. For example, you could plot the heights and weights of a group of people, or their ages and blood pressures. The scatter plot is most useful to see if there is any systematic or causal relationship between the two measurements. Typically, regression lines (I will cover this in the next chapter) are added to see if there is a relationship between the two measures. Figure 3.7 is a scatter plot showing the average daily rate and rooms sold for a 500-room hotel for each night in 2012. Ideally, if the revenue manager were doing their job, there would be a positive relationship between these two measures. What do you think about this revenue manager's ability to manage price according to demand (is it about the same as my ability to generate random numbers)?

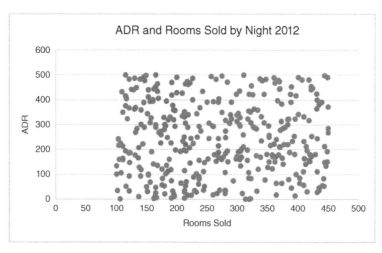

Figure 3.7 Scatter Plot

Heat maps. Heat maps are a graphical representation of data where the individual values contained in a matrix are represented as colors. The intensity or shade of the color visually represents the values of the category, and generally more intense colors indicate higher values. There are two kinds of heat maps. One overlays on an image like a map (think about radar mapping for weather forecasts) or a webpage (where the intensity of colors represents the amount of views in that section). The other is known as a tree map, which is a way of displaying hierarchical data using colored, nested rectangles. Figure 3.8 shows a tree map of changes

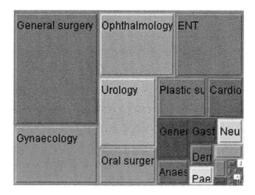

Figure 3.8 "Heatmap incito" by I, Colinmcfarlane
Source: Licensed under CC BY 2.5 via Wikimedia Commons, https://commons.wikimedia.org/wiki/ File:Heatmap_incito.png#/media/File:Heatmap_ incito.png.

in wait times for patients of English Primary Care Trusts. The shadings represent positive and negative changes (darker color is an increase in wait times), and the size represents the number of patients served.

Sankey diagrams. Sankey diagrams demonstrate a flow by representing the volume or amount of flow by the width of an arrow. They are traditionally used to diagram the flow of energy or materials through a system or the flow of costs through a process. More recently, they have been used to diagram flow of traffic through a website, and can be a very strong visual indicator of how guests are using the website, and where they might be getting hung up. There could possibly be a use case for using them to display pedestrian traffic patterns through the hotel or casino property, to identify opportunities for marketing or operational improvements. One of the more well-known Sankey diagrams (although it technically predates the official naming of Sankey), is Charles Minard's Map of Napoleon's Russian Campaign of 1812. It is a flow map, overlaying a Sankey diagram onto a geographical map. The flow is the number of soldiers in Napoleon's army. You can clearly see the impact of the march on his numbers, and why he got into trouble (Figure 3.9).

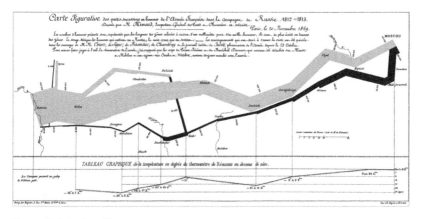

Figure 3.9 Sankey Diagram

CREATING POWERFUL VISUALIZATIONS

Routine reports are created from a variety of sources and tend to be generated and distributed automatically once they are built, but analysts will always be called upon to present a synthesis of information from various sources or the results of a special analysis. Access to a flexible visualization tool is not enough in these scenarios. It is also important to understand how to create a simple but powerful visualization to support your story and inspire action.

Here are six tips for creating visualizations:

1. **Determine the purpose of your visualization.** It sounds simple to say, but rather than dumping a bunch of data into a graph, start by defining exactly what point you want the visualization to support. Exploration happens during the analysis; when you create visuals for a presentation, you need to be more purposeful and more streamlined.

2. **Consider your audience.** How well do they know the subject? What information are they expecting to get out of your presentation? What type of questions will they ask? Do they like to dig into the data or just want the highlights?

3. **Pick the visual that best represents the data.** Flashy is not always better. The visual needs to clearly demonstrate the story in the data, not mask it with fancy graphic effects. I'll show some examples later of what could work and what definitely doesn't.

4. **Keep your style and formatting consistent.** Viewers can get easily distracted by formatting inconsistencies. They will struggle to process the changes and lose the point of your story. When you go from graph to graph, stay consistent so viewers can stay with you.

5. **Don't forget to label.** Seriously. There is nothing more frustrating than looking at a graph and not knowing what it represents. Label everything so you can spend time on the interpretation of the information, not interpretation of the graph.

6. **Show comparisons.** Multiple visualizations, either on the same graph or near each other, are a very powerful way to make a point. Without cluttering the visualization, try to get comparisons on the same visualization. If this is not possible, remember tips 4 and 5, so that when you move from graph to graph, the viewer can easily interpret the comparison.

Think carefully about how the data and visualizations are connected. We default to certain chart formats when we see certain

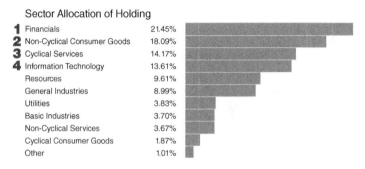

Sector Allocation of Holding				
▪ FINANCIALS	21.45%	▪ NON-CYCLICAL CONSUMER GOODS	18.09%	
▪ CYCLICAL SERVICES	14.17%	▪ INFORMATION TECHNOLOGY	13.61%	
▪ RESOURCES	9.61%	▪ GENERAL INDUSTRIES	8.99%	
▪ UTILITIES	3.83%	▪ BASIC INDUSTRIES	3.70%	
▪ NON-CYCLICAL SERVICES	3.67%	▪ CYCLICAL CONSUMER GOODS	1.87%	

Figure 3.10 Traditional Pie Chart
Source: Image from Visual Business Intelligence, www.perceptualedge.com.

Sector Allocation of Holding

1	Financials	21.45%
2	Non-Cyclical Consumer Goods	18.09%
3	Cyclical Services	14.17%
4	Information Technology	13.61%
	Resources	9.61%
	General Industries	8.99%
	Utilities	3.83%
	Basic Industries	3.70%
	Non-Cyclical Services	3.67%
	Cyclical Consumer Goods	1.87%
	Other	1.01%

Figure 3.11 Stacked Bar Chart
Source: Image from Visual Business Intelligence, www.perceptualedge.com.

kinds of data, such as percentages. These default formats might not be the best representation of the information. Consider Figure 3.10 and Figure 3.11.

Figure 3.10 is really more of a spreadsheet with a picture next to it. It is not easy to determine how the two pieces of information (numbers and picture) are related. The pie chart is so small that it's difficult to relate the percentages to each other. Now look at Figure 3.11. It's the same information, but in a stacked bar chart. This is a visualization. The information is connected to the picture, and it is crystal clear what the relationships among the data points are.

The two figures that follow are an example of a situation where "flashy" formatting is actually distracting from the main point of the story. In the first picture (Figure 3.12), the 3-D effect masks the real relationship among the departmental expense categories, and the pointy bars make it much more difficult to see the exact values. In Figure 3.13, a simple bar chart helps to make the relationships clear.

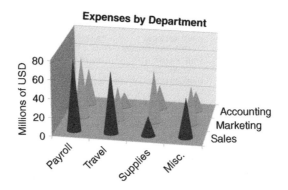

Figure 3.12 Flashy Effects

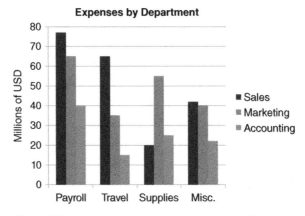

Figure 3.13 Simple Bar Chart for Clearer Relationships

CASE STUDY: VISUALIZATIONS IN HOSPITALITY, DAVID TURNBULL, SNAPSHOT ANALYTICS

CASE STUDY

I caught up with David Turnbull, Cofounder and Chief Operating Officer of SnapShot, to get his perspective on the state of hospitality data visualization and the opportunities available to hotels and casinos. Located in Berlin, SnapShot provides a cloud-based hotel analytics tool that presents a comprehensive overview of a hotel's data in a powerful yet intuitive dashboard.

Here is my interview with David.

1. What kind of data, data visualization, and analytic capabilities does the average hotel or casino have?

Considering the volume of performance, market, user, and customer-generated data created on a daily basis, as the demand management chart in Figure 3.14 displays, hotels are extremely high producers of data. Yet, they perform below par in terms of analytics capability, due to the sheer scale and complexity of their data and technology infrastructure.

In 2016, the current trend is to convert existing historical facing reporting into "visuals" due to the growing influence of off-the-peg business intelligence solutions like QlikView and Tableau.

Hotels have traditionally, from a data and technology planning perspective, been highly (PMS) vendor reliant. This, of course, reflects, especially in Europe, the highly fragmented and independent nature of the

Demand Management Cycle

Figure 3.14 Demand Management for Hotels

(continued)

(continued)

market. The impact of this is that the majority of data is collected, stored, and analyzed in Excel with very low focus on visualization.

Analytic capability is typically outsourced to third-party vendors, such as descriptive tools like Rate Shoppers or first- and second-generation predictive tools like Revenue Management Systems. However, these are typically confined to one source or channel of data, highly focused on historical performance as the main driver, and are of use for a limited or specific subset of the organization's audience.

The problems operators, owners, and asset managers are actually trying to resolve would be more accurately handled by focusing first on data warehousing and data aggregation, as taking this approach would force stakeholders to determine:

- What types of data do I have (big, small, structured, unstructured)?
- How do I currently collect and store it?
- What manual and automated processes do I have to analyze the data?
- What manual and automated processes do I have to predict and implement the decision?

The average hotel or casino should be able to lay out a technology and distribution landscape that looks like the one in Figure 3.15, but it probably looks more like the one in Figure 3.16.

2. When you have conversations with your clients, what kinds of capabilities tend to be on their roadmap?

Sadly, the perceived "OTA fight" in recent years means independents through global brands are often distracted by short-term hacks to try and restore the balance between OTA and brand.com, when in reality a deeper and more fundamental review of their business model, customer behavior, and intended technology infrastructure should be conducted.

What is understood is that hospitality businesses are being strangled by the lack of a single source of the truth platforms that all stakeholders can access. This growing demand for centralized access to data has

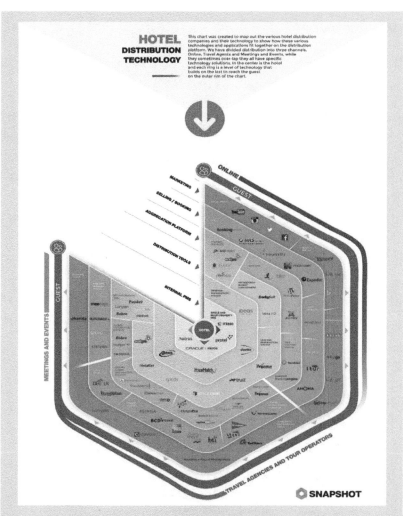

Figure 3.15 Technology and Distribution Landscape Ideal
Source: Image courtesy of Anton Hell, HIT Consult.

increased the implementation of organization-wide analytics tools focused on financial (bottom line) performance.

These financial tools provide much needed 360-degree oversight of the business. However, they typically rely on data from one source (PMS), focus only on historical performance, and are too generic to appeal to all stakeholders (commercial, operations, finance, management, ownership, asset management).

(continued)

(continued)

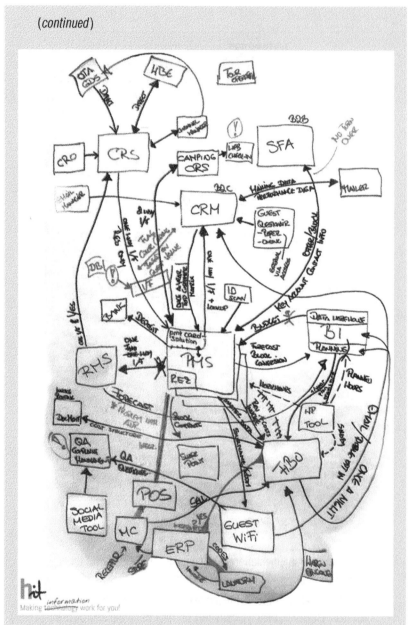

Figure 3.16 Technology and Distribution Landscape Actual—Hotel Picasso
Source: Image courtesy of Anton Hell, HIT Consult.

3. What are the most sophisticated companies doing in the area of data, data visualization, and analytics?

Christian Chabot, CEO of Tableau, one of the market leaders in data visualization, recently said that data analytics software will soon be as commonplace as Excel, which implies that these tools will in the near future become highly commoditized.

The competitive edge will be given to those who can use this data the fastest. Accor Hotels' Senior Vice President, Global Revenue Management, Pricing, and Analytics, Agnes Roquefort, said, "It isn't big data we're after but fast data," and that is exactly where hotels need to be looking.*

If you look at the technology revamps being conducted by brands like Accor and IHG, through to smaller innovators like citizenM, as of the publication of this book, they have all recently gone through significant data aggregation projects.

These companies' main focus has been on building in-house platforms that both integrate data without direct reliance on a third-party vendor and have useful application interface layers on top for easy connection with relevant technology and service providers.

By doing so, they are starting to define the frequency and perspective of their data and analytics needs into clear buckets of requirements:

- Predictive analytics (forecasts)
- Streaming analytics (monitoring and problem detection)
- Streaming business intelligence (real-time dashboards)
- Reporting

4. Where do you think the biggest opportunity for hotels and casinos is in this area? What are most companies missing out on?

As an industry, we do appear to have our heads stuck in the sand, failing to recognize that the insights gained from our current tech infrastructure and Excel approach to storage and analysis are disproportionate to the time and resources spent. A hotel's ability to make solid, informed decisions is based on the relevant team's skill with a particular program, rather than their experience and knowledge of the industry.

---

* Martin Soler, "How to Choose Big Data Analytics Tools for a Hotel," SnapShot, March 1, 2016, http://blog.snapshot.travel/how-to-choose-analytics-and-data-visualization-tools-for-a-hotel.

(*continued*)

(*continued*)

Lennert de Jong, Chief Commercial Officer of citizenM, recently said, "Data becomes the glue of the organization and I see it as the job of the current leaders to fix this. We should not have data discrepancies between our finance systems, PMS, forecasting systems, and CRM. Why would finance only report on occupancy, ADR, and distribution costs, and the marketing department on repeat figures, demographics, et cetera?"*

The bigger opportunity for hotels and casinos is to implement data aggregation and analytics tools, not to produce fancier management reporting (merely a byproduct) but to also enable them to take action on a much wider range of data sources.

This increases the focus on real-time, perishable data that when converted into insights, directly influences the customer experience, such as by predicting potential issues and bottlenecks in the operation before they are reported back by the customer.

5. How do you advise your clients to get started in this area?

This is a massive education process, and it starts at the owner and C-level throughout the organization. As our Hotel Picasso diagram in Figure 3.16 demonstrated, this is a great exercise on how you can educate management teams about their current technology infrastructure and where the bottleneck(s) exist—they all lead back typically to a blackbox with a three-letter acronym.

At SnapShot, education was the first initiative we launched back in 2013. From the grassroots level (hotel schools) to the C-level, we have developed a series of online and offline education bootcamps and MOOCs [massive open online courses] (via Coursera and our university partner, ESSEC, in Paris) to drive the message and need for data and customer designed infrastructure planning.

On an operational level, it's important to get senior leadership at the property and regional level to recognize the pains by asking simple questions like, "How many versions of your 2016 budget did you create?" or "How many collective hours per day are spent by the reservations, sales, revenue, and banqueting departments daily on data collection and preparation?"

---

* "The Future Is Now: Lennert de Jong on Predictive Analytics for Hotels," SnapShot, April 12, 2016, http://blog.snapshot.travel/predictive-analytics-for-hotels-the-future-is-now-lennert-de-jong.

To promote our SnapShot Analytics tool, we ask hotel general managers to get their commercial teams to work together on an analytics exercise as follows:

- Select yesterday stay date
- Collect and prepare all available data related to the hotel's performance
- Perform an analysis of the data
- Determine the findings and trends
- Visualize the findings and trends
- Consider the requirements to repeat this exercise for the past and future 90-day windows

The objective for the team is to review this exercise and discuss how easy it was to visualize the findings and present the data in a cross-dimensional manner that immediately gains understanding and promotes action.

6. What kind of data should hotels and casinos focus on collecting for maximum impact?

In an OTA-dominated business, the service delivery, customer experience, and public reputation of a hotel are the key drivers in the generation of first-time and repeat business. As part of any hotel's or casino's redesign of its technology infrastructure, I would recommend that hotels place significant investment into the collection, storage, and analysis of in-house customer behavior data, both retrospective and real time, with a focus on providing unique (branded) and consistently high customer experiences.

A significant investment is required to capture this data (sensors, RFID); however, it is the starting point in the journey (supported by data scientists) to learn the fundamental behaviors and needs of the customers and to take action to deliver superior guest experiences.

The knock-on effect of this on reputation, pricing, as well as augmented real-time analytics to support and boost direct booking conversion will all contribute (mid to long term) on boosting direct conversion.

7. What kind of technology would you recommend for a typical hotel and casino to support their data, data visualization, and analytical efforts?

(continued)

(*continued*)

Advanced generic tools like Tableau are ideal because they already arrive as an Excel killer with a wide range of features and can theoretically be implemented by people with low knowledge of analytics tools. But this is also where they are the hardest to implement since using a generic tool means you have to do all the heavy lifting yourself. For example, choosing which stats to show, what's important and what's not, whether the information should be shown as a pie chart, a bar chart, or in a column may all seem trivial when selecting a solution software but becomes hard work when you actually set them up.

When considering a generic analytics solution for your hotel, make sure you thoroughly investigate whether the tool can be customized to every potential metric you may want to measure. The more you know before starting, the less likely you'll be to get stuck later.

On the other hand, hotel-specific analytics solutions (such as SnapShot Analytics, Juyo Analytics, and LodgIQ) have already taken care of the hard part. They're designed to present relevant information in the best possible way. Hotel-specific analytics solutions can save time because they are designed to handle the difficulties of aggregating hotel data. These analytics providers also know the industry, so the visualizations are designed to represent data in the most useful way for hotel management.

What's more, the better hospitality-specific analytics solutions also have ongoing partnerships with PMS providers and other data sources, vastly accelerating the implementation process.

A final note on generic versus hotel-specific analytics solutions should be made on the topic of predictive analytics and prescriptive analytics. Hotel-specific solutions often already have either predictive analytics or prescriptive analytics built in. This creates an opportunity for hotels to develop massive (and highly actionable) business intelligence.

Hotel-specific solutions are usually the better option for small to medium-size hotels and groups. Generic tools are customizable, but they're often challenging to customize or integrate with data sources like PMSs, a job normally only available to very large hotel chains that have the resources to launch such a project. Hospitality-specific data analytics tools are faster and cheaper to set up and are vastly more powerful and responsive.

CONCLUSION

Data visualization tools are putting more power in the hands of the business user, while reducing the burden on IT to create ad hoc reports and maintain dashboards. Advances in technology, including complex data management, are facilitating more access to more data than ever before. New capabilities like mapping and animation, as well as a self-service approach, are empowering the business to explore relationships and answer questions without requiring support from IT or analytics.

Remember, the data is what it is. You are the one who puts context around it. When you get good at providing that context, you will transform what people think. This is, obviously, a big responsibility. Darrell Huff said, "If you torture the data long enough, it will confess to anything." This is scarily true. It's up to you to make sure you are maintaining the neutrality of the data. Let it tell you what it is; don't force it. Not that you can't take some license to show it in a light that supports your story, but be careful, and be respectful.

The concept that a broader set of individuals across the organization can have access to data and analytics that were formerly the domain of IT or data scientists is known as "democratization of data." With the clear shortage of data science talent, the idea that a broader set of resources can perform some of these functions is quite attractive to organizations today.

Recently, the term "citizen data scientist" has become a popular way to describe the persona that is enabled by the access to data analytics that I describe in this chapter. The citizen data scientist is not necessarily formally trained in business intelligence or statistics and might not be in a role purely involving data analytics. They do understand the business and are familiar with the data. Now they are able to perform data manipulation and basic analyses through wizard-driven, highly visual interfaces. Most experts agree that enabling citizen data scientists will not replace the need for educated and trained data scientists, but it will greatly increase the efficiency of data preparation and speed up routine analyses. The right tools are what make this possible. There is an interesting blog post on this topic, titled "How the Citizen Data Scientist Will Democratize Big Data," at www.forbes.com.[3] Think about whether enabling citizen data scientists will help you to overcome resource challenges in your organization.

Much of what I described in this chapter is about looking back on historical data rather than predicting what may happen in the future. In the next chapter, I will describe the difference between this historical view and predictive analytics and introduce you to the types of advanced analytics that will help your organization move from reactive to proactive decision making.

ADDITIONAL RESOURCES

- 7 Considerations for Visualization Deployment, www.sas.com/en_us/whitepapers/iia-data-visualization-7-considerations-for-deployment-106892.html.
- Visualization Best Practices (All Analytics), www.allanalytics.com/archives.asp?section_id=3365.
- Great reference site for visual inspiration: Perceptual Edge, www.perceptualedge.com.
- Stephen Few, "Save the Pies for Dessert," Perceptual Edge, August 2007, www.perceptualedge.com/articles/visual_business_intelligence/save_the_pies_for_dessert.pdf.

NOTES

1. Portions of this chapter taken from Kelly McGuire, Telling a Story with Data, Hotel Business Review, www.hotelexecutive.com/business_review/3723/telling-a-story-with-data.
2. From HSMAI Insights Video Series "How Will Revenue Management Look Different in 2020?" www.hsmai.org/knowledge/multimedia.cfm?ItemNumber=22136.
3. Bernard Marr, "How the Citizen Data Scientist Will Democratize Big Data," Forbes, April 1, 2016, www.forbes.com/sites/bernardmarr/2016/04/01/howthe-citizen-data-scientist-will-democratize-big-data/#257f316e4557.

CHAPTER 4

From Reactive to Proactive Decision Making: Advanced Analytics in Action

An unsophisticated forecaster uses statistics as a drunken man uses lampposts—for support rather than illumination.

—Andrew Lang, author

Data only has value when you can turn it from information to insight. That is the topic of this chapter. All of the best data management solutions with the latest, most flexible visualization tools will only provide so much insight. True insight is derived when you can use all of that data to uncover key relationships and employ them to predict and plan for the future. That is the role of advanced analytics. Advanced analytics are complex mathematical algorithms. Many managers suffered through their calculus and statistics classes in high school and college, if they even had to take any, and haven't wanted to look back since. The very idea of advanced analytics can be intimidating. Now that you have a vision for a strategic analytic culture, established in Chapter 1, an understanding of how to capture, store, and process your data from Chapter 2, and have learned about opportunities in data visualization in Chapter 3, this chapter will help you get past this intimidation, and give you enough of an understanding of the techniques and their value to help you guide your organization toward a competitive advantage gleaned from the smart use of your second most important asset, your data.

You don't have to have a master's or PhD in statistics to understand where and how advanced analytics can help your business. However, you do have to be a master's or PhD in statistics to build a model from scratch, with the correct method, parameters, data formats, and statistical significance. Some of these techniques involve really hard math. That's what the statisticians are for. However, they don't know your business like you do. My goal in this chapter and the ones that follow is to help you have better conversations with your analysts, vendors, and team regarding analytics projects. I hope to help you identify what kinds of skill sets will best support your analytics program, and to find the right talent to fill those jobs. I define techniques in business language, describe how they are best applied, and give examples. You don't have to build the models, but you should be able to have a conversation with the people who build them for you—and you should be able to make sure the models are doing what your analysts said they would do.

REACTIVE TO PROACTIVE DECISION MAKING

Executives and managers have many questions about their businesses. What happened? Where is the problem? How many, how often, where? What actions are needed? What if these trends continue? What's the best that can happen? What will happen next? Why is this happening?

If you think about it, the first four questions are really descriptive-type questions. Of course, you want to understand what sales were last night, how many covers there were in the restaurant, what the labor costs are, and if you're performing to budget. These questions are very important to keep a finger on the pulse of business, and to evaluate whether programs you put in place are having the impact you expected. However, these are *reactive* questions. To answer them you look at historical data, a snapshot of the past. They will help you fight a fire, but they are limited to past performance.

The second four questions involve concepts like "What if?," "Why?," "What's next?," and "What's the best that can happen?" These questions are predictive in nature. They are forward looking to help you anticipate trends and identify opportunities. Answering these questions can give you a competitive advantage, and it is these questions that are answered by advanced analytics.

The diagram in Figure 4.1 represents a continuum of analytic capability from data to optimal decisions. The first six bubbles represent reactive decision making based on descriptive analytics. I addressed the data foundation in Chapter 2, and talked about the reporting and alerts in Chapter 3. For this chapter and the remaining chapters in the book, I'm going to talk primarily about the last four bubbles. As you move from the reactive bubbles into the proactive bubbles, the organization starts to become more forward looking. Techniques like statistical analysis, forecasting, predictive modeling, and optimization add tremendous value, but are more complex and require different technology and skill sets to execute.

FROM REACTIVE TO PROACTIVE WITH ANALYTICS

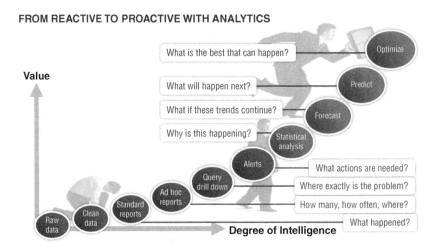

Figure 4.1 Analytics Continuum from *Competing on Analytics*
Source: Davenport and Harris 2007.

Let's discuss each of the proactive bubbles in more depth. In the following sections, I provide a definition and some key points about each of the advanced analytics categories in the bubbles. This will help you to differentiate these techniques and begin to understand how they can be used. Then, in the remaining chapters of the book, I provide function-by-function examples of where these techniques can be applied. By the end of the book, you should have the tools to build a roadmap toward a strategic analytic culture.

STATISTICAL ANALYSIS

There are two main types of statistical analyses, *descriptive* and *inferential*. Descriptive statistics is basically a summary of the characteristics of the *population* represented by your data. This includes things like counts, maximum, minimum, and most frequent values, averages (mean), median, distribution (percentage breakdown), and standard deviation. Mean and standard deviation are generally used for continuous data (revenue, guest counts), whereas percentages are generally used to describe categorical data (gender, hotel class). Most businesspeople are quite comfortable with descriptive statistics and can interpret them properly. They are useful for understanding some basic demographics of your data, to *describe* your data, but they do not allow you to make any predictions, conclusions, or *inferences* about that data. Descriptive statistics form the basis for business intelligence.

Inferential statistics are used to draw meaningful conclusions about the population or scenario that your data represents. The important concept behind inferential statistics is that you are not always able to collect information about every member of a population (i.e., every potential guest of your hotel). Inferential statistics allow us to make generalizations about a population based on what can be learned from a subset, or sample. These inferences could be answering yes or no questions (hypothesis testing), describing associations within the data (correlations), estimating numerical values from the data (estimation), or modeling relationships within the data (regression). Care needs to be taken when gathering the sample of the population, because, if not carefully chosen, the group could contain some bias that could cause errors in your interpretations. For example, if you ask only guests who took cabs from the airport if the hotel was easy to find, you will miss the opinions of the people who had to navigate to the hotel for the first time themselves.

Before I describe these inferential statistics methods, I want to take a minute to talk about standard deviation (in case your memories of your high school math class have gotten a bit fuzzy over the years). Standard deviation is a very important statistical concept. The standard deviation represents the amount of variability in the data, or how "spread out" the observations are from each other and from the mean (average). A low standard deviation means that the individual observations in the data are relatively close to the mean. A higher standard deviation means that the values can be quite spread out. Consider two data sets: one with the values of [0, 0, 0, 100, 100, 100], and one with the values of [45, 45, 45, 55, 55, 55]. The mean of both data sets is 50: (300/6). However, the standard deviations are quite different. For data set 1 it's 54 and for data set 2 it's 5.4.[1]

Why is this important? Well, if the values represented the high temperature across six days, you'd need a very different wardrobe for each set of days, even though the average high temperature was 50 degrees. To use a potentially more relevant example to this conversation, if you were comparing two data sets with a mean that was relatively the same, you might be tempted to treat the two populations they came from the same, or assess their success similarly. If the standard deviation was high, you would be missing the fact that there was wide variation in the sample set, indicating inconsistency or diversity in your population. For example, if you noticed that average check-in times at the front desk for the morning shift versus the afternoon shift were relatively the same, and stopped there, you might miss the fact that the afternoon shift was relatively consistent across all the employees, but the morning shift had one stellar employee that was very fast, pulling the mean down, whereas her less well-trained colleagues were creating long lines while struggling through basic functions in the PMS.

Standard deviation is important in inferential statistics because it is used to assess how confident the researcher can be in the results of their statistical analysis. Most statistical analysis is based on predicting an expected value of the variable of interest. The standard deviation is used to describe the margin of error around that expected value (again, formulas are not critical for this conversation, but a quick Internet search will get you plenty of information on this). You need to ask for that margin of error, also called a confidence interval, when you are evaluating the results of an analysis. If the data is particularly volatile, or variable, sometimes referred to as *noisy*, it is more difficult to be confident in that expected value.

Hypothesis testing (yes/no questions) involves determining if there is enough statistical evidence to say whether something is or is not the case. For example, you could ask the question "Are guests more satisfied after the renovation?" (by comparing average satisfaction before and after a renovation), or "Do parties of two have a higher average check than parties of four?" Hypotheses tests are generally measured using a p-value, which is a test of whether your data provides enough support to suggest that "yes" answer. Generally, statisticians look for a p-value that is less than 0.05. A p-value of 0.05 says that you are 95% confident that the answer is yes, and smaller p-values increase the confidence. P-value is a good metric to remember. It is used in many statistical analyses and will be something that your analysts should know and be able to report to you. As you can imagine, there is a good deal of research about where the p-value comes from and how it is calculated. You can look that up if you want. The important point is that it's one of those things that if you ask about it, your analysts will assume you know way more than you may know, and won't try to put one over on you.[2]

Correlation measures the relationship, or association, between two variables. In technical terms, it is used to describe the strength and direction of the linear relationship between two quantitative variables. For example, there could be a correlation between the number of spa treatments and lunch covers in the restaurant or a correlation between the hotel's aggregate rating and the average daily rate. Correlations can either be *positive*, whereas one variable increases so does the other, or *negative*, whereas one variable decreases the other increases. The key metric associated with correlation is the correlation coefficient, which is positive or negative depending on the relationship between the variables, and will be a number between negative one and one. The higher the absolute value of the number, the stronger the correlation.

One of the biggest rookie mistakes in all of statistics is interpreting a correlation between two variables as causal—in other words, after running a correlation analysis between ADR (average daily rate) and aggregate ratings, and finding a significant relationship, saying that high aggregate ratings cause a high ADR. Correlation only proves a relationship, an association, and does not imply any causation. Be very careful with this yourself, and pay attention to what others are telling you. You will see this happen all over the place!

Estimation comes up with an *effect size* estimate and a *confidence interval* (low value/high value) around the estimate when an outcome is relatively unknown. For example, there are many unknowns associated with the duration of a large project like a renovation. Estimation could take a statistical look at other similar projects and provide an estimate of the project duration, with a confidence interval that summarized the range of likely values for the duration. When the confidence interval is statistically derived, it means that there is a 95% chance that the project duration will fall within that range, and the effect size estimate is statistically the most likely duration. In estimation, the confidence interval replaces the p-value (if you think about it, it's a similar concept, turning the p-value into a range of data instead of a singular probability). The trick with estimation is that if there is a lot of "noise" in the data—a high standard deviation—then the confidence interval, which is calculated based on the standard deviation, can be so large that it is not very usable. This is why whenever your analyst is giving you an estimate of a value, you should ask for the confidence interval. If it is wide, then the estimate is not very likely to be accurate, and you better plan against the risk of high variability. If it is narrow, then you can be more confident about planning against that value.

Regression is one of the most commonly used statistical analysis techniques. It is a mathematical model that estimates the relationships among two or more variables. In technical terms, regression establishes the way a dependent variable (the variable you want to predict) is impacted by one or more independent variables (the "predictor" variables). Unlike in correlation, with regression the point is to show causality, that the independent variables have some influence over the value of the dependent variable, or that changes in the independent variables cause changes in the dependent variable.[3] See Figure 4.2.

Regression is used when you want to understand the relationship between the independent variables and the dependent variable or when you want to use the independent variables to predict the dependent variable.[4] For example, you might want to understand what variables are most strongly related to guest satisfaction. In this example, overall satisfaction is the dependent variable, and the independent variables are things like satisfaction with the room, price paid, how long it took to check in, which services they used, how long they stayed, or how many times the guest visited. For this analysis, the analyst includes every variable that your business knowledge tells you could be a driver of guest satisfaction, and the output shows which variables have a significant relationship with satisfaction, and how strong those relationships are. Identifying the variables that drive satisfaction would tell you which programs could be put in place to better manage those elements of the service. For example, if the analysis showed that check-in time and room cleanliness were the strongest predictors of overall satisfaction, you could be pretty confident that adding more front desk agents during peak periods, and more training for housekeepers, would improve guest satisfaction.

Alternatively, you may want to make a prediction of a future result using a set of known dependent variables. For example, you may want to predict the performance of a new hotel development project using

The REG Procedure
Model: MODEL1
Dependent Variable: Weight

		Parameter Estimates			
Variable	DF	Parameter Estimate	Standard Error	t Value	Pr > |t|
Intercept	1	−143.02692	32.27459	−4.43	0.0004
Height	1	3.89903	0.51609	7.55	<.0001

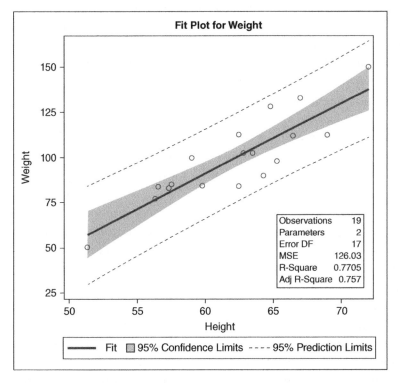

Figure 4.2 Regression Output
Here height is used to predict weight. You can see from the chart on the top, the p-value (<.0001) of height as a predictor variable is significant. The chart shows the actual observations of height and weight (circles), and the line is the set of weight predictions that the model would make at each height value.
Source: Image courtesy of sas.com.

what you know about your existing hotels. The dependent variable would be a performance metric (revenue, profit). You would first run a regression analysis to see which of the variables that your business knowledge says could predict hotel performance are actually statistically significant predictors, such as location, market size, number of competitive hotels, number of rooms, and so on. The regression output gives not only which variables are significant, but also a model to use for future analyses. You could then use values of those significant factors for a proposed hotel in the regression model to calculate an expectation of performance. Very useful, right?

A regression model is formulated as an equation, where the dependent variable is expressed as the aggregate (sum-product) of the independent variables adjusted by a coefficient (called beta or β). When the regression analysis is run, the math determines which of the proposed independent variables are significantly related to the dependent variable, and the coefficient values for the independent variables are calculated. Using our hotel performance example, your regression equation might look like:

Revenue = intercept term + 0.34 × (hotel size) + −0.45 × (distance from airport) + −0.34 × (number of competitors) + 0.53 × (number of Fortune 500 companies in the area) + error term

If you wanted to predict the revenue for a proposed hotel location, you would enter the relevant values for hotel size, distance from airport, number of competitors in the area, and number of Fortune 500 companies in the area. Obviously, this is a simplification of the many factors that contribute to expected hotel revenue, but you get the idea.

The p-value associated with each of the betas, the coefficients, for the independent variables, will tell you if they have a significant predictive relationship with the dependent variable. The p-value should be less than 0.05. The measure that is used to determine how good the equation as a whole is in predicting the dependent variable is R-squared, which is a value from 0 to 1. There is a good deal of information available on how to calculate and interpret R-squared. The higher the R-squared value, the more likely it is that you found all of the variables that explain the dependent variable. So, the higher the better. However, this is open to some interpretation. For example, researchers in biology or chemistry look for

R-squared values in the 0.8 or 0.9 range, whereas social scientists are happy when they find R-squared values of 0.5 or even less. If you are going to be betting business results on regression models, make sure you ask the analyst what the R-squared is, and have a discussion about what that means for the reliability and completeness of the model.

I talk about other types of regression in the predictive modeling section.

FORECASTING

Forecasting is the use of historical data to predict the direction of future trends. In business applications, forecasting is generally used to assist in the planning process, so it is most commonly used to make a prediction of revenue or demand for a product or service (see Figure 4.3).

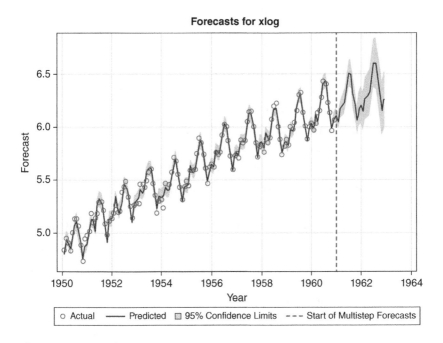

Figure 4.3 Forecasting Output

Circles are the actual observations; the line is the forecasted value, predicted into the next four years.
Source: Image from SAS ETS courtesy of sas.com.

There are two categories of forecasting methods, *qualitative* and *quantitative*. Qualitative forecasting techniques are subjective, based on the opinions and judgments of experts. They are most appropriate when past data are not available (like new product forecasting), and are usually applied to intermediate or long-range decisions.

Quantitative forecasting models are used to forecast future data as a function of past data. They are most appropriate to use when past numerical data is available, and when it is reasonable to assume that some of the patterns in the data will continue into the future. These methods are generally applied to short- or intermediate-range decisions.

The key to a forecast is its ability to make an accurate prediction. The method and the parameters associated with that method should be selected with accuracy in mind. Factors to consider when selecting a forecasting method are:

- **Amount and level of detail of the data.** When data gets *sparse*, as in very few historical observations are available, accuracy is impacted. Also, some forecasts are better for *aggregated* data, data that is summarized, and others are better for *disaggregated* data, data broken into lower levels of detail.

- **Amount of seasonality.** If there are regular day of the week or monthly patterns in the business, certain forecasting methods will be more appropriate.

- **Volatility in the data.** If there is a lot of noise in the data, meaning observations jump around quite a bit and there are very few detectable patterns, it will be more difficult to use for prediction.

- **Special events, outliers, or exogenous factors.** Certain forecasting methods deal better with unusual observations or factors that influence the patterns that are not easily visible in the historical data (like oil prices, unemployment rates, or weather).

Here are high-level descriptions of some of the most popular methods:

- **Naïve approaches.** This category uses simple methods to predict future values. For example, the average method uses a straight average of past values as the forecast and the naïve approach uses the most recent value as the future value. These methods can be adjusted by a drift (adding change between first and latest observations) or seasonality (prediction is the last observed value from the same season). These approaches can be used with any sort of data where past data is available. It will be most accurate when the numbers are relatively stable, with no seasonality or variability, or if the patterns in the data are relatively difficult to predict. Naïve approaches are frequently used as benchmarks for more complex methods. If the complex method does not prove more accurate than one of these methods, then it makes more sense to use the less complex forecasting method.

■ **Time series methods.** These methods use historical data, but add more complexity for pattern detection and pattern changes, helping to account for elements like trend and seasonality. Methods can be as simple as a moving average, an average of a specified number of previous periods, or more complex with terms and parameters to account for trend or seasonality, like exponential smoothing and ratio-to-trend. Most are designed to smooth out the volatility in the data for a more stable forecast. For time series methods, the decision of what forecasting method to use depends on whether you suspect that there is either trend (upward or downward movement) or seasonality (changing demand patterns by time period) or both in the data. You can determine this by graphing historical data and observing any patterns, although some forecasting packages will automatically test for this on any data set.

■ **Causal/econometric methods.** These methods account for additional information beyond historical data that might influence the variable that's being forecast. For example, the number of conventioneers in town might impact demand for a restaurant, or gas prices might impact demand for a roadside hotel. These variables are known as exogenous (outside of historical data) variables. Methods here are generally regression based (see my previous discussion of regression). Econometric modeling is generally based on supply and demand relationships, predicting the price sensitivity of demand, the switching behavior in the face of available alternatives, or the impact of certain financial policies on gross domestic product. Extending to hospitality, it can be used to predict room demand or optimal menu item pricing for restaurants.

▪ **Artificial intelligence methods.** As technology has advanced, providing sufficient processing power to solve larger and more complex math problems, additional complex forecasting methods have been developed. These methods have been designed specifically with big data in mind, and tend to straddle the line between forecasting and predictive modeling. These methods are very good at detecting patterns in large numbers of inputs, particularly when exact relationships are unknown. You might hear terms like neural networks, expert systems, or belief networks. These are all artificial intelligence methods. Because these are all big data–type methods, they can sometimes fall into the overfitting trap that I discussed in Chapter 2, where they perfectly predict the present but can't predict the future.

Forecast Accuracy

There are many ways to measure the accuracy and performance of forecasts. Each method has advantages and disadvantages, so most forecasters will use a combination of methods to get the complete picture. I outline the most basic metrics as follows. Other, more complex forecasting error measures are based on these principles and are designed to overcome some of the weaknesses I identify in the following list.[5]

▪ **MAD (mean absolute deviation).** This measure is the average of the absolute value of the difference between each forecasted value and the actual value for that period. There are two issues with this. First, the measure is a number, like 20. Well, if you have 2,000 rooms, that's a pretty accurate forecast. If you have 40 rooms, not so much. Second, because it's an absolute value, it does not provide any information on the direction of the error. If the values are balanced between lower or higher than the actual, that's okay. If they are mostly positive or negative, that's not good—and with this metric, there's no way to tell the difference.

- **MAPE (mean absolute percentage error).** This measure adjusts for the problem of scale just described by expressing the mean absolute error as a percentage of the total forecasted value. This is the most common way to describe forecasting error. It still doesn't account for the bias in your forecast—whether it consistently under- or overforecasts—but it does account for the relative magnitude of the error.

- **Tracking signal.** This measure provides a relatively real-time update to the direction of the forecasting error. Generally, this is calculated by dividing the sum of the errors by the MAD. It provides a directional percentage figure. If this value begins to become either largely positive or largely negative, you need to worry about bias in the forecast. Many use both the MAPE and a tracking signal to monitor forecast accuracy.

To add an additional layer of complexity, there is a bit of an art to interpreting these errors as well. As a favorite analytic hospitality executive pointed out to me recently, "I could tell you that my forecast error was 9%. Well, that's incredible if I'm forecasting hotel room demand or even revenue a year or so out. It could be very bad if I am forecasting occupancy the night before arrival. You need to understand the type of forecast and the horizon of the forecast to evaluate the forecast accuracy."

Obviously, the more accurate the forecast, the better your decisions will be. Given the breadth and depth of forecasting methods, finding the best one for each problem could clearly take a long time. Technology, like the SAS Forecast Server, can automate the process of selecting the best forecasting method and optimizing parameters for that method. The testing iterations are performed in seconds. The selection is based on a combination of accuracy measures. Even with this tool, forecasting can be a bit of an art along with the science. Make sure your analysts are able to explain why they picked the methods and the accuracy measures they selected.

I know it isn't the sexiest topic these days (at least to some), but I love the science of forecasting. For example, in revenue management, it is easy to get excited about new price response modeling approaches—and I certainly share the excitement. But an A+ price elasticity model on top of a C– forecast yields a C– result. We talk about forecasting all the time at Marriott; we're pretty good at it, but we can be better—and we will continuously improve. I've been in revenue management for 20 years; if there is an aspect of revenue management that is more important than forecasting, I have yet to find it.

—Dave Roberts, Senior Vice President, Revenue Management
& Revenue Analysis, Marriott International

PREDICTIVE ANALYTICS

Forecasting is a specific case of predictive analytics, but there are many other conditions, patterns, or behaviors that you may want to predict other than understanding how trends will continue into the future. For example, you may want to predict what offer a guest is most likely to respond to, or their future value to the firm. You may want to know when a guest is exhibiting behavior that signals that they are about to switch their loyalty to another brand, or what content on the website is most likely to result in a conversion. These are all applications of predictive analytics. Today, predictive analytics are commonly associated with data mining.

Logistic Regression

This is a specific type of regression where the dependent variable is binary (zero or one), and the output of the regression model is the probability of an event occurring (a value between zero and one). The model is built using observations where an event (a booking or a response to a campaign, for example), either occurs or does not. Then, for future events where the outcome is unknown, entering the values of the independent variables provides a probability that the event will occur in that circumstance. This is also known as a *score*, so you will hear analysts or statisticians talking about *scoring* the guest database. They mean calculating the probability or likelihood for each guest to take a particular action.

For example, you could build a model to predict whether a guest will respond to a specific campaign (Figure 4.4). The independent variables could include demographic variables like their location, age, or loyalty status, as well as stay history, most recent stay, response to previous campaigns, lifetime value, and preferences. Based on the values of the independent variables, the model would give a probability of the guest responding to the campaign. You can see the usefulness of this type of technique in all kinds of analyses. Like regression, there will be a *p*-value associated with the coefficients for each of the independent variables so you can determine whether they have a statistically significant relationship with the dependent variable. Unlike in linear regression, R-squared is not used to determine how well the model fits the data. In fact, statisticians have not come to agreement on a single method that best describes the fit of a logistic regression.

I know it's a bit strange to quote myself in my book, but since I asked other analytic hospitality executives to weigh in on their favorite techniques, I wanted to tell you mine.

Logistic regression is my favorite analytical technique. Being able to predict the probability of something occurring is so broadly useful, that I keep running into new use cases for this technique. This is a tool that every analyst should have in their toolbox, because they will always find new ways to apply it.

—Kelly A. McGuire, Vice President, Advanced Analytics,
Wyndham Destination Network

Cluster Analysis

This category of predictive models is used to find groups of observations in the data that behave similarly, or share similar characteristics, and then categorize future observations accordingly. Segmentation is the most common use of cluster analysis in hospitality. Segmentation analysis finds groups of guests who share similar demographic characteristics, behavioral patterns, or value. For such an intuitive concept,

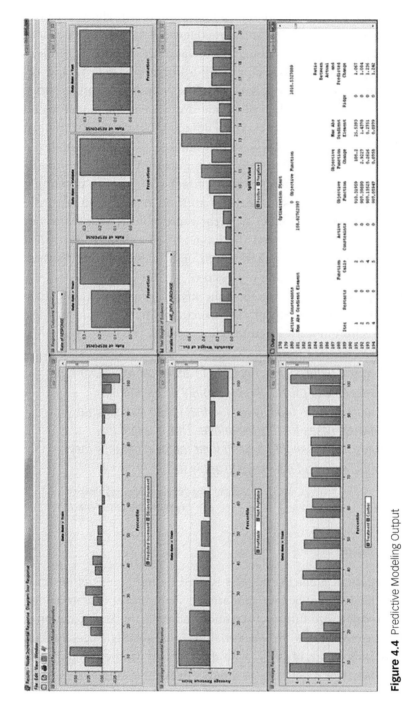

Figure 4.4 Predictive Modeling Output

This is the incremental impact of a marketing treatment. The two shadings represent the control and predicted impact of the treatment, respectively.

Source: *Image from SAS Enterprise Miner, courtesy of sas.com.*

98

there is actually a broad range of options for clustering. Factors to consider when deciding which method to use include:

- How distinct the differences between clusters should be
- Whether you want to force the model to cluster based on a specific characteristic (lifetime value, age), or let it find groupings naturally
- What types of variables you want the model to consider (only demographic, only behavioral, all variables)
- Whether the model will force each observation into only one cluster, allow observations to belong to multiple clusters, or output a likelihood for each observation to belong to every cluster

As you can tell from this brief overview, cluster analysis, like forecasting, is a bit of art and science. You should discuss the problem you are solving with the analysts in specific detail so they can choose the right cluster model for the solution you desire.

Data Mining

This term refers to a large class of models that are specifically designed to find patterns in large data sets when the researcher does not have a predetermined idea of potential relationships in the data. Data mining can be descriptive or predictive. Just as I described earlier, descriptive data mining explores the data for patterns or relationships. Predictive data mining makes inferences using the data. The biggest advantage of data mining over other predictive or statistical methods is that most data mining algorithms handle many more predictor variables than regression (200 or more). The artificial intelligence methods I described in the forecasting section are also considered predictive data mining methods to be used on extremely large data sets.

Common data mining techniques include:

- **Classification.** A broader category of modeling similar to clustering, where the algorithm evaluates observations to determine what group they belong to.
- **Decision tree.** A form of predictive modeling, where a model is created to predict the value of a target variable based on several input variables. Decision trees overcome the limitations of some predictive models, which can consist of the number or

type of variables that can be included, making them very useful for extremely large data sets.

■ **Intention mining.** Determines the users' intention from their behavior in interacting with a computer system, particularly a search engine.

It is important to understand the implications of the exploratory nature of data mining. Unlike the statistical methods and some of the predictive methods I described earlier, there is typically not a predefined hypothesis in data mining. Exploratory means that the researcher does not know what to expect from the data, so the methods are designed to survey large data sets, detect patterns, and classify observations. This means that if not carefully validated, the data mining technique can produce results that may appear to be significant, but do not predict future behavior and cannot be reproduced on a new sample of data. For example, a data mining–based forecasting technique could perfectly model the conditions in the historical data set, producing a very low forecasting error when compared to actuals, but yield huge errors when applied to future dates. The best way to overcome this is to hold out a test data set that is not part of the data you use to build the model. The data mining model can be applied to this test data set to see if it produces the same results.

OPTIMIZATION

Optimization is a specific mathematical technique that solves for the decisions you need to make to get to the best possible answer to a specific objective, accounting for all of the constraints unique to the problem. One of my biggest pet peeves in all of analytics is the overuse and misuse of the terms "optimization" and "optimal." If you haven't used a mathematical optimization problem, you are not "optimized." If you have to look at a chart or graph to find the answer yourself, you are not getting an "optimal" decision from that solution (no offense meant, I know you are pretty good at using data to make decisions, but you see where I'm going with this—it has to be from an optimization algorithm to be truly optimized or optimal).

All optimization problems involve the following elements:

- **Objective.** The equation that describes the desired outcome of the problem, always written as a goal of minimizing or maximizing. For example, in price optimization modeling for revenue management, the goal is to maximize revenue. The objective equation is expressed in terms of *decision variables*.

- **Decision variables.** These are the outputs of the optimization problem. They represent the decisions the model recommends to achieve the best possible outcome. In other words, these are the factors you can manipulate to achieve the best possible result. The revenue management optimization algorithm's output is the price to charge (by date, length of stay, and room type) that maximizes revenue.

- **Constraints.** The constraints are how you express the operating conditions under which the problem should be solved. For example, you can't sell more rooms than the hotel has, so the capacity of the hotel is a constraint. Also, you will not sell more rooms than there is demand for, so the amount of expected demand by segment, or by willingness to pay, is also a constraint. The number of PMS terminals behind the front desk could be a constraint in a labor scheduling optimization, because you can't schedule more agents to check guests in and out than there are terminals for them to use to do that.

Optimization problems are solved by testing different values for the decision variables, subject to the constraints, over and over until the objective is achieved. The process of solving the problem through these iterations is managed by an optimization *algorithm*, which is basically a set of rules that are followed in calculating the answer to a problem. At each iteration, the algorithm must verify that no constraints are violated and compare the answer to the previous iteration, to see if it is better. The algorithm stops when the best possible answer is found (Figure 4.5).

Optimization problems are among the hardest problems in mathematics. The complexity of the problem, and the number of iterations it takes to solve, requires highly specialized algorithms and

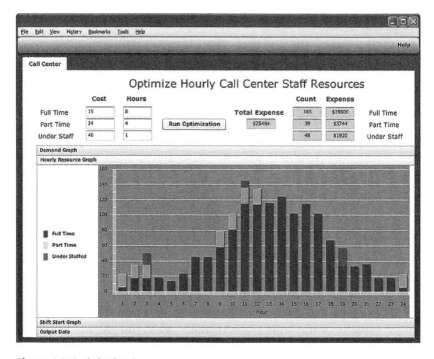

Figure 4.5 Optimization Output

The optimization recommends the right staffing levels and indicates where there will be staffing short-ages, which will cause waits. To set the constraints, analysts enter the hourly wage for employees and how many hours they can work. The model minimizes expense.

Source: Image courtesy of sas.com.

intensive processing power. Some mathematicians spend their entire careers just figuring out how to solve these problems faster and more efficiently. Even so, in some cases, using traditional technology infra-structure, solving the full problem can take days or weeks. I talk more about this issue, and how advances in technology have helped to over-come it, later in this chapter.

If the solution you are considering is not based on an optimization problem and solved using an optimization algorithm, it will not pro-vide an "optimal" or "optimized" answer. If you are only looking at a graph of historical data, or a forecast of expected demand, you are not getting an optimal solution. If your analyst is expected to derive the answer by looking at reports or forecasts, you are not optimizing (and yes, I said it again, it's that important to me).

Optimization is my favorite analytical technique because it provides an answer that can be easily operationalized, the best answer for the problem at hand. When we build pricing solutions, we focus more time on building a robust optimization model rather than trying to get an extra percent of accuracy on our forecasts and demand models. Our users need a price recommendation, and that's delivered by the optimization.

—Jeremy TerBush, Senior Vice President, Global Analytics,
Wyndham Destination Network

MACHINE LEARNING

"Machine learning" is a term you have likely heard associated with a wide variety of problems, and has probably been pitched by some of the analytics vendors you have come in contact with. Machine learning started as a branch of artificial intelligence, but separated from that field in the 1990s, moving toward a discipline more focused on statistics and probability theory. Today, machine learning refers to any algorithm that is developed on a set of test data and then deployed on unknown data to perform the same task. The algorithm "learns" the new data and is able to automatically perform the same analysis on new data sets. Regression, clustering, decision trees, factor analysis, logistic regression, and neural networks are all classifications of models that can be considered machine-learning algorithms. The idea is that as the algorithms see new data observations over time, they become more accurate with predictions.

Machine learning is highly related to data mining, and even uses many of the same algorithms. However, data mining is typically focused on exploration and discovery of previously unknown properties or relationships in the data. Machine learning, on the other hand, uses known properties or relationships in the data to predict properties or relationships for new data added to the data set. This distinction between exploration and prediction is crucial to understanding how and where to use machine-learning algorithms. They are deployed in production software environments, like websites, revenue management solutions, or marketing systems. Data mining is used to develop the machine-learning algorithms, but data mining can also be used for ad hoc analyses. While some of the algorithms that are classified as machine-learning algorithms can be used for ad hoc analyses, they don't technically become machine-learning algorithms until they are put into production.

Machine learning is used broadly across many industries. Some common applications include search engines, recommender systems (like Amazon or Netflix), advertising, detecting credit card fraud, and natural language processing.

TEXT ANALYTICS

Speaking of natural language processing, text analytics, which leverage this technique, while not new, have become more widespread since the advent of the social web. Text analytics can be used to mine the content of any unstructured text document, either created on external sites like Facebook, Twitter, or TripAdvisor, or created internally like call logs or open-ended questions on a guest survey. There are several methods available to quantify the contents of these unstructured text documents. These methods are based on natural language processing, a type of algorithm that understands language in context and can interpret or infer meaning from it. Natural language processing is most effective when it is applied natively, as opposed to translated text, which is why it is important for a global industry like hospitality to work with software that has the largest available portfolio of languages in their text analytics package. There are several primary categories of text analytics:

- **Content categorization.** This identifies key topics and phrases in electronic text and sorts them into categories. It eliminates the manual work of reading and tagging documents, giving you much faster results. Text documents can be organized and tagged for search, making it easier to find, sort, or process the content. This approach also makes it easier to assign certain issues to specific departments that can resolve the issues. It also makes it easier for internal teams to find specific content stored in the text repositories.

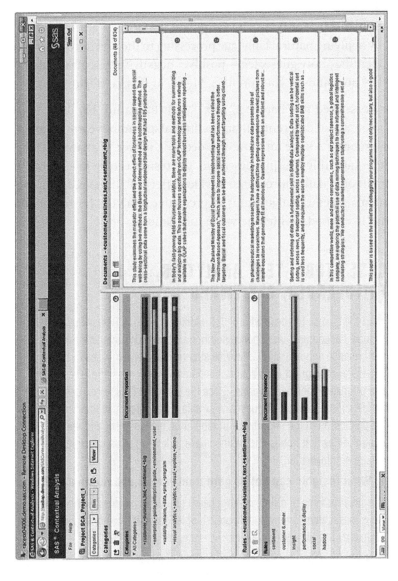

Figure 4.6 Text Mining Output

Shown here in black and white, the bars and text would in actual use have sentiment indicated as neutral (blue), positive (green), and negative (red).

Source: Image courtesy of sas.com.

- ■ **Text mining.** Similar to data mining, text mining uncovers related concepts in large volumes of conversations. It surfaces key topics that can be used in future analyses, like predicting or understanding guest behavior.

- ■ **Sentiment analysis.** This helps you understand guest opinions by applying natural language processing to the text documents. It identifies how guests feel—positive, negative, or neutral—about key attributes of your product, brand, or service (Figure 4.6).

As I described in Chapter 2, text data is by nature big data, so it needs to be stored differently than traditional quantitative information and will require a large amount of processing power to analyze. Once the data is quantified, as just described, the results can be incorporated with traditional data sources into a wide variety of analyses, including revenue management algorithms or predictive analytics for retention, response likelihood, or lifetime value calculations.

CASE STUDY: TEXT ANALYTICS, R. J. FRIEDLANDER, REVIEWPRO

I had the chance to speak with R. J. Friedlander, CEO of ReviewPro, a cloud-based guest intelligence solution that provides reputation performance and operational/service strengths and weaknesses to help hotels increase guest satisfaction, ranking on review sites and OTAs, and ultimately increase revenue. Since his company focuses on gaining insights from volumes of guest review data, I was interested to know his perception of the importance of reputation management and the opportunities that hotels and casinos have to leverage this valuable source of information.

1. What insights can hotels gain from review and rating data?

The sheer volume of online reviews being published by guests on a daily basis makes them an invaluable source of feedback for hotels across all segments, from budget to luxury.

First and foremost, review analytics provide hotels with a deeper understanding of reputation performance, as well as their strengths and weaknesses. By using this actionable insight to prioritize operational and service improvements, hotels can deliver better experiences for their guests, improve satisfaction, boost rankings on review sites and OTAs, and increase revenue.

Review data also helps hotels understand what guests are saying about competitors, which they can learn from in order to differentiate themselves and to gain an advantage over their rivals. Today's advanced technology makes it possible to compare performance on a group, brand, or individual hotel level and, more important, drill down to the details to make changes where they will have the most impact on results. Savvy hotel marketers are also using benchmarking insights to identify the strongest sales messages and guide website or promotional copy.

2. How important is reputation management?

Almost no one disputes the importance of a hotel's online reputation. Hoteliers largely understand the impact of reviews on both consumer and business travel, and the influence they have when travelers are choosing which hotel to stay in and how much they are willing to spend at a given hotel. The results of numerous industry studies show that guests are more likely to book a hotel with positive reviews, and that their impression of a hotel can improve if they read an appropriate management response to a bad review. According to a Cornell University study (Anderson 2012), using ReviewPro's data, a one-point increase in a property's Global Review Index™ can lead to a:

- 0.89% increase in ADR
- 0.54% increase in occupancy
- 1.42% increase in RevPAR

The question, however, is about the importance of reputation management. Although many hoteliers today monitor and measure online reputation, the key is to know how to improve it to exceed guest expectations, maximize ADR, and outperform competitors. What used to be an orientation toward online reputation management has now shifted to prioritize reputation improvement. This change is driven by recent advances in technology that make it easy to leverage the combined analytics of online reputation data with that of direct feedback from guest surveys to identify and prioritize resources, to drive service excellence, and to maximize revenue.

(continued)

(*continued*)

3. Why can review and ratings data be challenging to analyze?

The complexity comes from the sheer number of websites (175+) where hotel reviews are being written (OTAs, review sites, etc.) combined with the number of languages (45+) that reviews are written in. For most hotels, the volume of online reviews proves difficult for them to analyze manually and requires the use of a reputation management solution. Valuable "big data analytics," a term that creates confusion for many hoteliers, is a reality today in the area of guest feedback. If hoteliers choose the right Guest Experience Improvement Solution, the technology can take care of the number crunching and analytics and remove the complexity to analyzing review and ratings data. Such technology should include not only average scores but also algorithms/indexes and advanced sentiment analysis to provide both corporate- and property-level users the information they need, in real time, so they can effectively leverage the insights guests are providing.

4. From your experience, what is the typical hotel or casino doing in the area of text analytics and reputation management?

The average hotels today are aware of the importance of their reputation, but how they manage their reputation can vary dramatically. A small, independent hotel with few rooms typically monitors reviews manually on several key sites such as TripAdvisor and Booking.com and may respond to some negative reviews in their own language. Hotels with a higher review volume are more likely to decide to invest in a reputation management tool and look to combine online reputation analytics with guest feedback analytics from post-stay surveys and manage this powerful guest intelligence with a single technology platform. They also realize the need to have a single text analytics system that evaluates positive and negative sentiment across both types of guest feedback. Further, most hotels have dedicated resources that coordinate things on both the corporate and property level, monitor and share internal key performance indicators, and oversee the ongoing performance of managers versus objectives.

5. What are the most sophisticated hotels and casinos doing?

The most sophisticated hotels are harnessing the true power of guest intelligence, which combines online reputation and guest satisfaction survey analytics, across their entire organization to prioritize operational and service improvements. The top performers on TripAdvisor and those achieving the best results are focusing on reputation improvement. They have a much broader approach to guest feedback, incorporating what is being said about their brand online with direct feedback from guests. Hotels are getting this feedback by sending customized guest satisfaction surveys—after the guest has checked out but also while the guest is still on the property—so that if there is a problem, they have time to fix it before the guest leaves.

We are seeing that organizations that make a cultural shift to become more guest-centric, ensuring that the right people are getting the right information, are achieving the most remarkable results in improving guest satisfaction and online reputation.

For example, Jurys Inn operates 31 hotels in the United Kingdom and Ireland, and they successfully created a guest-centric culture across the entire organization, which they called the Happy Guest Program, to increase engagement of all employees. They completely overhauled their guest feedback program using ReviewPro's Guest Experience Improvement Solution. Within 10 months, the TripAdvisor ranking for 28 of their hotels increased from an average of 3.5 to above a 4-star rating.

6. When you talk to hotels and casinos about reputation management and text analytics, what capabilities are they most interested in? What does a typical roadmap look like?

Generally speaking, text analytics to process written feedback for sentiment has existed for a number of years and the accuracy has consistently improved. Undoubtedly, there is huge potential value for hotels with detailed insight into what guests liked and didn't like about their hotel experiences. Our text analytics system was built from the ground up for the hospitality industry and that makes a difference. All of the categories and concepts were designed specifically for hotels and restaurants, to measure guest sentiment and provide insight into where improvement and training need to be focused.

Hoteliers want text analytics to provide them with the specifics to be able to take action and make improvements on the property. They want to be able to see what concepts are trending, both positively and negatively, and where the biggest changes have been. As is often the case, hotels

(*continued*)

(*continued*)

are interested in understanding their strengths and weaknesses in comparison to competitors, and so competitive analysis is a requirement for text analytics too.

We've seen that hoteliers want to avoid information overload and only want to see feedback that is relevant for their department. That's why it is important to provide the option to create customized views, depending on the user's role within the organization. For example, a housekeeping manager could use advanced text analytics to identify the key concepts of cleanliness that are trending up or down and, more important, understand why.

Hoteliers also want to be able to use insight from text analytics to make forecasting improvements based on factors such as seasonality. By giving the option to analyze feedback on specific dates, hoteliers can identify issues that happened in the past and use this information for planning and improving future periods ahead.

7. Where do you think this area is headed over the next few years? What opportunities are on the horizon?

As previously mentioned, there is going to be a clear evolution to focus on overall guest satisfaction improvement rather than just measurement. Travelers are becoming increasingly savvy and demanding. The challenge will be for hotels to keep ahead of the curve by effectively leveraging guest intelligence to deliver remarkable experiences and drive higher guest satisfaction.

Decisions that impact guests are often made at the head office, but the guest satisfaction battle is won or lost on the property. It's essential that the right people within the organization are getting the right information at the right time. New mobile apps, conceived for on-property use by hoteliers on the go, make it easier to manage guest feedback from anywhere and receive alerts in real time so hotel staff can act quickly to ensure that guests leave the hotel happy.

It is critical for hotel organizations to train, support, and engage their staff. It's all about creating a cultural shift to evolve everyone in the organization to become more guest-centric. Brands that take advantage of technological advances to be more efficient and share information more effectively will make it possible for hotel staff to free up more time to spend doing things that have a positive impact on guests.

There is also a clear opportunity for properties to exploit big data to outperform competitors by implementing the right strategy. Data becomes powerful when the analytics combine insight from a variety of sources and systems. It is critical that guest intelligence platforms are flexible and open and that they can integrate seamlessly with other systems and technologies. For example, hoteliers should demand that their guest intelligence data be able to integrate into their revenue management and customer relationship management (CRM) system to leverage the full potential of guest feedback in both optimizing pricing and building rich guest profiles.

Guest profile information gathered from satisfaction surveys is incredibly rich and valuable for CRM activities. Sophisitcated hotels will synchronize guest survey data with their CRM systems to be able to personalize promotional offers and the guest experience on the property.

MAKING IT WORK—ANALYTICS AND TECHNOLOGY

Analytics and technology go hand in hand. Obviously, most of the analytical methods I just described are designed to solve problems that are too complex and too large to calculate by hand. (Anyone who has learned to calculate a regression model by hand understands this fact intimately—if you haven't had the pleasure of transforming X'Y matrixes by hand, consider yourself fortunate). The larger the data sets, the more complex the analytics, and the more processing power is required. Along with the technology innovations I described in Chapter 2, which allow for faster, more flexible, and more scalable data storage, have come advances in the execution and delivery of analytics, making it possible to turn all of that complex data into meaningful, actionable insights. In this section, I describe innovations in the execution of analytics that provide better, more detailed answers faster, as well as innovations in solution delivery that make analytics more accessible for businesses. Finally, I close the chapter by describing the next frontier of analytics, streaming data, and real-time analytics.

Innovations in Executing Analytics

As I alluded to several times in previous discussions, emerging algorithms designed to handle big data will require increasingly large amounts of processing power to execute at the speed of business. Think of the definition of *big data* from Chapter 2: "exceeds an organization's storage or compute capacity." Big data is of no use unless you can turn it into insight. For that you need big analytics. Every piece of the analytics continuum. from reporting to advanced analytics, has been impacted by big data. In reporting, billions of rows of data need to be quickly rendered into a report form, and users want the flexibility to slice and dice, and drill down into the data according to their specific needs. Advanced analytics like forecasting and optimization require complex math executed by multiple passes through massive data sets.

Without changes to the technology infrastructure, analytic processes on big data sets will start to take longer and longer to execute—even if you can capture and store that big data. Businesses today can't be run by pushing the button and then waiting hours or days for an answer. Today's advanced analytics need to be fast and they need to be accessible. This means more changes to the technology infrastructure.

Analytics companies like SAS have been developing new methods for executing analytics more quickly. The following is a high-level description of some of these new methodologies, including why they provide an advantage. Once again, the intention is to provide enough detail to start conversations with IT counterparts (or understand what they are talking about), certainly not to become an expert. There is a ton of information out there if you want more detail.

1. **Grid computing and parallel processing.** Calculations are split across multiple central processing units (CPUs) to solve a bunch of smaller problems in parallel, as opposed to one big problem in sequence. Think about the difference between having to count an entire jar of M&Ms yourself as opposed to splitting the jar into 10 stacks and asking 10 of your friends to count and report back. To accomplish this, multiple CPUs are tied together, so the algorithms can access the resources of the entire bank of CPUs.

2. **In-database processing.** Most analytics programs lift data sets out of the database, execute the "math," and then dump the data sets back in the database. The larger the data sets, the more time-consuming it is to move them around. In-database analytics bring the math to the data. The analytics run in the database with the data, reducing the amount of time-consuming data movement.

3. **In-memory processing.** This capability is a bit harder to understand for nontechnical people, but it provides a crucial advantage for both reporting and analytics. Large sets of data are typically stored on the hard drive of a computer, which is the physical disk inside the computer (or server). It takes time to read the data off the physical disk space, and every pass through the data adds additional time (note that the math behind the analytics requires multiple passes through data). It is much faster to conduct analysis and build reports from the computer's memory. Memory is becoming cheaper every day, so it is now possible to add enough memory to hold large data sets "in-memory," speeding up the calculation of answers or rendering of reports.

To give you an idea of the scale of the impact, SAS applied these methodologies to render a summary report (with drill-down capability) from a billion rows of data in seconds. Large-scale optimizations, like risk calculations for major banks or price optimization for thousands of retail products across hundreds of stores, have gone from hours or days to minutes and seconds to calculate. As you can tell, the advantages are tremendous. Organizations can now run analytics on their entire data set, rather than a sample. It is possible to run more analyses more frequently, testing scenarios and refining results.

INNOVATIONS IN SOLUTION DELIVERY

Solution providers are innovating the way that technology is delivered as well, and this has an impact on solution decisions that hospitality and gaming companies make. While we are talking about technology innovations, it is worth defining available solution delivery options in order to understand the advantages and disadvantages of each.

Hoteliers are likely hearing a lot about solutions delivered via *the cloud* versus requiring the technology to be managed on-site or *on-premise*. Cloud-based solutions are accessed via the Internet, the applications are *hosted* in a remote site, and the technology environment is managed by the vendor. On-premise solutions, on the other hand, require the company to invest in the hardware and IT resources to manage the solution and the technology environment themselves.

At a high level, there are two different types of cloud solutions:

1. **Software-as-a-Service (SaaS).** These cloud-based solutions are complete end-to-end software packages that are standardized for the entire user base. While they can be configured, generally, the software is the same for all companies that access it. The application sits on a layer above the individual users' databases. Security is maintained between the users' databases, but all databases access the same application layer. Salesforce .com is probably the best-known example of a SaaS application, but many hospitality solutions today are delivered SaaS (Avero's Slingshot™ application and IDeaS Revenue Solutions suite of products are well-known examples).

2. **Hosted.** A hosted, or managed, solution is a proprietary solution for each customer that is effectively the same as having an on-premise solution, except it is located in a remote data center and managed by the vendor. This enables a more proprietary, customer-by-customer application delivery, but without the organization having to own and manage the technology infrastructure or resources.

Four advantages of a cloud solution over an on-premise solution are:

1. **Reduced burden on IT.** The vendor assumes all responsibility for maintaining the environment, including regular maintenance, upgrades, data transfers, or managing memory and storage capacity.

2. **Guaranteed service levels.** Cloud providers guarantee a minimum up-time for the solution, and build in the mechanisms required to achieve this. You have the security of knowing the system will be available when you need it.

3. **Implementation speed.** Particularly for SaaS applications, the time to implementation is dramatically reduced for cloud solutions.

4. **Security.** Most cloud providers have extensive data encryption and cybersecurity measures in place. In fact, some financial services companies use hosted solutions to manage credit card fraud activity, and are able to meet all of their both internal and external regulatory security measures to ensure that credit card numbers are not stolen, and the consumer's privacy is respected.

Three advantages of an on-premise solution over a cloud solution are:

1. **Control.** An on-premise solution is 100% in the control of the company that uses it. The data flow in and out is controlled by the company, as is the system configuration. Many companies see their data as a strategic asset, and do not want it to be managed by a third party.

2. **Regulatory issues.** Some industries' data is highly regulated (casinos, for example), and these regulations prohibit some data from ever leaving the facility where it is created. While the data centers for cloud solutions may have every protection mechanism in place, these companies are simply not allowed to leverage them. This is particularly an issue for customer data.

3. **Cost.** While the up-front cost of many on-premise solutions may be higher, the long-term costs can be significantly less. For hosted solutions, you can pay all of the up-front hardware and software costs plus an ongoing maintenance fee for the solution. SaaS solutions are frequently subscription-based, which means they charge a regular fee while the software is being used. Over the life of the solution, these can be significantly more than up-front software costs for an on-premise solution.

Here are some of the differences between pure SaaS and a hosted solution:

- The time-to-value of SaaS solutions, or any out-of-the-box solution, can be significantly shorter than any proprietary option, even including custom-built hosted solutions. The implementation process is standardized, so the solution can be up and running much faster. There generally are standardized training materials available, as well as extensive support mechanisms for users at every stage of the life cycle.

■ SaaS solutions are multitenant, meaning that all users share a common application layer (although each company's data is kept separate). This means that upgrades happen simultaneously and automatically for all users. They are included in the monthly subscription fee, so do not require additional services fees. This means you are always using the latest version of the software package.

■ SaaS applications are standardized to an industry or an application, so they do not offer a lot of room to customize to meet unique or highly specific customer requirements. Some companies have unique requirements that would make a proprietary solution highly valuable (for example, a unique operating constraint like the capacity of a kids' club or a minimum occupancy requirement driven by other on-site services). These unique requirements are difficult to accommodate in an SaaS application, and if they are incorporated, they become generally available to any user of the application. A proprietary hosted (or proprietary on-premise) solution could incorporate any unique business processes or operating constraints, turning the solution itself, not just the application of the results, into a competitive advantage.

■ SaaS applications include specific user interfaces and workflows. There is some flexibility, but in general, users must be trained on and conform to the methodology as laid out by the application. When a company decides to use one of these applications, the change management can be extensive, and the opportunity for company-specific business processes is either reduced or must be developed within the context of the application. For a company brand new to such a system, this can be an advantage, as business processes are baked into the solution implementation, so there is no need to invent new ones. For a more mature company that desires to upgrade their capabilities, this can be burdensome and restrictive.

CASE STUDY

CASE STUDY: ADVANTAGE OF PROPRIETARY SYSTEMS, WYNDHAM DESTINATION NETWORK

In my group at Wyndham Destination Network, all of our analytical systems and solutions are built internally, and we have invested in the people and the technology to do that. This is an important strategic decision for us. The main driver for this decision was that the pricing problems in vacation rental and time-share exchange were different enough from "traditional" revenue management problems that no commercially available solution fit. Once the company invested in the resources to build the pricing solutions, it was natural to keep innovating internally on any new problems that come along, rather than working with vendors.

This creates several advantages for us, particularly in such a complex environment. First, all of the solutions are purpose built for the specific problem. While we can, and do, use what we learned from previous projects, we can also adapt to the specific operating conditions of the business unit we are working with. Second, our development cycles are astoundingly fast (from a former vendor's perspective), because we only have to solve that exact client's problem, not make the solution flexible enough to handle a multitude of different flavors of the problem. We can add value very quickly, which makes our stakeholders more willing to work with us on current and future projects.

"Given the option, I prefer to build solutions internally," said Jeremy TerBush, Senior Vice President of Global Analytics, Wyndham Destination Network. "We know our business better than anyone else, and we know what will drive value. That level of control over the development gives us the flexibility to design the right solution for that very specific scenario, and to be very nimble as our understanding of the problem improves. It also provides our team the most interesting work and helps them continue to grow within the business. Anything from building a report to automating a process to building an entire pricing system is core to our analytical strategy and has been instrumental in our success. This required investment in people and technology, and a commitment from senior leadership to continue to support that investment, and it has more than paid off for us."

REAL TIME AND STREAMING

The move to digital has given hospitality companies a platform to interact with guests in real time, or near real time, as guests are browsing the web or using an app. This same technology facilitates personalized recommendations in context during face-to-face interactions. Real-time decisioning is now being used across hospitality and travel. Many interactions are based on business rules, such as "if the guest clicks here, show them this banner ad." The competitive advantage will come when analytics are infused into the real time interactions, to predict the next best offer that will cause the guest to take the action you desire in that moment. Real-time engines typically work by understanding the context of the interaction, and looking up a score or analytic result that is matched to an offer or communication sent back to the guest in the moment. The action that the guest takes as a result of the interaction is recorded in the database, so that future actions are improved. These real-time interactions can take place through the website, kiosks, mobile apps, or even face to face at the front desk or concierge—any place where the guest can be identified through a device that is integrated with the real-time decision engine.

The next big innovation in real-time analytics is streaming analytics, or analytics on the edge. In this application, the data is analyzed before it even hits the database. It is analyzed, in fact, as it is being created. This dramatically speeds up time to results. You've probably heard the phrase "the Internet of Things." This is the concept that devices are connected to the Internet and are generating volumes of data about their condition and the environment around them. Think about manufacturing lines that have interconnected machines with parts that wear out, or a car that is a giant system of interrelated components that need to sense not only their operation, but the conditions of the road and the driver. In hospitality, we will soon have room service trays that can tell us when they are set outside the door, or lighting and HVAC systems that capture guest preferences and provide opportunities to improve energy efficiency, even faucets that can tell us when they are leaking. All of these individual components are creating and reporting data.

Analytics that can watch this data as it streams by and instantly make decisions will be the difference between detecting a pump failure before it happens and the next oil spill. These types of analytics are just emerging, and are best suited for very large, very fast-moving data sets like machine sensors, website tracking, or data usage for mobile devices. You will hear a lot more about this issue as the Internet of Things goes mainstream, so it is important to be aware of the opportunity. I speak more about this in subsequent chapters.

CONCLUSION

The term "analytics" is used to describe a wide variety of techniques ranging from traditional business intelligence applications to advanced predictive modeling and optimization. While an analytic hospitality executive, or an aspiring analytic hospitality executive, does not necessarily have to be able to develop and execute these modeling techniques, they do need to work closely with the people who do. Therefore, it is very important to have a basic understanding of what they are and how they can add value to your business.

In this chapter, I talked about some common advanced analytic techniques, including statistical modeling, forecasting, predictive modeling, data mining, and optimization. I also talked about innovations in the execution of analytics that make it possible to execute these complex techniques on larger and larger data sets. You should be prepared to have better conversations with analysts and IT to help guide an analytics strategy for your organization. In the rest of the book, I'll go functional area by functional area in the hospitality and gaming enterprise to describe how analytics are commonly and best applied within these areas. In combination with the overview I provided here, you should gain from the following chapters a good understanding of where the potential exists in your organization to leverage these techniques, and how to make the right investment in data, analytics, technology, and people.

ADDITIONAL RESOURCES

▓ Thomas H. Davenport, Jeanne G. Harris, and Robert Morrison, *Analytics at Work: Smarter Decisions, Better Results* (Boston: Harvard Business Review Press, 2007).

▣ John C. Chambers, Satinder K. Mullick, and Donald D. Smith, "How to Choose the Right Forecasting Technique," *Harvard Business Review*, July 1971, https://hbr .org/1971/07/how-to-choose-the-right-forecasting-technique. There are some good processes outlined in this article, but it was written in 1971, so there are portions (particularly the section on how long it takes to develop the forecasting method and how expensive the technology is) that are quite dated.

▣ Jared Dean, *Big Data, Data Mining and Machine Learning: Value Creation for Business Leaders and Practitioners*, May 2014, www.sas.com/store/books/categories/business-leadership/big-data-data-mining-and-machine-learning-value-creation-for-business-leaders-and-practitioners/prodBK_66081_en.html.

▣ Darrell Huff, *How to Lie with Statistics* (New York: W. W. Norton, 1954; reprint, 1993).

NOTES

1. The formula for standard deviation is the square root of the sum of the variance. Variance is the absolute difference between each observation and the mean. If you want to learn more about variance, look it up, but it's not important for our conversation here. There's a formula in Excel—you just need to know how to interpret it.

2. The geekier of my analytic hospitality executive readers will appreciate the inclusion of the following debate, which may or may not impact my advice to sense check your analysts by asking for a p-value. My technical reviewer (and good friend) pointed me to an ongoing debate in the statistical community that suggests that the reliance on p-values as the sole measure of statistical validity is probably causing the community to accept the results of studies that simply aren't valid. In a nutshell, the p-value simply states that there is only a 5% chance that the study results occurred randomly—that's not a zero percent chance. If the wrong research method was used or the wrong sampling was employed, the chances are much greater that you created a scenario to support your conclusions rather than described a condition of your population. The community is suggesting that even with a p-value, the methodology needs to be carefully evaluated. Good advice. If your analyst uses this argument with you, give them a raise. See Monya Baker, "Statisticians Issue Warning over Misuse of P values," *Nature*, March 7, 2016, www.nature.com/news/statisticians-issue-warning-over-misuse-of-p-values-1.19503 for more.

3. You still have to be very careful assuming causation even with regression. Academics and pure statisticians will tell you that even with regression reverse causation is also possible. For example, aggregate ratings may have a significant relationship when used to predict average daily rate, but if you made aggregate ratings the dependent variable, average daily rate could also show up as a significant predictor variable. Be sure to think this through when using regression as well. *Never* say that correlated variables have causal relationships, and be cautious implying that with regression as well. There should be some strong theoretical or practical reason behind the direction of the relationship between the two variables (which causes which).

4. Regression technically belongs in both statistical analysis and predictive modeling. I'll acknowledge this again in the predictive modeling section.

5. For the sake of clarity, because I did find that some of my revenue management students found this concept confusing, to test the accuracy of your forecasting method, you forecast the values for periods that have already occurred, and then compare the results of your forecast to the actual value. I can see how "forecasting" for an

event that already happened can be counter-intuitive, but if you think about it, how else would you be able to understand the ability of your method to predict future values? This concept is also applied to testing the results of a predictive model. You use a *hold-out sample*, which is a set of data similar to the data you use to build the model but that was not included in that set. You can run the predictive model on this hold-out sample and see how well it does with data it hasn't already "seen." This is very good modeling practice and something to keep in mind as you are evaluating your analysts' work.

CHAPTER **5**

Analytics for
Operations

*Quality in a service or product is not what you
put into it. It's what the customer gets out of it.*

—Peter Drucker

In the next five chapters, we will go function by function in the
hospitality organization and describe how analytics can help these
functions meet their goals and move their businesses forward. I start
by describing the purpose of that function and the kinds of challenges it
currently faces. I talk about the available data, challenges associated with
collecting the data, and new data sources that could hold great potential
for that function. I will outline the type of analytics that can be used to
support typical business goals for that function, and provide suggestions
for both common and potential use cases for analytics in that function.

I provide some benchmarking information about what I believe
is the minimum being done with analytics in each function, what an
average hospitality or gaming company is doing, and what the most
sophisticated players are taking on. Fair warning: I have not conducted
an empirical study in this area. I think it would be very interesting to
do so. These are merely my own observations based on what I have
seen both within hospitality and outside of it. Take this information as
a directional indication of how you should be planning your analytics
program.

I always get asked about technology investments, including which
systems are required, which are the best, and what companies are
typically investing in. I will provide some directional guidance in each
chapter for the best technology investment areas and a little bit of advice
on what to look for in those systems. I have purposely kept this high
level and relatively light. Technology moves so quickly that any specific
recommendations will be outdated before this book is even published.

I have asked technology vendors to contribute their perspectives on
where the hospitality and gaming industry is in their use of data and application of analytics in each functional area (you will notice that I have

already featured two technology vendors in the previous chapters). I am certainly not advocating for any of their technology solutions, but keep in mind that vendors talk to many different types of hospitality and gaming companies across the globe, and so they have a holistic perspective on where the industry is and where the potential for advancement lies. I picked people who I trust to give (relatively) unbiased opinions.

I am a firm believer that we need to break down departmental silos, so after you have an opportunity to think about how data and analytics are applied function by function, in the final chapter of the book, I talk about how the functional areas should think about leveraging one another's data and analytics for more holistic decision making.

As you no doubt already realize, analytics programs are frequently among a company's most protected competitive advantages. Analytic hospitality executives often cannot talk in specifics about their modeling techniques, applications, and results. Where possible, I've included testimony and examples from leading hospitality companies. These inspirational examples are designed to help you build a program that you can turn into a competitive advantage. After all, it's not about who can build the most elegant and robust model, it's about what you do with those results that will make the difference. Most companies' "secret sauce" is also how they infuse the analytics into their operations to make decisions and take action, not just in the techniques they choose or the models they build. In each chapter, I also provide some examples of operationalizing analytics, focusing on a key business process for that function. Frequently they contain research and best practices that are more holistic than just the implementation of analytic results, so that you can think broadly about developing an analytics-supported business strategy.

I'll first talk about the operations department, which is at the heart of delivering the guest or patron experience. Then I'll address marketing, sales, revenue management, performance analysis, and gaming.

OPERATIONS

Operations in hospitality and gaming represents a wide variety of guest-facing functions on property, as well as the supporting infrastructure at the regional or corporate level. I refer here to front desk, concierge, and housekeeping, as well as food and beverage, banquets and catering, retail, spa, and other related services. I separately address the gaming floor specifically in Chapter 10, and I address pricing and revenue management for all outlets in Chapter 8.

Operations has two unique challenges. The first is that they are the group that executes the guest experience when the guest is on the property. This means that they have the challenge of satisfying guest needs while the guest is in the experience, and they often must make decisions about the best course of action for serving the guest while the guest is right in front of them. This is fast and immediate. Second, operations has the most cost pressure of any department, since managing the variable costs associated with line level labor and perishable products are the responsibility of this function. Perhaps more so than any other area in the hotel or casino, operations feels the pressure to balance the guest experience with the need to minimize costs.

Operations departments frequently leverage technology to facilitate service delivery, and so the technology footprint in operations can get quite complex. Different systems manage the process of checking guests in and out of rooms, tracking and charging spa appointments, calculating guest reservations at restaurants, and ringing out retail customers. Housekeeping might deploy an automated system to keep track of which rooms have been cleaned. Maintenance could be automating the service requests and resolutions. There are phone systems, in-room technology like televisions or automated lights and blinds,

Figure 5.1 Operations Must Balance Cost
and Guest Experience

mini-bars, elevators, digital signage, and so on. Any systems that collect guest charges need to be integrated, and respond fast enough to reconcile the guest folio when guests depart, especially if they walk right from charging their breakfast at the restaurant to the checkout counter. Now organizations are talking about keyless entry for rooms and tracking location to deliver real-time recommendations. All this is just to execute the service experience, let alone analyze it!

This complex technology environment provides valuable data about the guests and the operations, but requires careful management and ongoing staff training. While IT is responsible for installing and maintaining these systems, operations feels the immediate impact of any technology failures, and must deal with the implications on the guest or patrons. Operations managers run a 24/7 business, and need to be focused on providing a safe and efficient environment for delivering an excellent guest or patron experience. They can't afford to be distracted by technology that is overly complex, difficult to manage, or hard to interpret.

In the hotel industry, the brands tend to recommend the technology that should be deployed at the site level, and they develop service systems and processes that align with the brand proposition. Hotel brands rarely own and operate the majority of the properties that carry their flags, so sometimes adopting the brand's technology recommendation is not required. Therefore, the brands must convince owners and franchisees to invest in these innovations in technology or processes in their properties. They need to be able to train management companies to deploy and operate these technologies. Contracts with the brands do not necessarily even require that owners redesign lobbies or deploy new in-room technology, even if that becomes the new brand standard. This creates an interesting pressure on the brands, which depend on consistency for their own reputations, to demonstrate the value of the investments in terms that the owners understand (like return on investment, cost reductions, or revenue increases).

The situation can be a bit different for casinos, which tend to both own and operate their properties. They may have more control over their technology implementation decisions. The current trend for the integrated resort type of casinos is to lease their food and beverage and retail space to third parties. This means that the casino does not control the technology investments for these operators. The reason this matters is that many casinos want to understand the full picture of their on-property patron activity. If they have no visibility into their patron activities with these third-party retailers, due to technology compatibility issues, they could miss an important piece of the puzzle.

OPERATIONS DATA

Operations generates some similar data across the various functions within the hotel. They capture labor costs for the line-level employees, and the costs associated with ordering the various products used in the delivery of service (food, room amenities). Many operational outlets also capture sales transaction information, including what was ordered, when it was ordered, how many people used the service, and what time the service took place. Consider, for example, a check at the restaurant, which has an open and close time, the number of people dining, and the food that was ordered. These transactions could also contain guest identifying information, depending on how the system is set up.

In fact, a good deal of crucial operations data falls into the categories of demand and time. Demand in this context means the number of people served or number of "jobs" executed at any given service area. For example, demand for the front desk is how many guests are checked in or checked out, or for housekeeping, it's how many rooms that needed to be cleaned. Demand in hotels and casinos is a function of occupancy (how many people are staying in the hotel rooms), but many hotels and casinos also serve guests who are not staying at the property. Demand can also be a function of events that are happening on property and in the local market, as well as current marketing promotions or even the time of year. Operations managers are generally very well aware of all of the factors that might influence demand for all of the outlets across the enterprise. The challenge is understanding to what degree these factors will influence demand at any given outlet for any given time period.

The Importance of Time in Operations

Time refers both to the *time of day* that something happens (a check-in or a spa appointment), but also refers to the amount of time it takes to complete a service, such as how long it takes to clean a room or park a car, which is also referred to as *duration*. Knowing the time of day is important for labor scheduling—making sure there are enough staff scheduled during each time period to serve expected demand during that period. Most operations managers are pretty good at understanding business flow at the time of day level. However, the amount of time it takes to complete the service, or any element in the service process, is frequently less well understood because it can be more difficult to capture. It is important, however, because the time to complete the service combined with demand (number served) represents the amount of work that needs to get done, which dictates the amount of staff that needs to be scheduled. Manipulating all of the levers that impact these two elements, demand and time, is the most effective way to take costs out of a labor schedule, while maintaining service levels.

When duration is fixed, such as the number of nights that the room is booked, the number of minutes in the spa appointment, or the amount of time a group can rent the function space, it is relatively easy to understand how much work will need to be done, and to manage the process accordingly. It is when duration is *variable* that things become trickier (and way more fun for us analytic hospitality executives). For example, checking in a guest is a relatively standardized process, but factors like special requests, computer challenges, or reservation issues can dramatically change the amount of time the agent must deal with the guest.

The branch of mathematics called *queuing theory* tells us that it is the variability in the service time—these occasions when the service deviates from typical patterns—that creates lines, disgruntled customers, or idle employees eating up payroll. Most of us don't need math to understand how this phenomenon can occur, as we've all experienced the frustration of standing in line behind someone who is asking a lot of complicated questions or creating extra work for the agent we are waiting for, while watching the line grow behind us. I talk a bit more about queuing theory in the analytics section of this chapter and spend a good deal of time on waiting lines, since they are so ubiquitous in our industry. Proper application of both queuing theory and waiting line management requires a good understanding of both the average duration and the variability around that duration.

Dining duration at restaurants is a very good example of variable duration. Guests do not book a table for a specified period of time. Once they are seated, there is generally an implicit agreement that that party is able to use the table for as long as they want. When the restaurant is busy, the amount of time that guests use the table has a direct impact on *throughput* for the restaurant, which is the number of guests that can be served during a certain time period. A table that turns every hour potentially generates much more revenue than a table that is used for three hours by the same party (yes, I know it can also depend on how much wine that three-hour table ordered, but you see my point). If the restaurant takes reservations, the problem gets harder. You need to have some idea of the amount of time a table will be used by any given party to know when you are able to book it again—however, if you estimate too long of a time, the table sits empty when it could be generating revenue. Estimate too short of a time, and you've got angry waiting guests who were promised a certain time for service (many of us have also experienced this personally).

The challenge is that there is generally very little technology that automates the measurement of duration, and what technology there is, is heavily dependent on user entry, and therefore, prone to user error. For example, the point of sale in a restaurant captures the time the check was opened and closed, which should be a good proxy for the total dining duration. However, the server generally opens the check at the time they are able to enter the first order—which could be long after the party was actually seated. Similarly, the server might be too busy to close out the check immediately after the party leaves, so the duration continues to increase until the check is closed. It gets harder in other areas of the hotel or casino. For example, there is generally no technology utilized to capture the duration of interactions at the front desk, concierge, or valet stand.

The best way to accurately capture variable duration is through a *time and motion study*. This type of study involves deploying people to time the service process with a stopwatch and note the exact time that certain events occur (see Figure 5.2—party is seated, party orders drinks, party receives drinks, etc.). This task is time consuming and resource intensive, but it does provide a very detailed view of the service process and highlights areas for improvement. Early in my

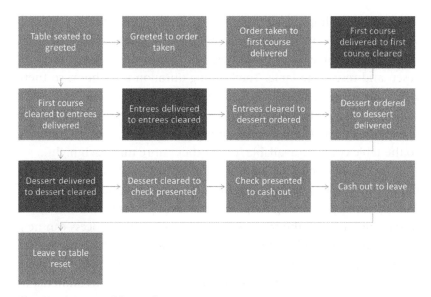

Figure 5.2 Stages of the Service Process
When you plan to conduct a time and motion study, generally the first step is to map out the stages of the service process that you want to time, such as those shown in this diagram. It is useful to note which are in control of the operation (light gray) and which are in control of the guest (dark gray).

career, I conducted a few such studies at restaurants. We looked at a few full-service restaurants, and also a few buffet-style restaurants. At the full-service restaurants, we noted that the time it took the server to drop off the check, take payment, and return it to the table was at times greater than the time it took the table to consume the entrees. Frequently, these parties were ready and waiting for the server to take their money, yet the server did not prioritize this activity.[1]

Besides being an interesting study in human behavior (we watched a gentleman dragging an oxygen tank and two plates full of crab legs stacked on top of each other. We also saw a lady build an assembly line to wrap her plate full of mufaletta sandwiches in paper napkins and drop them in her purse for later), the service process at the buffet also offered areas for immediate improvement in controlling duration and increasing the number of guests that could be served. Despite there being a long line for service at peak times, it was taking a long time for the staff to clear and reset tables. This stage of the service process is completely under the control of the staff, and represents a huge opportunity to improve throughput. Imagine if the buffet restaurant were open for four hours with a line the entire time. Say the guests occupied the table for 45 minutes, but it took 15 minutes to clear, reset, and reseat the table. Total dining duration is an hour, so there would be four turns per night for each table. If the reset and reseat time was reduced to a minute or so (remember, this is a buffet, so the setup is relatively simple), total dining duration becomes 46 minutes, so the table could be available for another entire turn each night.

The other useful benefit of a time and motion study is the opportunity to stop and watch the service process and demand flow. Managers can get so caught up in the details of execution that they fail to see the forest for the trees. Stopping to watch the process can help to identify opportunities to improve efficiency. Even little things like noticing that the service station is too far from the floor or that there aren't enough trays to bus tables can result in small investments or changes that make big differences in efficiency. Often, your staff will not be able to articulate these issues because they have simply become too used to dealing with them.

In high-volume services where seconds matter, these time studies can also make a difference. Fast food companies, for example, use these types of studies extensively to justify major investments in processes that can shave seconds off service delivery—whether it is technology, design and layout, business process, or training. Time and motion studies are used in manufacturing assembly lines as well, where they can shave days off delivery times. They are useful anywhere there is a multistage production or service process, and where technology is not able to capture the duration of each stage.

Customer Satisfaction

In addition to sales and cost information, hotels and casinos also collect satisfaction information from guest surveys. Guest surveys have evolved over time, but the value of understanding reactions to the service experience remains the same. Many say that with the emergence of review sites, a "24/7 Focus Group" has been created online, which is making guest surveys obsolete. I would argue that because you can't control the conversation topics in these review sites, nor can you control who responds, you need both the online information and your more structured guest survey to form a complete picture of guest satisfaction. The structured format of survey data allows you to gather exactly the information you want or need to know from exactly who you need to hear from, not just what the guests who like to write online reviews feel like talking about. Solid survey design ensures that the guests are answering the questions you asked, rather than an alternate interpretation of the question that you didn't intend. Augmenting that information with the elements of the service that guests commented on in freeform gives you a full picture of the success of your operational efforts.

Emerging Data Sources

In addition to the traditional data sources I just described, operations departments are starting to look carefully at the data generated by review sites and social media outlets. Operations was on the front line of the explosion of reviews, ratings, and social commentary. As mistakes were widely exposed, and they were suddenly forced to execute service recovery in front of the entire world. By necessity, hotels and casinos have become very good at monitoring and responding to reviews and social posts. They are also using data from reviews and ratings to help improve service and facilities. There is still more opportunity to mine the content of these text documents, to un-cover additional opportunities to incorporate the voice of the customer into the service delivery process.

Another emerging area of opportunity for operations is the location data generated by mobile devices. Not only does knowing where a guest is at any given moment facilitate communication "in the moment," but it also allows operations to track traffic throughout the property. This could help to identify opportunities for targeted marketing, placement of slot machines or other types of service offerings, adjusting operating hours, or fixing signage.

In 2014 and 2015, most of the larger hotel companies announced plans to provide room keys on smartphones. Operationally, this presents a few challenges in terms of staff training and guest logistics, but it also represents an opportunity to start collecting location data. The key will require logging into the hotel app, and enabling location services, which will allow operations to access guest location information in and around the hotel.

The next large, complex source that will impact operations is "the Internet of Things." As I mentioned in Chapter 4, this is the term that is used to describe the condition that is created when devices are connected to the Internet and begin to deliver status and diagnostic information about themselves. For hotel and casino operations, this means the HVAC system in each room would be streaming information about temperature fluctuations in the room. Same for the television, lights, and water. Imagine if the room could tell you it requires maintenance—a leak, a lightbulb, something rattling in the HVAC—so that maintenance can be scheduled before the guest even notices. In order to save energy, the HVAC could detect when the sun is shining into the room, and automatically close the drapes, or open them back up again, if that's what the guest wants, when the key is near the door. Room service trays could call for pickup after they are set outside the door. The industry is just now scratching the surface of the potential enabled by the Internet of Things. It will, however, require more technology investment by hotels and casinos, so the full realization of this opportunity may still be a bit far away.

ADVANCED ANALYTICS FOR OPERATIONS

There are many interesting analytical applications in operations at the intersection between maintaining the guest experience and controlling costs. First, I will talk about the analytical opportunities by the major categories I covered in Chapter 4, then I will identify some common operations goals and the analytical techniques that should be applied to address them.

In this chapter and the ones that follow, I'm going to focus on advanced analytics applications as opposed to discussing the descriptive techniques at the start of the analytics continuum (see Figure 4.1). Most departments already have a set of key performance indicators (KPIs) that they track internally to measure performance. I want to demonstrate opportunities to influence those KPIs through advanced analytics. That is not to say that hotels and casinos have perfected the KPIs they should be tracking. There is always an opportunity to improve measurement. It is particularly important because many KPIs that are tracked in these various departments (cost of sale, RevPAR, conversions) are also the basis of measurement for bonus and incentive plans. Peter Drucker also said "You can't manage what you don't measure." Of course, the opposite is also true. You very diligently manage what you are being measured on. Defining the right KPIs in the right way is very important to ensuring you get the outcomes you want from the business.

With the improvements in data access and data visualization, hospitality companies have opportunities to rethink how they will track performance and measure success. As analytics evolve, you will find new measures as well. While there are industry standards, driven either by common practice or by regulatory reporting requirements, to a certain extent, the KPIs you track and how they are defined can also be a strategic decision based on the company's long-term business plan and unique operating conditions.

And now that I've gotten myself out of the tricky and lengthy task of defining KPIs for you, on to advanced analytics for operations!

Statistical Analysis

As I described in Chapter 4, using survey data, with overall satisfaction as the dependent variable and the individual elements as the predictor variables, regression models will identify which elements are significant predictors of guest satisfaction and which are most impactful. This way, service operations managers can be laser focused on the elements of the operations that have the biggest impact.

The effectiveness of process changes or program options can be evaluated using hypothesis testing. For example, you may want to know if promoting a bar special in the room increases traffic to the bar.[2] You could put the information in a randomly selected group of rooms, and not in others, and then evaluate whether more guests took advantage of the bar special from rooms where it was promoted, or whether bar sales are significantly higher when the information is in the room versus not. This is also known as *A/B testing*. In order for this to be effective, you need two randomly selected groups—one that gets the new treatment, and one that does not. You also need a carefully defined and easily measurable outcome, and a statistically significant sample size (which can be as small as 30, according to statistical rules that you can look up—called the *assumption of a normal distribution*). A/B testing is so valuable, that you'll definitely see it come up again in subsequent chapters. In fact, as you'll read in Chapter 11, Dave Roberts, Senior Vice President of Revenue Management and Revenue Analysis at Marriott International, says nothing significant should be launched without extensive A/B testing and he believes it is analytics' responsibility to ensure that the entire organization is fluent in it.

Forecasting

Forecasting is probably the most useful, and widely used, advanced analytic application for operations. Many operations managers are responsible for producing budget forecasts, which are an expectation of revenue generation by time period for the year ahead. A demand forecast for any department in the hotel is very useful for labor planning, product ordering, and service process design. Most forecasts for operations involve seasonality, for time of year, day of week, and time of day impacts. Forecasts might also need to be at a detailed level, or based on a hierarchy of relationships. For example, forecasting the number of steaks that will be ordered is useful for product ordering. However, with an extensive menu, forecasting each product means a lot of very detailed forecasts. This means that demand forecasts for operations can become quite complex very quickly.

Operations might also find *unconstrained demand* forecasts useful. This forecasting method predicts the amount of demand that existed for your service, regardless of whether there was space to accommodate it. These forecasts are useful for outlets that have a capacity constraint—like the number of tables and seats in the restaurant or the number of spa appointments. Previous history is "constrained" or limited by this capacity—in the historical data, you will never actually "see" more demand than was able to be served, even if the restaurant turned guests away. An unconstrained demand forecast statistically adjusts for this occurrence, and allows you to forecast what "might have been." This means that you would know if you should hire more technicians for the spa or expand the restaurant. I cover unconstrained demand in more detail in Chapter 8.

When forecasting for labor scheduling, it's most important to forecast the entity that drives the work. This might be harder to do from a data perspective, but ultimately, it will result in a more accurate forecast. For example, an overall nightly hotel occupancy forecast is less useful for scheduling housekeepers and front desk agents than forecasting the number of arrivals and departures by time period would be. Arrivals and departures are what actually dictates the work that the front desk does. Similarly, a revenue forecast for the restaurant is helpful directionally, but it is actually the cover count (people to be served) that drives the work. The time period for the forecast should also be considered. For example, the number of guests that will check out on a day is helpful for the housekeeping schedule, because all of those rooms need to be cleaned by the end of housekeeping shifts. However, forecasting the number of covers per day for a three-meal period restaurant is not as helpful. Restaurants need a more granular schedule, because demand can vary widely by meal period, or even by hour or half hour period. Of course, the challenge is in the data. The smaller the time increment, the less historical data there is, and therefore, the more difficult it is to build an accurate forecast. Forecasters need to balance accuracy with the usefulness of the forecast.

Disaggregation is a useful forecasting method in the cases where there are small amounts of data that roll up to an overall number. With this technique, the forecast is performed at the higher level (e.g., covers by meal period), and then split up into smaller increments (e.g., covers by half hour) using percentage allocations according to typical historical patterns. For example, a restaurant could forecast that they expect 150 covers for dinner on a Saturday. The analyst would then use historical arrival patterns to understand what percentage of guests typically arrive at each half hour increment, and then the overall, or *aggregated,* forecast is split according to these percentage increments (10% of total demand arrives between 11:30 a.m. and noon, 30% between noon and 12:30 p.m.). This method can help balance the need for more detailed forecasts with the challenge of decreasing accuracy as the number of observations becomes smaller.

Predictive Modeling

One of the more interesting predictive analytic applications (at least for me) that is not yet widely used in hospitality or gaming operations is *simulation analysis*. Simulation allows you to model complex real world systems in an artificial environment so you can test options before you implement them and they impact the guest experience. Simulation is most useful for multistage processes where each stage depends on the outputs from the previous stage. For example, think about a kitchen. There are a certain number of stations in the kitchen with a set staff. Each station produces certain menu items. When an order comes in, it is split among the various stations, which prepare the individual items, and then the order is pulled together to deliver to a table. Each station has a varying amount of work to do depending on the content and timing of the checks, and how long it takes to prepare each item. However, all of the items for each course on each check need to be ready at approximately the same time.

A simulation analysis could model series of orders of typical sets of items and test to see whether certain stations get overloaded or have slack. This would allow the restaurant to test a new menu to make sure it doesn't overload the kitchen, test new kitchen configurations, or test a new piece of equipment, simply by adjusting the parameters of the simulation. As you can probably tell from reading this, the time and motion studies I described previously are required to build an effective simulation. The two key simulation inputs are the time it takes to complete each task in the process, and the arrival process of the entity you are modeling (guests, orders, cars, etc.). The first needs to be specific to the operation; the second can be analytically modeled according to some standard distributions. There are commercially available simulation packages, but they generally need to be configured by a trained and experienced analyst.

Another type of predictive modeling that can be useful to operations is *queuing theory*. Queueing theory is a branch of analytics that predicts the behavior of lines. As it turns out, this modeling is among the most complex mathematical techniques, because it needs to account for *uncertainty*. I've talked about uncertainty before. Also called *variability*, uncertainty basically means that a task or measure changes each time it happens. It doesn't take exactly the same amount of time to check in a guest or serve a table or park a car every time you do it. When tasks are performed in sequence, the variability at each stage can create massive waits and long lines. Queuing models can predict what will happen under a variety of service conditions, ultimately determining the best way to design a service process to better manage waits. They can also help you to evaluate which interventions will have the biggest impact on reducing waits. I talk more about waiting and queues later in this section.

Optimization

Operations most typically uses optimization for labor scheduling. Remember from Chapter 4 that optimization tells you the decisions you should make that result in the best possible outcome, considering all of the business constraints. For a labor schedule, the goal is to minimize labor cost. The constraints can include the number of guests that are expected, the number of staff that are available, the number of hours they can work, break schedules, special requests, equipment or process design constraints, a guest-to-staff ratio, a desired service level, and opening and closing hours. The output of the labor schedule can either be the number of staff required each period to serve demand or an actual employee schedule that also respects employee availability and labor laws. Because labor can be so expensive for hotels and casinos, I have a special section later in the chapter where I discuss the integrated analytics process associated with building a cost-effective labor schedule. Optimization can also be used to allocate a development budget, set operating hours, or determine the best use of space on the casino floor, which I cover in more detail in Chapter 10.

Analytics by Business Goal

Operations has many business goals. Some are specific to departments or functions, others span the enterprise. Table 5.1 shows some of the higher level operations goals and the analytics that help to achieve each goal.

Table 5.1 Analytics for Operations

Operations Category	Top Operations Goal	Analytics
Guests	Increase guest satisfaction	Regression to identify key drivers of satisfaction
	Reduce wait times	Queuing theory, simulation
	Increase spend	Predictive modeling to identify opportunities to cross and up sell, promote high-profit items, or encourage add-on purchases.
Labor	Reduce labor costs	Forecasting, optimization, simulation analysis
	Improve hiring and retention	Data mining and predictive analytics
	Increase employee satisfaction	Regression to identify key drivers of satisfaction
Facilities and Material	Reduce waste	Menu item forecasting
	Improve revenue-generating capability of key outlets	Capacity management, pricing, simulation analysis
	Reduce food cost	Menu item forecasting, supply chain analytics
	Decrease carbon footprint	Energy forecasting

Of course, operations must also function within the broader organization, so their goals should be considered in light of what the enterprise is trying to achieve. I speak more about how to accomplish this in Chapter 11, when I describe opportunities for cross-departmental data integration and decision making. Obviously, this goes for every functional area in the hotel or casino, and it is easy to forget as you are driving toward an incentive-related goal, fighting fires, or dealing with an angry guest right in front of you.

WORKFORCE PLANNING AND OPTIMIZATION

Every hospitality operations manager, no matter what department they work in, has been caught short-staffed, and faced the wrath of guests who had to wait—or worse, guests who walked out because they didn't want to wait. On the other hand, every manager has also been called onto the carpet over labor costs above target levels—which impacts bonuses and salaries. Labor scheduling in hospitality is a delicate balance between maintaining the guest experience and minimizing the highest controllable cost on the P&L.

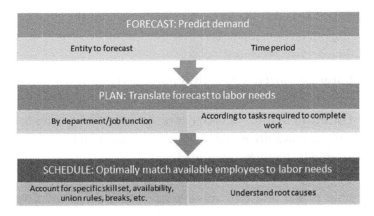

Figure 5.3 Labor Scheduling Process

Scheduling labor for hotels and casinos, in my opinion, has traditionally been too much art and not enough science. The gut feel of experienced managers is always valuable, but most labor scheduling, when done manually, has a healthy bias toward whatever happened most recently—did you get yelled at last week by a waiting guest, or are your costs running a little high this month? Further, with all the moving pieces in a labor schedule, finding the right answer is a problem that is really too large and too complicated for a human to figure out without the aid of advanced analytics. Bringing some science into the labor scheduling process can help managers achieve this delicate balance between reducing costs and maintaining the service experience, and save them time as well.

Scheduling labor is a three-part process (Figure 5.3). Analytics can be brought to bear at each stage of the process, getting those managers back on the floor where they belong!

Forecast

The first part of the labor scheduling process is to forecast demand. An accurate and credible demand forecast is the foundation for a cost-effective and service-focused labor schedule. In fact, in my opinion, the majority of the benefits of an analytical approach to labor scheduling will be achieved in the demand forecasting step, if it is done properly.

In order to ensure that the forecast is appropriate for the labor you are scheduling, operations managers first need to make several decisions about their service processes:

- **Forecast entity.** What drives the amount of work—is it cars to park, rooms to clean, guests to check in?
- **Duration of job.** For each entity, does the time it takes to serve vary significantly enough that the duration and the variability around it should be accounted for?
- **Time period to forecast.** How much does demand vary by time period and how do you schedule your labor? Can you stagger shift start and end times? Do you have part-time workers who can cover busy periods?

The hospitality and gaming labor scheduling problem is particularly challenging because of this complex combination of number of entities, pattern of arrival times, and the time it takes to serve the entities. Let's look at an example of why entity, time period, and duration matter in hospitality labor forecasting. The number of occupied rooms in the hotel might be a good enough forecast for scheduling housekeepers, but even though demand at the front desk is related to occupied rooms, occupied rooms are not driving the amount of work at the front desk. Work at the front desk is driven by checking guests in and out, so it's actually arrivals and departures that impact the number of front desk staff needed. Think about how long it takes housekeepers to clean rooms. Does it take significantly longer to clean a check-out room than it does to straighten one for a guest who is staying over? If so, then perhaps the number of departures is a valuable forecast for housekeeping scheduling as well. While housekeepers can be assigned a number of rooms to clean over their entire shift, activity at the front desk can vary hour by hour, as guests arrive and depart. For housekeepers, a daily "rooms to clean" forecast (accounting for the time element associated with room type and checkouts versus stayovers) would be sufficient for an accurate schedule. For the front desk, if you calculate that you expect 100 check-ins on Monday, there's a huge difference between 100 check-ins at 10 per half hour and 100 check-ins that show up at 3:00. You will need a forecast of check-ins and checkouts by hour, half hour, or even 15-minute period to ensure agents are scheduled to match guest arrival and departure patterns. Otherwise, you could end up with long waits and low satisfaction scores.

Plan

The next step in the labor scheduling process is to match the forecast to labor needs. In this step, managers determine how many employees it will take to meet expected levels of work that need to be done without overscheduling. This calculation can be as simple as establishing a standard operating procedure or a "rule of thumb." For example, many restaurant managers make the assumption that one server can handle four tables, or ten covers, at one time. If the demand forecast calls for 20 covers in an hour, the manager can assume that they will need two servers in that hour. While this level of assumption might be "good enough" for some hospitality scenarios, there are definite advantages to taking a more analytical approach. Questions managers should ask themselves are:

- Is there a difference in the amount of time it takes to serve or process different types of entities, for example a two-top versus eight-top in the restaurant, check-in versus checkout, suite versus standard room? (*Note:* The answer to this question could change your forecasting plan as well, which means you may need a more granular definition of the entity.)

- How much variability is there in the amount of time it takes to serve an entity? Dining duration can be highly variable, whereas a check-in might be relatively predictable in duration. If you schedule to the average when the time is variable, you will end up with either idle workers or long lines and angry guests. I discuss variability more later, in the section on queueing.

- Does serving different types of entities require different skill levels or different types of employees, for example, a facial versus a massage, a blackjack dealer versus a roulette dealer?

- How long am I comfortable having guests wait for service? Is a 20-person line at the front desk okay? Will guests accept a 30-minute wait at the restaurant?

■ How much work can I realistically expect from my employees? A front desk agent might be able to check in 12 guests per hour, but can they really keep up that pace hour after hour without a break? Or even within that hour, is there another task they must do besides checking in guests that will impact their ability to serve the 12?

Answering these questions helps to set the standards for the amount of work each staff member can reasonably do per period. If the service times don't vary greatly, you can simply use arithmetic to figure out labor needs. When you're confident that a housekeeper can clean 14 rooms a shift, or a valet can park 30 cars an hour, matching the number of employees to the demand forecast is a relatively simple matter. It can be easily automated according to the demand forecast. If service times are more variable (think about dining duration in a restaurant), queuing theory or simulation analysis might be required, which will add one more step into your labor needs analysis. As described previously, these techniques model the impact of highly variable service times and complex, multistage processes, accounting for factors like employee utilization and tolerable wait times. They also let you model scenarios without interrupting actual operations, so you can test the impact of adding or removing servers, or raising and lowering utilization assumptions. Unlike forecasting, these analyses do not have to be run frequently. You can employ them during the initial analysis of your service process and implement the results in the labor schedule. Then you would only need to update the initial results if something in your service process changes (new menu, redesigned parking area, new key technology).

Schedule

The final step is to translate a labor needs plan into an actual schedule. This is where an employee name is associated with a shift. Managers typically do this task by hand—and it can be quite time consuming to figure it out manually. Scheduling of this nature is a classic optimization problem. Applying this technique not only derives the best possible answer to minimize costs while maintaining service levels, but also saves managers time. The optimization will automatically take into account all constraints that must be met in order to create the schedule, including employee skill and seniority, scheduling availability and preferences, minimum and maximum shift length, union rules, desired service levels, and labor regulations (i.e., breaks).

Labor scheduling is a good example of a multistep process where analytics can provide significant advantages at every step in the process. Remember, for such a complex process, it is not necessary to start with the large, interconnected analytical system. In fact, that is probably the wrong decision. Applying analytics to small, defined sections of the problem can provide immediate benefits, while helping the team to get used to interpreting and taking action on results. Then you can phase in the next analytical application once the staff has had a chance to adapt and work out any issues with the first one.

▶ NOTE

Right after college I managed a family-owned restaurant in New Orleans. We were open for lunch and dinner five days a week with about 60 seats and a front of house staff of around 14. Since the entire management staff (which was basically the owner and me) was so hands on, we never really took the time to look at data for anything other than reconciling the books. We figured that we were there, so we knew what was going on. However, being a budding analytic hospitality executive, one day I looked back through our lunch data and made a simple bar graph in Excel of average lunch covers per day of week. Much to our surprise, our lunch covers on Tuesdays were higher, on average, than any other day of the week. Yet, we always scheduled the fewest servers on Tuesday, because we assumed that the beginning of the week was slower than the end of the week. I always thought that the reason Tuesdays were a bit chaotic was because it was the first day back after our weekend. It turned out the chaos was because we were actually busiest on Tuesdays. This very simple analysis helped operations to run more smoothly.

Now, I know what you are thinking—this is way more basic than where most operations are today. Just remember, it was a very small restaurant, and it was a while ago. The point is that even a simple data analysis can challenge assumptions, and provide insight that helps to make better decisions.

QUEUES

The image in Figure 5.4 will look all too familiar to operations managers. Given how ubiquitous queues are across all kinds of industries, and the very real problems that queues cause (service delays, disgruntled guests, loss of revenue from guests choosing not to join or leaving queues), there has been a great deal of research into how queues behave and how to reduce or eliminate them most efficiently. As I mentioned in the analytics section, queueing theory is among the most complex areas in math. This is because the uncertainty and variability in any service system, where arrival patterns and service times differ, requires some pretty advanced modeling to solve. As a result of all of this research, there are some standard (complicated) formulas that can be used to evaluate queues. Simulation, as I described, is used when the system becomes so complicated that it can't be solved in a closed-form equation.

The advantage of queuing math or simulation is that it can help you evaluate that balance between guest experience and controlling costs. The inputs to a queuing formula generally are the number of servers, the service time, and the arrival pattern of the guests. The way these inputs are used in the formula depends on the queue configuration. The outputs include the number of guests that can be served in a certain time period, and the duration of the wait, if there is one. By modeling the waits using these mathematical formulas, managers can understand the impact of staff reductions on wait times, or the improvement that can be gained by investing in technology that reduces service time. Managers may be willing to essentially require a short wait

Figure 5.4 The Ubiquitous Waiting Line

at the front desk from time to time because the cost of never having a wait, in terms of staffing, is so significant. Conversely, it could be that a relatively small investment in staff or technology can result in dramatic improvements in waiting times.

There are five essential features of a queuing system:

1. **The calling population.** This is the group from which guests are obtained. The calling population isn't homogeneous. It is comprised of many market segments and many guests or patrons with different needs.

2. **The arrival process.** This is the rate at which guests arrive to the service system and if necessary join the queue. This can vary by time period.

3. **Queue configuration.** This refers to the way the queue is designed. For example, single line, single server, a snake line to multiple servers, and multiple lines to multiple servers.

4. **Queue discipline.** This refers to the rules that govern the order in which guests or patrons are selected from the line. For example, the available server could simply take the next guest in line, or pass over that next guest in favor of a guest with a more immediate need or a higher status.

5. **Service process.** This final feature describes the process of delivering service. This could range from self-service to a multistage server process.

The queueing formula you use depends on the characteristics of these essential features. The good news is that there are some basic rules of thumb about queue behavior that have been established that you can work with before you hire a queueing specialist or build a simulation. The calling population should be analyzed to determine what the diverse needs of the population are, and decide how the service process should match the needs of the population. The arrival process is typically modeled in queueing math according to a known distribution, but operations managers can also observe when there are peak periods and slow periods and begin to deploy staff accordingly. These are relatively simple analyses that can be repeated as business conditions change. However, one of the biggest decisions that needs to be made is how the queue should be configured and how the service process will be designed. The reason these decisions are so important is that they frequently involve making design choices that once made are expensive to change.

THE IMPACT OF QUEUE CONFIGURATION

Queue configuration, the third feature, is worth delving into in a bit more detail because it has an impact on not only waiting time but also on consumer behavior. This is a great example of operationalizing analytics, demonstrating how you need to consider the entire process when you evaluate how analytics will be deployed within it to support performance improvements. It is very important for managers to understand this impact, since it can be difficult to change the queue configuration once the design has been implemented. The impact of queue configuration on waiting time and consumer behavior has been widely studied, and there are some basic rules that can be considered when planning a service process that will include a queue.

There are three basic options for traditional queue configurations, with some variations. First, there is the multiple server, multiple line configuration where patrons line up in front of the individual servers, as in a grocery store. The second option is a single snake line with multiple servers, and the third is the "take a number" option, where guests wait for their turn without standing in line. Each line style has benefits and drawbacks.

- **Multiline, multiserver.** The multiline, multiserver system requires the guest or patron to select which line to join (Figure 5.5). The benefits and drawbacks to this line style are (Fitzsimmons and Fitzsimmons 1994):
  - Service can be differentiated. With this set up, you can have a priority line for VIP patrons, or segregate check-in and checkout. This means that patrons with smaller demands or greater priority can be served quickly and removed from the service system.
  - Division of labor is possible. More experienced agents can be assigned to VIP customers or an expert barista can be assigned to the specialty lane.

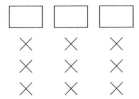

Figure 5.5 Multiline, Multiserver System

- *Balking,* deciding not to join the line, is deterred with this style of line. The lines in front of multiple servers can appear shorter than a single snake line, so joining patrons may be less likely to leave.

- From a consumer behavior perspective, this line style permits jockeying—line switching—which can help waiting patrons feel more in control of the wait. However, it can also be very frustrating for patrons to watch the line next to them seem to move much faster than the one they are in.

- **Single-line, multiserver.** The single line, multiserver system is where the guests or patron joins the end of a single long queue that feeds into multiple servers (Figure 5.6). There are several items to consider with to this type of system (Fitzsimmons and Fitzsimmons 1994):

  - The average time spent waiting in this queue configuration tends to be less than in any other format.

  - The line perfectly preserves the first come, first served service order, guaranteeing fairness. Waiting guests join the back of the queue and are served in the order they arrive.

  - There is no anxiety from worrying that you joined the slowest line.

  - With only one entrance to the queue, cutting in line is more difficult, and reneging (deciding to leave) is also made difficult.

  - Privacy is enhanced because there is no one standing immediately behind the person being served.

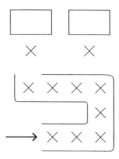

Figure 5.6 Single-Line
Multiserver System

- **Take a number or virtual queue**. In this format there is no physical line. Guests check in and receive an indication of the order they will be served (Figure 5.7). There are a few advantages to this format (Fitzsimmons and Fitzsimmons 1994).
  - If guests are free to wander around instead of being restricted to the line, they may feel encouraged to make additional purchases in retail stores or gamble a bit more.
  - The arrival order is masked to a certain extent, so if you want to change the service order, guests may not notice. This is a risk as well as an advantage, because guests can be quite observant when they are protecting their place in line.

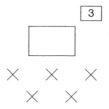

Figure 5.7 Take a
Number, or Virtual Queue

Alternative Queue Designs

After understanding the implications of the standard queue design, you can apply that knowledge to alternative designs. For example, many hospitality and gaming companies utilize separate queues for priority guests or patrons. This type of queueing system removes one or more servers from the general system and also removes a subset of guests. Depending on the number of priority guests, and the design of the system, this could result in increased waits in the regular line, with slack (idle servers) in the priority line. However, if the two lines are close in proximity to each other the idle, priority servers can serve guests from the regular line when there are no priority guests. Hotel front desks and airline check-in counters employ this design, and the priority check-in servers will call guests from the regular line when they are idle.

Adding a self-service option is another alternative queue design. Airlines also attempted to speed up service times and reduce waits by adding kiosks to the check-in process. These kiosks act as additional servers. The risk, of course, is that if customers are not comfortable with the usage of the kiosks, or the interface is not intuitive, more servers are required to provide assistance at the kiosks. Even with kiosks, you can still end up with queues during peak periods.

Another alternate queue design is the multistage wait process. This is where the service process is broken up into stages, and there is potentially a wait before each stage—as opposed to having one server take a single guest through every step in the process. The department of motor vehicles in some states is a good example of this type of wait. The first server checks paperwork and routes you to the appropriate area (license renewal, driver's test, license plate). If you are getting a new license, for example, the next server enters your information, verifies ID, and passes you along to the server that operates the camera. That server takes your picture, processes the driver's license, and passes you along to the cashier, who takes payment and hands over the new license. There could be a queue in front of each stage. Multistage queues provide the perception of progress to the waiting consumers. As each stage is completed they feel as though they are moving forward. It also allows for servers to become specialists at certain tasks, which has some advantage in terms of speed and training. The process has to be relatively complex, possibly with alternative routings, to make this type of staged wait feasible. Amusement parks employ this method with some of the themed rides. Waiting guests move through various themed areas where the "story" of the ride begins before the patrons actually get to the ride. A restaurant might think about using this method to reduce the time guests spend at the table. They could offer appetizers or dessert and after dinner drinks at the bar, which has the advantage of getting guests off the tables, while using some of the free space in the restaurant.

MANAGING CONSUMER PERCEPTIONS OF THE WAIT

As important as it is to manage actual wait time, and the efficiency of the service process, it is equally important to understand and manage consumers' reactions to the wait experience. David Maister, in *The Psychology of Waiting Lines*, conceptualized two Laws of Service and eight propositions about the psychology of waiting. His first law of service deals with expectations versus perceptions. If consumers receive better service than expected, they will be highly satisfied and very likely to pass along their good impressions to other consumers. The reverse is also true. If service is worse than expected, they become extremely dissatisfied and pass along bad word of mouth.[3] Maister's second law of service states that first impressions can influence the rest of the service experience. This means that if guests become irritated during the wait for service, they will be less satisfied with the service itself. It behooves service managers to make the wait as pleasant as possible for consumers. This is where Maister's eight propositions come into play.

These propositions describe the impact of the conditions of the wait on the consumers' perceptions during the wait. Operations managers should pay attention to these eight psychological propositions when they design the waiting experience.

1. **Unoccupied wait time feels longer than occupied wait time.** Most of us would probably agree that having something to do during a wait makes the time seem to pass much faster than an idle wait. Think about how you can amuse your guests or patrons if they must wait. Video screens at check-in playing ads for the services at the property, or passing through the waiting area with complimentary appetizers are good examples of small ways to occupy the wait. Of course, if the video is short and on a loop, the third or fourth time the patrons see the same sequence might become counterproductive.

2. **Preprocess waits are perceived as longer than in-process waits.** Consumers are always anxious to get started with their service experience. They become more tolerant of waits if they know that the service experience has started. If a server acknowledges the table as soon as they are seated, even if it's just "Welcome, I will be right with you," consumers can relax knowing that their dining experience has begun. Think about what you can do to make the guests feel like they are getting started, even if they are technically still waiting. Maybe there is paperwork to fill out or a waiver to read when the guest is waiting for a spa treatment, for example.

3. **Anxiety makes the wait seem longer.** It is easy to become anxious during a wait. Guests might not be sure what line they are supposed to be in. They could perceive that line next to them is moving faster. They could think that they missed an opportunity by standing in the wrong place. Service staff should always be conscious of reassuring the guests that they are in the right place and that they will be served. Signage is helpful, but also having one server doing line management provides the personal touch and lets guests ask questions (potentially, it could even satisfy proposition number 2, also). At the front desk of a large conference hotel, having an employee at the back of the line simply verifying with guests, "Are you checking in?," and "Are you a rewards member?" could help to reduce anxiety, particularly if the lobby area is crowded. Think about what your guests may be worrying about while they are waiting, and take steps to remove that worry.

4. **Uncertain waits are longer than known, finite waits.** Consumers wait more calmly if they know how long they should expect to wait. There is a big difference between "we will begin boarding soon" and "we will begin boarding in 15 minutes." The certainty associated with the duration of the wait makes the wait more tolerable. Where possible, hotel and casino operations managers should attempt to define the wait.

5. **Unexplained waits feel longer than explained waits.** Understanding the causes for waits changes expectations. You

expect to wait longer in the taxi queue on a rainy day, or longer in line at the grocery store on a weekend morning. Think about the difference between sitting at the gate ten minutes past boarding time when no one has acknowledged the delay, versus when the gate agent announces that the inbound flight has just landed and as soon as they deplane and service the plane you will be on your way. Open communication about wait times and reasons behind waits are preferable to ignoring the problem.

6. **Unfair waits feel longer than equitable waits.** There is nothing worse than watching someone cut in line in front of you, seeing a party you know arrived after you get seated before you, or watching a car speed down the shoulder of the road and cut into traffic far ahead of you. This is infuriating for guests and makes them pay much closer attention to the duration of the wait. If you are going to give priority to certain guests, either make sure it's explained (clearly marked priority lines, and how you qualify for priority) or hidden from the other waiting guests.

7. **Consumers will wait longer for a more valuable service.** Consumers are willing to wait longer for services they perceive as valuable. They'll accept an hour wait for a table at your marquis restaurant, but will be very irritated by a line at the coffee shop. Keep this in mind when you notice where waits occur in your property, particularly when a service experience is ending and patrons are just waiting to pay and leave. How long does the wait to exit the plane after landing feel? Definitely longer than the wait during boarding.

8. **Solo waits feel longer than group waits.** Waiting in a group is more distracting because members of the waiting party are engaged with one another. Train your staff to be conscious of solo guests, or where possible, create a group feeling in the wait experience. Just be mindful that solo guests may not feel like being interacted with, so there's a delicate balance between understanding what they are going through and irritating them with the wrong kind of attention.

NOTE

I was very intrigued with this concept of improving the perceptions of the wait experience during my PhD research. We know that because dining duration is uncertain, taking reservations at a restaurant can negatively impact the number of guests you are able to serve. If you are not able to accurately forecast how long guests will use the tables, you can end up with empty seats when guests have finished long before the next party is due to arrive. There are a few ways to manage this situation, but it is most efficient from a capacity management perspective to have guests waiting to be served as soon as the previous guests are finished with the table. This keeps all seats full and generating revenue. If you have to have a wait, then you run the risk of impacting satisfaction with the entire experience, as Maister's propositions described. Maister's propositions, while intuitively logical, have not all been empirically tested. For my dissertation research, I decided to test the occupied versus unoccupied wait time proposition, to see if the kind of activity waiting patrons engaged in during the wait made the wait feel shorter, more pleasant, or more acceptable. I ran a series of experiments where I tested several different activities on different duration waits with different types of services at the end of the wait. Disappointingly (for an academic researcher), I found no significant differences between activity types. I merely discovered the rather intuitive result that people hate to wait. They would prefer not to, but if they have to, they'd rather have something to do (McGuire et al. 2010). Still, it was a good learning experience in research design and data analysis, which is what the PhD dissertation is supposed to be.

Please, please, please no matter what queueing design you ultimately deploy, and how you design the wait experience, please, clearly indicate how guests or patrons enter the line and where they need to be to receive service. There is nothing more frustrating than approaching a front desk or entering a cafe when you don't know where you are supposed to stand, who you are supposed to talk to, or what you can to do make sure you get taken care of before the hundreds of other guests who seem to be charging ahead of you!! And consider guests' comfort as much as possible during the wait. Provide sufficient space so that guests or patrons are out of the way of each other and the service staff. An uncomfortable wait can increase irritation, and also reflect negatively on the service experience.

BENCHMARKING OPERATIONS ANALYTICS CAPABILITIES

As I mentioned in the chapter introduction, I often get asked about what the most sophisticated companies in hospitality and gaming are doing in analytics, or how the typical company is thinking about this area. I have not done an extensive study on this, but I can provide my impressions from my years working with leading hospitality and travel companies. This should serve as a guide for those who are embarking on or rethinking their operational analytics programs. Your own decisions, of course, should be based on your company's capabilities, operating conditions, and market strategy.

Beginners. Operations departments that are in early stages of analytical capability operate in a highly manual environment. They have difficulty getting access to the data they need to make operational decisions proactively, so they are likely relying on the (hopefully good) instincts of the managers. Reports can take days to pull together, so it is only possible to react to sales and service trends long after they've happened. Managers are likely using summary reports from the selling systems to track trends, but these reports are simply static snapshots of performance information. Some of these operations are collecting and reviewing guest surveys, but it is a manual process or a benchmarking exercise to calculate bonuses. Some may be using a reputation management vendor to help them understand trends in guest reviews and ratings, and to monitor and respond to service issues.

Average. The typical operations department is able to look at their data at a pretty detailed level. They are probably using some sort of business intelligence application to identify trends and uncover the factors that might be driving costs. Depending on the operations department and the skill level of the resources in it, they might be doing some basic forecasting analysis to predict demand patterns or revenue trends. Food and beverage operations could be using a program like Avero Slingshot™ to provide some intelligence about menu item category sales, server performance, cost patterns, and outlet performance. They are likely consuming the results of reputation management analyses, and probably have a monitor and respond program in place for tweets and reviews. They are actively collecting and reviewing satisfaction data. These companies have gotten good at understanding and using data, but really aren't leveraging much advanced analytics like predictive modeling or optimization.

Most sophisticated. The most sophisticated operations groups in hotels and casinos are heavy users of very sophisticated forecasting techniques. They use forecasting for labor scheduling, financial planning, and supply ordering. Teams analyze survey data at a very detailed level, understanding and managing the drivers of satisfaction. They are likely gathering and mining their own text data for insights about reputation, service improvement opportunities, and guest sentiment. They are doing extensive modeling of the service process before implementing any new designs or technology. This could involve queuing math, optimization, or simulation analysis. These organizations are partnering with marketing to implement location-based programs on property. They are probably also using this location data to track traffic patterns, and make operational adjustments based on traffic flow at different times of the day. They do A/B testing on the signage around the property to understand what marketing treatments drive conversions. This can also extend to the digital menu signboards at restaurants.

I have heard of major hospitality companies using the advertising space on menu boards to adjust the flow of orders into the kitchen to take advantage of slack. For example, if the grill is getting too many orders during a busy lunch period, the signboards might advertise salads or cold sandwiches to drive orders to an area of the kitchen that has slack. This type of operational adjustment requires real-time access to operational data, and predictive modeling to evaluate the impact of shifting traffic.

■ ■ ■

I have seen McDonald's present on their process for testing new kitchen designs or drive through layouts. Remember, for a quick-service restaurant like McDonald's, seconds matter. Any new piece of equipment, layout change, or process adjustment that saves seconds has a huge payoff in throughput and revenue across their system. McDonald's does time and motion studies to understand the performance of all of the options. They have a team of operations researchers that model the new process using optimization and simulation analysis, so they can understand how the new system will perform under a variety of operating conditions. They implement in a test group of stores and observe performance in the real world. All of this is done before they recommend the change to the franchise community. This is a great example of advanced analytics adding value to an operational process. With tight margins and an international reputation, there are big risks for McDonald's when they take a new process or system live in their restaurants. The analytical modeling and testing can give McDonald's operations confidence in the effectiveness of their new programs.

I hosted a webinar with Marriott as part of the SAS/CHR series "Insights and Innovations for Hospitality," which described how Marriott redesigned the lobbies at Courtyard by Marriott to be more modern and more functional. Analytics played a role during all phases of design by providing insight from focus groups, surveys, and concept testing. It was, frankly, a fascinating discussion.[4] I encourage you to look into it. There is a reference to a white paper summarizing the discussion at the end of the chapter. The point here is that a large global company like Marriott doesn't launch new designs because they think they look cool. There is purpose and function to new programs like this, and they have been extensively tested before they are implemented, and after as well.

TECHNOLOGY AND PEOPLE INVESTMENTS

There are some basic technology investments that would benefit operations, and of course, there are analytical resources required to support analytical technology investments. I will outline the types of systems and personas that I believe are worth the investment, depending on what stage of analytical capability the organization is in. The decision of which vendors to work with, and what specific technologies you should implement is, clearly, up to your business strategy and budget.

Technology

There are some basic, must-have technologies for operations and a few items that can be placed on a roadmap as sophistication grows. As with any other technology area, the roadmap items turn into must-haves as technology evolves and industry adapts, so don't wait too long before making the basic investments, or you will get behind.

The Basics

Business intelligence. Every department should have some way of viewing their data that is accessible, fast, and scalable. System generated reports, like those that come from a point of sale system, do not provide a sufficient level of detail, and Excel can quickly get bogged down. Many vendors provide purpose-built business intelligence applications for specific hospitality or gaming operations departments that have certified data integrations and department-specific KPIs and reports. These solutions can be cost effective, since these days they tend to be delivered in the cloud, so they require minimal on-site investment.

Forecasting. Can you tell that I am a fan? To start, operations departments do not need a complicated or sophisticated forecasting application. Despite the limitations of Excel, you can use it to develop basic trends, projected at a high level into the future. As the organization becomes more comfortable understanding how to interpret and use these trends, they can add more advanced forecasting capability.

Reputation management. Operations cannot get along these days without a system that monitors social activity, and provides the ability to respond to service issues in real time. Whatever program you are using should be able to provide some basic idea of guest or patron sentiment, key topics of conversation, and some competitor information. Again, offerings in this area tend to be very accessible, as they are cloud based and purpose built.

Next Steps

Flexible business analytics. After operations has mastered the basics, it's time to grow analytical capabilities both in sophistication and usage. The purpose-built, departmental business intelligence applications are great to get started, both from a functionality and cost perspective. However, they are limited to one area of the business, and tend to provide precanned reports without a lot of flexibility. As the variety of business personas and business problems grow, the organization will likely outgrow the problem-specific business intelligence applications. There are data visualization applications that provide the flexibility to design custom reports, as well as offer some light analytical capabilities like forecasting or correlation analysis. This gives end users more flexibility to analyze their data, and to visualize cross-departmental information in the same platform. The tradeoff for flexibility is that these solutions do require a bit more time and effort in data preparation. The effort pays off, but needs to be planned for.

Advanced forecasting. A sophisticated analytical forecasting tool will provide more accuracy and more detail to forecasting projects. More detailed forecasting can improve ordering, form the foundation for a sophisticated labor management program, and help with identifying problem areas in the operation. This requires good, clean, detailed data, which is a challenge, and it also requires a specialized resource that understands analytical forecasting techniques. I address that in more detail in the following section.

Time and motion study. At this stage, hotels and casinos could consider conducting a few time and motion studies. These studies are time consuming, but relatively inexpensive. Select a service process with several stages, like the restaurant, and hire an intern or some contractors to time each stage. The analysis of this data will help you to identify inefficiencies in your processes, and ultimately provide opportunity to improve throughput and revenue. You will also have data to use in more complex analyses like simulation or queuing math, should you decide to go down that path.

Advanced

Advanced analytics platform. The more advanced operations department should have a fully integrated advanced analytics platform that delivers predictive modeling, forecasting, and optimization. Analysts will be able to apply the right technique to any problem the operation uncovers, on a single source of data.

Workforce planning and optimization. This is a good stage to invest in a fully functional planning and optimization solution for the workforce problem. Forecasts are produced at a detailed enough level to drive a deployment plan and an optimal schedule that considers labor laws, time-off requests, and staff availability.

Simulation analysis. Operations analysts could leverage a process-oriented simulation analysis that provides a graphic user interface–driven methodology for designing steps and configuring the elements of the service process. This is an area that companies that consistently innovate in their service design will want to invest in to support new service development. Simulation packages can help test new processes or layouts before they are deployed in the actual service environment. As I discussed earlier, there are some specific data requirements for simulation analysis, including arrival patterns and service duration by stage, which involve some effort to collect. Still, the results can be quite useful.

Location-based or real-time technology. Particularly for large integrated resorts, any location-based data collection and interaction systems, or real-time analysis technology can be very helpful. In the next chapter I talk about how marketing leverages this technology for one-to-one communication, but operations can use it for analyzing traffic patterns to improve flow, adjusting layouts, influencing traffic through digital signage, or deploying staff to reduce waits or relieve congestion.

People

Operations departments should first invest in a resource that is very strong in building operational reports. This resource should understand how to clean and manipulate data, and how to turn that data into visualizations that tell a business story. He or she can help to build and update routine reports, and can also perform ad hoc analyses according to the needs of the department.

A forecasting analyst will also be a good investment for most operations departments. As I suggest previously, there are many forecasting problems in operations, so this resource can support multiple departments with many different types of forecasting analysis. A forecasting analyst will likely also know techniques like correlation, regression, and statistical analysis, so he or she could also support analyses like identifying the drivers of satisfaction.

Of course, this investment depends on the size and scope of the organization. At the property level, most mid- to large-size hotels could benefit from a reporting analyst. If those hotels already have a revenue management department, it is possible to slightly expand the functions of that group to include operational forecasting or report building. Large casinos and corporate hotels can make investments in centralized operations support functions, with multiple resources to support reporting and analytics.

Large corporate entities, particularly those that are active in innovating in-service processes, would see benefit from investing in an operations research department, like I described with McDonald's, to support testing and innovation. An operations research team is specialized and expensive, so this function could also be outsourced if it is not used all the time. Keep in mind that if the organization doesn't "own" the development process, it is easy for the modeling to become disconnected from the organizational goals, so be sure you have a good project plan in place.

CASE STUDY: ANALYTICS OPPORTUNITIES IN OPERATIONS, BERNARD ELLIS, INFOR

Bernard Ellis, Vice President of Industry Strategy for Infor, provided the following perspective on analytical opportunities in operations, which I've summarized here. The full case study with examples can be found in Appendix 1.

Infor builds beautiful business applications with last-mile functionality and scientific insights for select industries delivered as a cloud service. With 14,000 employees and customers in more than 200 countries and territories, Infor automates critical processes for industries, including healthcare, manufacturing, fashion, wholesale distribution, hospitality, retail, and the public sector. Infor software helps eliminate the need for costly customization through embedded deep industry domain expertise.

Hotels have been practicing revenue optimization relatively effectively for the last decade or so, to the point where revenue managing rooms has become a game of small incremental adjustments. Particularly recently, with rates at historic highs, there just isn't that much farther to go in driving room revenue. Yet, all of the revenue optimization expertise at hotels, and casinos, tends to be narrowly focused on managing room rate. It's time to move to a broader enterprise-wide effort to move the needle on revenue and profits, what I call Hospitality Enterprise Optimization.

This may sound very similar to Total Hotel Revenue Management or Total Hotel Profit Optimization, where revenue management techniques are applied also to all ancillary revenue sources, like spas, restaurants, and retail. This is important, of course, but hotels need to also be focused on the costs associated with bringing in that revenue. Hospitality enterprise optimization (EO) doesn't just limit itself to the demand management side of the picture, though, but also examines the costs associated with delivering the experience that actually earns the revenue, which can sometimes be much greater. As its name would suggest, it has as its universe the entire hospitality enterprise. Any input, output, or business practice that can be made to yield a more optimal result by applying observation, science, and technology is fair game for EO.

The biggest barrier to hotels achieving this vision of EO is the simple fact that today it's rarely someone's job to pursue it. Service operations analysts may be doing their best to drive efficiencies, and revenue management and marketing may have carefully targeted the market mix that's expected, but each department's analysis tends to be limited to its own silo, driven by its own KPIs and incentives. As revenue managers continue to gain more trust in the automation of their routine forecasting and optimization tasks, they should have more available time to find new questions to answer and new optimal results to deploy. This will be especially true if the distribution landscape in the post-parity world isn't so much about the endless goose chase of matching prices and mastering the shell game of constantly changing commission models, but rather about broader marketing reach and savvy, for which most hoteliers are more than willing to sacrifice margin.

CONCLUSION

Operations is a fast-paced, high-stakes department in hospitality and gaming. Operations is challenged with delivering an excellent guest experience while controlling costs to optimize profits. This all happens in real time, in front of the guests, with line-level staff and a myriad of interdependent, integrated technologies. Analytics can help operations achieve that balance between excellent guest experience and cost control by facilitating demand forecasting, setting staffing levels, finding efficiencies in the service process, and putting the right information in the hands of the decision makers.

All of this needs to be seamless to the guest or patron. They should be able to navigate the experience with ease, with limited waits, and find what they need without having to look too hard. Disney has provided a good example of streamlining the service experience with their MagicBands. There's a great article from *Wired* magazine (see Additional Resources) that describes the development process and the goals of the program. I have yet to personally experience the MagicBand, but, as an analytic hospitality executive, I can appreciate several aspects of the program. First of all, the amount and diversity of data that Disney can potentially collect through this program is staggering, and very, very valuable. And we all know that Disney is very good at data and analytics. Also, however, as a former operations manager, and current frequent hospitality and gaming patron, I very much appreciate the guiding philosophy behind the program, which is to facilitate a magical Disney experience.

In the *Wired* article, Disney speaks about removing friction from the service experience. When designing the MagicBand program, the team looked at every single tiny detail of the highly complex Disney experience to find places to remove transactional interactions, waits, logistical problems, and anything mundane that could potentially distract the guest from the magical Disney experience. Payment information is stored on the band. It can track a place in line, or serve as a room key at the resorts. More important, Disney realized that it's not just about developing what the band can do, but also it should be about how it got implemented and used across the estate. Disney placed a laser focus on how the guest actually uses the band. It had to be easy to carry or wear. Usage points must be clearly marked, it must be intuitive to use, and it *must* work *every time*. Before Disney could even think about what could be done with the volume of data that is generated by the program, they certainly needed to live up to the frictionless promise.

I tell this story as a reminder that despite how tempting it is to offer the latest, coolest technology, automating the in-room experience, integrating with wearables, or allowing keyless entry with smartphones, you must consider how the guest will experience this service. I hear the occasional debate in industry circles about automating certain aspects of service in hotels and casinos. I think this is a fruitful area of research, which I frequently remind the students I mentor, but there are some aspects that are intuitively logical. Guests are getting used to technology interventions in their lives, from pay at the pump to self-checkout to ATMs. There is likely a tolerance, or even desire, for some automation in their service processes. However, the hospitality industry has been very reluctant to implement technology like check-in kiosks or web ordering for room service, arguing that their guests expect a certain level of in-person service. This debate swings both ways—on one side, the discussions are all about seeming relevant by providing super-cool technology regardless of function. On the other side, traditionalists insist that guests want in-person service, and technology to replace people would remove all that is special about their service.

I didn't intend to create a diatribe on human vs. machine in the conclusion of my operations chapter, but it went there, so bear with me. Technology always has the advantage of providing consistency in the process. These days, it also has the advantage of convenience and even familiarity. The more you can automate the mundane, standardize data collection, and remove friction from the guest experience, the more you can focus on using the creativity and passion of your best employees and brand ambassadors to enhance instead of just execute. Automation then provides the additional benefit of a foundation of clean, credible data for your analytics programs.

My charge to those in hospitality who design service experiences is to get creative about where technology can be added to streamline and enhance. Approach this with the same analytical rigor that Marriott approached their lobby design, so you can be sure you are set up for success. Understand all of the use cases, and test and learn. If it goes wrong, it can go very wrong. After my move to New Jersey, I started flying out of Newark airport. In Terminal C, all of the food and beverage ordering is done on iPads, and requires credit card payments. I have seen nothing but trouble from this—I've even had trouble myself, and I work in technology. This results in irritated passengers and exasperated servers. Be very careful, but definitely don't be afraid.

This discussion of guest experience is a natural transition to the next chapter, where I talk about marketing analytics. Of course,

operations must execute whatever marketing promises, which is a
topic that I address in Chapter 11.

ADDITIONAL RESOURCES

- "Data and Analytics, "The Blueprint of Service Design," www.sas.com/en_us/
  whitepapers/data-analytics-blueprint-service-105102.html.
- "Disney's One Billion Dollar Bet on a Magical Wristband," www.wired.com/
  2015/03/disney-magicband.
- "Right People, Right Jobs, Right Time: The Art and Science of Labor Planning,"
  SAS white paper from the Cornell/SAS Webcast Series "Insights and Innovations in Hospitality and Gaming," www.sas.com/en_us/whitepapers/right-
  people-right-jobs-right-time-104379.html.

NOTES

1. Note that I conducted these studies at restaurants in the United States, where servers
   are not expected to wait until the party has asked for the check to deliver it. Our
   recommendation was to proactively drop off the check when it was clear that the
   table had finished with their dining experience. In other parts of the world, this
   would be considered rude. It was also surprising how much time elapsed between
   the time the check was dropped off and when the server returned to process
   payment, a time during which the guests are ready to hand over money and leave.
2. The reason you may want to test this rather than just do it is that there is a cost associated with printing the information, and with having the housekeepers place the
   information in the rooms and maintain the information consistently.
3. Maister developed these service laws long before review sites became popular. I am
   sure he would see these sites as proof of his service propositions.
4. I can't thank my friend Bill Minnock enough for offering this case study up for the
   webcast and for making his team available. It was a very interesting discussion about
   concept development and multiple research methods.

CHAPTER **6**

Analytics for Marketing

Half of my advertising is waste, I just don't know which half.

—Henry Ford

Marketing is quickly emerging as the next area of opportunity for driving value through analytics in hospitality. The crowded digital marketplace and increasing competition for the consumer have intensified the importance of better guest intelligence and smarter marketing actions. Recently, many hospitality companies have launched personalization initiatives, with the intention of mining guests' expressed preferences and behaviors to design more individualized interactions. This is a highly complex initiative doomed to fail if not built on a solid foundation of data collection and analytics.

Gaming companies have been calculating and tracking customer value for many years. The gaming industry is largely built on identifying and nurturing high value gamers, while still generating revenue from the rest of the patron base, so it is important to have a view of the potential of all casino patrons. Even with this ongoing focus on patron value, the marketing area in casinos has still been evolving in recent years. The proliferation of nongaming options, particularly in destination gaming markets like Las Vegas and Macau, is requiring that casinos understand the complete picture of patron spend, the so-called 360-degree view. Personalization is also of interest to casinos. As competition increases, any edge that shifts patron share of wallet can make the difference.

While digital has had broad impact across hotels and casinos, marketing has probably been the function most impacted by this shift. Consumer behavior has changed rapidly over the last decade, largely driven by the digital transformation. The way that hospitality and gaming companies must engage their guests and patrons, as well as the opportunities to communicate the brand promise and brand value, have fundamentally changed. Channel complexity has increased, and with reviews and ratings, service triumphs and failures are out there for the world to see. Success depends on the ability to navigate the messy digital environment, as search, PPC (pay-per-click), web traffic, Google Analytics, and SEO (search engine optimization) become household words for marketing. Complexity is growing. Skill sets are evolving. The landscape is getting more complex, and more crowded.

Marketing is fundamentally about demand generation. Marketers own the relationship with the individual guests and are responsible for building programs that result in bookings. Marketing has traditionally been thought of as a creative discipline, rather than an analytical discipline, but this reputation is rapidly changing. Particularly with the challenges associated with digital, most companies today realize that marketing needs to be a marriage of creativity with analytical rigor (really, all of hospitality and gaming should be, right?).

In the following sections, I cover the data, analytics, resources, and technologies that will help transform your marketing organization from pure creative to a winning blend of art and science.

MARKETING DATA

The guest is at the core of marketing's responsibility, so guest data is at the core of marketing data. Marketing should be concerned about collecting as much *relevant* information about the guests as possible. This includes demographic (age, gender, geography), psychographic (personality, values, opinions, attitudes, lifestyles), and behavioral information (recency, frequency, value).

Building a Guest Profile

There is a constant debate in hospitality about the composition of a guest profile, and the best way to collect the data. Many hotel companies use loyalty programs expressly for this purpose. A loyalty program effectively rewards guests for allowing the hotel to access and track their information. This means that loyalty programs must be designed with enough value to the guest that they are willing to allow this information to be collected. For example, many hotels offer free upgrades, access to specialized check-in experiences, or additional amenities as the guest collects loyalty status. These programs can become very expensive for hotels, so it is important to carefully analyze the value you can get from the guest data as you design a program.

Loyalty programs have become relatively commonplace, practically a "me too" requirement. In fact, many frequent travelers are members of multiple programs, and strive to achieve just enough status with each program to satisfy their desire for upgrades and amenities. This behavior creates loyalty to the loyalty program, rather than loyalty to the brand itself, meaning that guests will happily switch to a program that offers them better benefits. Research suggests that fostering feelings of loyalty to the brand is what results in valuable outcomes from guests like likelihood to recommend, likelihood to return, and increased spend.

 NOTE

Dr. Breffni Noone, Associate Professor, School of Hospitality Management at Penn State, and I recently conducted some research on the role of attitudinal loyalty in prepurchase evaluations, and we found that as attitudinal loyalty increased, sensitivity to negative reviews decreased, meaning that the guests who felt loyal to the brand did not pay as much attention to negative reviews (Noone and McGuire 2016).

Many hospitality and gaming companies are working on ways to incorporate brand experiences into their loyalty programs, so that guests are exposed to the brand while collecting points. For example, Kimpton Karma™, Kimpton's loyalty program, rewards guests for attending their wine hours or posting comments on social media. This encourages guests to experience the on-property activities that are core to the brand promise, and talk about them publically, presuming that this exposure will generate those valuable feelings of loyalty, as well as encourage other potential guests to try the brand.

There are companies today that promise that they can mine social media and web interactions to round out guest profiles. A guest doesn't even need to give you a complete profile for you to know all about them, including interests listed on Facebook, contact information, family and friends, pictures—think about all of the information about you that's available in social channels. This is very tempting, of course, but I suggest extreme caution in how you approach gathering and using guest information, particularly the personal information

Figure 6.1 Is loyalty the holy grail for hotels and casinos, or is it an expensive "me too"?

they reveal on social channels, even though they've released that publically.

In 2012, British Airways announced that they were going to start using facial recognition software to identify their most valuable passengers at the airport, from profile pictures on social media.[1] Their intention was to be able to provide better service to their best customers, but there was an extremely negative reaction from the passengers. Consumers are very sensitive to how their information is collected and used. My suggestion is to err on the side of caution and to only use information that your guests believe that they could have provided (even if they didn't), and if you do collect information from the guest, be sure to use it responsibly. Just because you can collect it doesn't mean you should. This line between relevant and engaging and creepy stalker is very thin!

As I mentioned in the chapter introduction, casinos also have a strong interest in building a robust patron profile. Rewards programs started in casinos primarily to identify the most profitable players, based on their observed and predicted gaming behavior, and to incentivize those patrons to continue to increase their share of wallet with that casino.

▶ **NOTE**

Harrah's Entertainment (now Caesars), pioneered the casino rewards programs with their Total Rewards™ plan. Every time the patron games on the casino floor, they present their Total Rewards™ card. The card collects gaming behavior (spend, frequency, game preferences, duration), and based on that play behavior, rewards patrons with points and benefits. In their initial analysis of the data generated by the program, Harrah's identified that their most valuable patrons, the backbone of their revenue and profits, were not the *whales*, or *high-rollers*, those patrons who spend thousands of dollars per hand, but rather, the frequent gamers in their locals' markets who would come weekly and spend several hundred dollars. This revelation, driven by the casino's analysis of the data collected by the card program, drove their business strategy. They focused on benefits that would attract and retain these high frequency gamers, and invested in markets with access to this profile of player (Davenport and Harris 2007). The key to the revelations for Harrah's was that the patrons were incentivized to allow the casino to track their gaming behavior, and match that back to a demographic profile. I will speak more about gaming-specific data in Chapter 10.

Both for hotels and casinos, the most important elements of the guest profile are any piece of data that generates an actionable result, something that could be used to cause the guests to behave differently, to explain a guest action, or help to understand a behavioral difference between one group of guests and another. These are the insights that would result in the hotel or casino treating one guest differently from another, or taking a specific action as relates to a particularly guest at that time. For example, a business traveler has different needs than a leisure traveler. Someone from China may want different amenities in the room than someone from Canada. A patron who is driving distance from the casino might be more likely to respond to a last-minute deal than a patron who needs to book a flight. This is pretty broad information, with obvious actions associated. As data gets more detailed, it becomes more challenging. How much does gender matter, for example? Certainly, it matters to ensure you are going to address the guest properly in non-face-to-face communications, but is there a relationship with behavior? How about age? Many argue that the millennial generation behaves very differently from previous generations, and has very different expectations for service, but how much does that impact how you would market to them, or how you would design your service offerings? Think even more detailed—income, title, industry, marital status, number of children, or education. Despite the fact that it has become much easier to store and process large volumes of data, there is still overhead associated with maintaining guest data, and resources required to manage it, as I discussed in Chapter 2. It is still important to capture only what can be used so that you don't incur a lot of overhead from unused data.

There are certain data points, like what products a guest prefers, how often that guest stays, how much they spend, and what their trip purpose is that are crucial for the analytics to identify the most valuable guests or patrons, calculate their likelihood to respond to certain marketing campaigns, identify guests who are likely to attrite, and identify acquisition targets. The information around these core behavioral metrics, like demographic or psychographic indicators, may or may not be useful. Some of what is useful will depend on your brand, your business strategy, and your market. Many argue that more is better when it comes to guest profile data. This is probably true, but there is no point in gathering and storing information if it will not ultimately lead to a better decision. I am not advocating for or against any of these data sources that I bring up here. In fact, I can think of circumstances where the same data might be highly relevant and/or not matter at all. The point I am trying to make is that every company needs to think about what data they want to collect in light of their own products and their own business strategies. One guest profile does not fit all, so to speak!

Campaign Performance

Marketers also collect data on the content and performance of campaigns, and can use this to report on past performance and predict future performance. Marketers should be monitoring response rates, to understand the percentage of the consumers who were sent the campaign who actually booked. They can also track click-throughs—how many consumers opened emails or clicked on a banner ad. Click-throughs identify whether you have the right content or compelling enough copy to attract attention. Collected at the guest level, they are also an indication of guests who are interested in this kind of promotion or property, even if they didn't book this time. Keeping track of guest interest will help to increase response rates in the future.

Emerging Data Sources

As the digital ecosystem evolves, so too do opportunities for marketing to collect new data. Hospitality and gaming companies are beginning to explore the following data sources.

Digital and Web Data

As the process of researching and purchasing a travel experience moved to the web, and now recently to mobile devices, marketers are having to collect and manage a whole set of new digital data. These can include keywords associated with search engine optimization, click stream data that tracks a guest's path through the website, including what they hovered over but didn't click on, and even information they started filling out but didn't complete. Synthesizing this data can tell you how effective your website is in generating and capturing demand, keep you abreast of competitive movements in keywords, and measure the effectiveness of pay-per-click programs. It can also help uncover guest preferences and interests, which can be used for remarketing.

Social and Text Data

Hotel and casino managers are becoming more accustomed to the data generated by review sites and social engagement, and well recognize the impact of social data on their businesses. In fact, as I sit writing this chapter in a beautiful all-inclusive resort in the Caribbean, I have had no less than four staff members encourage me to write a review on TripAdvisor mentioning their name specifically—interesting strategy from the resort to encourage positive reviews. (But thanks, Biakely, JC, Jorge, and Mr. New York—I've had a fantastic time!) There are many emerging opportunities to collect and act on this social data.

Dr. Breffni Noone, Dr. Kristin Rohlfs, and I wrote a paper several years ago in which we helped hoteliers think about how social data

Information Flow		Time Scope	
		SHORT TERM Tactical	LONG TERM Strategic
	INBOUND Consumer-Generated Content	(1) Inform promotions and pricing decisions	(3) Inform pricing, distribution, and CRM strategy
	OUTBOND Firm-Generated Content	(2) Drive short-term demand and build brand awareness	(4) Drive customer development and retention

Figure 6.2 Identifying Opportunities to Use Social Data
Source: Noone et al. 2011.

could be used for decision making. While we identified many areas of opportunity that hotels and casinos are now taking advantage of today, the basic premise still holds true that the easiest way to manage the data from these social channels is to start with the business problem you are trying to solve and think about how social data and social channels can contribute to a better solution. Figure 6.2 details a framework to evaluate opportunities to leverage social data, considering the direction of the social interaction and the time frame of the decisions you are trying to make.

Data generated in social channels can be traditional quantitative data, but is more likely to be unstructured, nontraditional data (I discussed the challenges associated with this data in Chapter 2). Quantitative data include ratings, which are essentially an aggregate score representing the opinions of all reviewers, numbers of Twitter followers, and Facebook friends. Unstructured sources could include text from reviews or posts, images, audio files, video files, and social network connections.

Social data is useful at the brand level, the property level, and at the individual guest level. Hotels and casinos can track reputation at the brand level or for an individual property. Mining the text data from all reviews from an individual property can provide insight into the elements of the product or service that are resonating most with guests or can identify service issues. Remember that social data is public data, so hotels and casinos can collect reputation data from the competitive set as well, and derive an apples-to-apples comparison of their reputation positions in the market, for an individual property or for the brand.

Many review sites also allow guests to post photos. Photos can provide interesting insights into what guests are noticing and valuing about their stay experiences. Some of my former Cornell colleagues did an interesting paper for the Cornell Center for Hospitality Research, where they used a technique called *photolicitation* to track the guest stay experience (Pullman and Robson 2006). They gave guests disposable cameras (remember those?) to take pictures of what made an impression, positive or negative, during their stay. The guests then provided commentary on why they took the pictures, which was analyzed to provide insight to management about areas for improvement and also areas that were successful in "wowing" the guests. This study was conducted in 2004, just before the widespread availability of smartphones and the proliferation of review sites. Today, this technique can easily be mimicked using the images that guests post on review sites, or if you want to do it more formally, ask guests to take pictures with their mobile phones.

Reviews contain information about the guests' experiences with your property, but they also can contain information about the guests themselves. Even if you don't know exactly who a guest is, you can find some clues from the way they talk or what they talk about that could be used for identifying trip purpose or doing some broad segmentation. This can be very beneficial in understanding how subgroups of guests use the property and how they value the different elements of the service. For example, the hotel could isolate the reviews that mention kids, couples, and business travel and calculate sentiment and popular topics for each group. This may explain reactions to certain hotel initiatives. For example, if there are many reviews about how much the kids love the pool, it could explain why romantic couples vacation packages are not so successful.

At an individual level, guest reviews could contain information about needs and preferences, which could be used to deliver more personalized offers and recommendations. If you have access to information about a guest's social network, and the influence they have within that network, you can identify social influencers and target them with information that they will hopefully broadcast (positively) to their social network. Identifying individuals within these social networking sites is a challenge, because you need to be able to connect them to their Twitter handles or TripAdvisor user names. This is another circumstance where incentives, like offering loyalty points for Facebook likes or for providing social identifiers, can help the hotel "buy" very useful information about their guests.

Location Data

Location data is also an interesting opportunity for marketers. It is possible for hotels to pinpoint exactly where a guest is at any given time down to a very granular level of detail—using the location services (GPS) in their smartphones and devices installed at the property, called beacons, that pick up a signal when the mobile device is in proximity. Generally, consumers have to give permission for this data to be used, first by enabling location services on their phones, and then by identifying themselves to the company through signing up for an app, Wi-Fi, or a program that connects devices on a network to individuals.

Many think of location opportunities at the individual guest level, incentivizing a guest to take a certain action based on where they happen to be standing—for example, sending a coupon for the retail store they are hovering outside of to incentivize them to enter and purchase something. Obviously, this is most effective when you can identify the guest and tie their current actions back to their profile, but there are some actions that can be taken without much identifying information that will add value.

There is also the opportunity to use the information in aggregate to gain behavioral insights. How do traffic patterns differ by time of day? What percentage of guests actually turn down the retail hall? Are non-hotel guests using certain portions of the property? When and where? These insights can be useful to understand the placement and content of internal advertising, adjust operating hours of outlets, or change the placement of certain banks of slot machines or table games.

ADVANCED ANALYTICS FOR MARKETING

Now that we have a better understanding of the available data, let's talk about techniques that can be used to gain insight from that data. First, I will talk about the broad categories of advanced analytics I introduced in Chapter 4, and then I will address common business goals and how analytics helps marketing to achieve those goals. Since digital intelligence is such an important topic for marketing today, I have a special section on it.

As I mentioned in the previous chapter, there are many key performance indicators that marketers should be tracking. I will not cover those here, for the reasons I discussed in Chapter 5. Keep in mind that digital has created some disruption in the traditional marketing metrics. As this area evolves, marketers have to constantly reevaluate how they are measuring the success of their marketing efforts, particularly those conducted through digital channels (which is nearly all of them these days, right?). I am certainly not an expert in this area, but I have been following the conversation, and it is a tricky one. There are many ways to manipulate digital metrics, and tying efforts to a return on investment (ROI) of any kind is also fuzzy. I encourage all analytical marketing managers to keep a close eye on this area, question everything, and experiment internally.

And now that I've gotten myself out of having to solve that particularly tricky issue, let's talk advanced analytics for marketing!

See Figure 4.1 for a reminder of the four categories of advanced analytics.

Statistical Analysis

Marketers should be heavy users of statistical analysis. Correlation analysis identifies which variables in the guest profile are related to which outcome measures. Regression, as I described in Chapter 4, identifies the factors that contribute to overall guest satisfaction and likelihood to return, and how much impact manipulating the values of those variables will have on overall satisfaction.

One of the most important uses of statistical analysis in marketing is *A/B testing* to understand the effectiveness of marketing treatments. A/B testing identifies which marketing content is most effective at driving desired outcomes. The content or treatment can be anything from images, to email titles, promotion content, or loyalty benefits. At a high level, with A/B testing, you design two alternatives, and then deploy them to a random, representative sample of your guest population. You measure the defined outcome for each treatment, and then use hypothesis testing to see which treatment results in a statistically significant better outcome.

NOTE

For example, you may want to test what subject line in an email results in more open emails. You need to narrow the choices down to a relatively small set of options (like two). So, maybe you pick "Best Vacation Ever" and "Time to Visit Paradise." The content of the emails should be exactly the same, as should every other component of the email (time of day it is sent, format of the email, who it is from). This way, you control for every other factor that influences the guest's decision to open the email except for the email title. Next, you need to ensure you have a random but representative sample of your guest database to deploy each promotion to. Here's where it gets a bit tricky. You want to be able to send the most effective email to a large group of qualified guests or patrons. First, you must randomly select a test group, a subset of the entire database who qualifies for the promotion, and then (virtually) flip a coin to determine which promotion each guest on the list gets (heads, it's best vacation ever; tails, it's paradise). Similarly, the website can do the coin flip when each visitor arrives during the A/B test to determine what content they will see. The open rate for the email, or click through on the website, is collected, and hypotheses tests will tell you which one had a statistically significant higher opening rate.

Digital has made it much simpler to conduct A/B tests. It's easy to quickly change out images on the website, and relatively inexpensive to send out a small group of emails before a larger group is sent. This means that all hotels should be using A/B testing to add rigor to their marketing efforts. There are relatively accessible programs and services that can execute these A/B tests.

The commercial head of a boutique hotel company in Europe told a group at a roundtable event that I attended that he learned a valuable lesson about the importance of A/B testing on the company's website when he "intervened" and asked the web designer to put a very cool drone picture of London with their hotel at the center as the picture on their website for their London hotel. He's in charge, so the web developer did what he said but put the picture through their regular A/B testing instead of making a wholesale change. That new image resulted in a 40% decrease in conversions as compared to the original, so it was quickly removed. The web designer knew that the site visitors preferred to see a close-up picture of the hotel than something flashy taken from a distance, and he quickly collected the data to prove it. The commercial director now says that absolutely nothing goes up on the website without checking with web development if there have been any prior experiments, or putting it through an A/B test, even if the chairman himself wants to make the change.

Forecasting

Marketing tends to be more of a forecast consumer than a forecast creator. It is useful for marketing to know what expected demand will be over a specific horizon in case they need to adjust promotion plans to generate additional demand during soft periods or restrict discounting during peak periods. Forecasting can also be used to predict the lift associated with a campaign based on previous experience with similar campaigns.

Predictive Modeling

Predictive modeling is probably the most heavily used category of analytics in marketing. Marketers use predictive modeling to calculate lifetime value, predict response rates to campaigns, segment guests, identify cross and upsell opportunities, identify the next best offer, or determine which guests are going to take their business elsewhere. Marketers are also extensive users of data-mining techniques for data exploration across large guest databases.

Segmentation analysis is a predictive modeling technique of particular importance to marketers. Segmentation splits guests into groups with similar characteristics, utilizing the clustering technique I described in Chapter 4. There is a wide variety of segmentation methods. The most basic are simple descriptive splits according to variables like age, geography, or income. This creates subsets of guests or patrons who share certain demographic attributes. This method is effective if you are trying to target specific geographic locations, like drive-in markets for casinos, and maybe you want to make a specific kind of offer within that geographic area, like a poker tournament. This kind of descriptive split has limitations. Just because patrons or guests live in a certain area, are a certain age, or prefer a certain type of game doesn't mean they share much else in common, doesn't necessarily predict whether they will be likely to respond to an offer, and doesn't indicate that they are an attractive prospect for your brand.

Analytical segmentation ascribes a bit more intelligence to the segmentation problem. There are various analytical techniques that can group customers on multiple dimensions, increasing the chance that they will behave and respond similarly. The modeler would enter any combination of attributes that they believe are important to distinguish among groups of patrons or guests. The model groups guests according to similar dimensions and reports the values. From this information, the modeler can understand "who" these groups are. For example, the analytical segmentation model might find a group of guests that lives within driving distance, is valued at about $200 per trip, and likes to play the penny slots. The model might show that this group typically visits twice a month, so the marketer's goal might be to increase their trip frequency by sending them special offers for slot tournaments or free play. The choice of analytical segmentation model depends on the data available and the goal of the model.

Scoring. You will probably hear the term *score* or *scoring* in conversations about predictive modeling and marketing. I described this in Chapter 4 as well. Basically, predictive modeling analyzes the variety of inputs deemed to be significant predictors of an outcome for each guest or patron in the database, and outputs a probability that a guest with a certain combination of values for those inputs will display that outcome. The actual outcomes in this case are binary—it happened or it didn't, yes or no. Using this yes or no outcome in the model development, the model can derive a probability of a future guest taking that action. For example, based on demographic characteristics, recent behavior, and lifetime value, the model would predict the probability, or likelihood, that the guest will respond to a specific offer. These behavioral scores, or probabilities, can form the basis for all kinds of marketing actions, as long as the company understands the outcome they are trying to achieve, and has the right data to predict that outcome. More important, once a guest is offered a certain treatment or intervention, the system should record their action, and use that updated data to improve the model for future analyses.

Optimization

Marketers can leverage a very specific (and, in my opinion, very interesting) application of optimization to improve campaign results. Hotels, and particularly casinos, tend to have multiple campaigns running at the same time. Guests or patrons might qualify for multiple campaigns, but due to contact rules and preferences, you can only send them one or a few of the available campaigns. The goal is to derive the best contact list for each campaign that maximizes overall response rates or profitability. This is where optimization comes in. The analysts set that goal, such as maximize response rates, minimize costs, maximize profitability, and enter the characteristics of the campaigns and the guests, which become the constraints for the optimization. Constraints can also include some information about best available rates, hurdle values, or discount thresholds so that any discounts do not violate the revenue management value calculation. The optimization algorithm generates as decision variables the list of contacts for each campaign that will ensure the best possible result, according to the goal.

Analytics by Business Goals

Table 6.1 categorizes typical marketing goals throughout the guest journey, and matches those to an analytical technique or category that provides a solution.

Table 6.1 Analytic Opportunities at Each Stage of the Guest Journey

Guest Journey Stage	Top Marketing Goal	Analytics
Discover	Profile guests	Segmentation
	Evaluate prospects	Lead scoring
	Reach right prospects	Acquisition models
Explore	Optimize promotion response rate	Offer/contact optimization
	Evaluate marketing mix	Marketing mix modeling
	Test marketing treatments	A/B, multivariate testing
Engage	Increase value of each guest	Cross-sell/upsell modeling
	Identify most valuable guests	Guest lifetime value modeling
	Incorporate guest feedback	Sentiment analysis, net promoter scoring
	Manage guest attrition/defection	Retention modeling, churn/attrition modeling

DIGITAL INTELLIGENCE

Since so much of marketing's role today is focused on digital channels and the digital experience, it is worth addressing the challenges and opportunities associated with this area. Marketers today extensively use Google Analytics to evaluate the effectiveness of their digital presence, but there are limitations to what can be accessed and used from this free application. For example, Google aggregates the data so that the organization cannot tie a session to a specific customer. You can track the performance of your website, your keywords, and your search position, but not use that information at the individual session, meaning the visitor level. The challenge, in general, with digital data comes in two parts. First is getting a handle on the unique data within these channels, understanding what it represents and how to analyze it. The second challenge is integrating this digital data with traditional or offline data.

Digital Marketing Defined

Digital marketing is an umbrella term for the targeted, measurable, and interactive marketing of products or services using digital technologies to reach and convert leads into customers and retain them. The key objective is to promote brands, build preference, engage with customers, and increase sales through various service, product, and brand marketing techniques, which mainly use the Internet as the marketing medium, but also use mobile technology. The fundamental concept in digital marketing is centered on inbound marketing, which is when customers contact the firm, also called the customer-centric approach, but it can broadly include communications through any digital channel.

Digital marketing activities include:

- **Search engine optimization.** The process of impacting the visibility of a website in natural or organic search—for example, by using phrases or words that are commonly searched for.
- **Search engine marketing.** Promotion of websites in Internet search engines, generally by paying for placement.

- **Content marketing (including e-books, CDs or flash drives loaded with content, and games).** A strategic marketing approach focused on creating and distributing valuable, relevant, and consistent content to attract and retain a clearly defined audience—and, ultimately, to drive profitable customer action.

- **Influencer marketing.** The process of targeting messaging (or content) at a set of individuals who have extensive networks with the hopes that they will advocate for you in your network.

- **Campaign/e-commerce marketing.** The process of organizing communications into a coordinated marketing effort to a targeted group of consumers.

- **Social media marketing.** The process of gaining website traffic or other brand, product, or service attention through social media sites.

- **Social media optimization (SMO).** The use of a number of social media outlets and communities, including RSS feeds, social news, bookmarking sites, and social networking sites to generate publicity to increase awareness for a product, brand, or event. SMO is similar to SEO in that the goal is to generate traffic and awareness for a website.

- **Email direct marketing.** Provides marketing messages directly to a consumer through their email address.

- **Display advertising.** This refers to advertising on websites. It includes many different formats and contains items such as text, images, flash, video, and audio. The main purpose of display advertising is to deliver general advertisements and brand messages to site visitors.

Digital marketing also extends to non-Internet channels that provide digital media, such as SMS and MMS, callback, and on-hold ring tones on mobile phones.

Digital Data Challenges[2]

Data is collected at every stage of the guest journey in a variety of systems and formats. The biggest challenge for marketing is to stitch together these fragmented sources of data, which come from online, offline, and even third-party sources. These data need to be pulled together in a format useful for both analytics and reporting. There are challenges associated with integrating this data, cleansing it, and ensuring it is analytics-ready.

Traditionally, data-driven marketers use the advanced analytics techniques I described earlier to perform sophisticated analyses, like regression, decision trees, or clustering, but they have been limited to using *offline data* (data collected through on-property interactions, or through reservation systems), primarily due to restrictions on access rights to online data from third-party technology vendors. Even if hotels get access to online data, commonly available web and digital analytics tools primarily aggregate and report on historical information and thus are not well suited to perform predictive analysis. In this aggregated environment, obtaining an omnichannel, integrated view of a single guest across the fragmented digital ecosphere has been extremely difficult. As a result, it has been practically impossible to get a data-centric, comprehensive view of the guest that could feed integrated marketing analytics, or more specifically, provide prescriptive recommendations for marketers. Enter digital intelligence.

Digital intelligence is defined as follows: The capture, management, and analysis of customer data to deliver a holistic view of the digital customer experience, which drives the measurement, optimization, and execution of digital customer interactions.

This requires that marketers focus on understanding the "who," "what," "where," "when," and the "why" of digital experiences, collecting detailed 1:1 data across channels, as opposed to aggregated snapshots channel by channel. As with any data project, it's also important to consider the downstream activities and use cases you wish to support.

For example:

- Predictive analysis to identify what unique behaviors or attributes in a visitor's digital journey are closely correlated with revenue generating events (like a conversion or upsell). These behaviors and attributes can then be identified and fostered for future visitors.

- Analytically forecasting website visitation by traffic source, and identifying which ad-centric channels have the largest effect in increasing overall traffic (attribution modeling). The ad strategy can be adjusted based on which channels are most productive.

- Predicting online and offline behavioral drivers of digital conversions using analytically driven segmentation techniques, and improving outbound and inbound targeting rules for future marketing communication and personalization efforts.

To support the opportunities outlined here, web and mobile data, if collected and prepared appropriately, can be merged with your company's or company-owned customer data, and then streamed into your analytics, visualization, and interaction automation systems.

Recent innovations in technology are making it possible for hospitality companies to move beyond the limitations of traditional web analytics (i.e., aggregated data and historical performance analysis as opposed to predictive modeling). Marketing departments can now integrate digital data with offline guest profiles, and use that complete picture of the guest in predictive modeling to support personalized content delivery, offers, and recommendations digitally as well as when the guest is on property.

Integrated Data for Digital Intelligence

New technology for collecting and analyzing digital interactions is becoming available that will help move the industry beyond traditional web analytics to a more detailed and flexible view of the consumer.

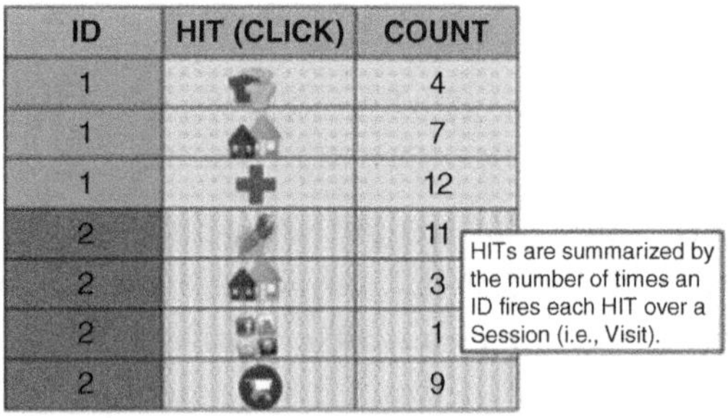

ID	HIT (CLICK)	COUNT
1		4
1		7
1		12
2		11
2		3
2		1
2		9

HITs are summarized by the number of times an ID fires each HIT over a Session (i.e., Visit).

Figure 6.3 Summarized Clickstream Data for Tracking Website and Campaign Performance
It is useful to understand aggregated activities on the website, but it cannot be disaggregated to track individual customer actions.
Source: Taken from: http://blogs.sas.com/content/customeranalytics/2016/03/22/web-analytics-vs-digital-intelligence-whats-difference/.

Data needs to be converted to one row per subject

ID	PREDICTORS											
	A	B	C	D	E	F	G	H	I	J	K	L
ID 1	0	0	4	0	0	7	0	0	12	0	0	0
ID 2	0	0	0	11	0	3	0	1	0	0	9	0

Each HIT ultimately becomes part of a column (variable/input)
Each ID becomes a row (observation/case)

Figure 6.4 Click Data at the Customer Level
This table becomes short and wide instead of tall and thin, but stores detailed activity associated with an individual instead of an activity.
Source: Taken from: http://blogs.sas.com/content/customeranalytics/2016/03/22/web-analytics-vs-digital-intelligence-whats-difference/.

The difference is in the format and storage of the data, moving from a clickstream view that focuses on channel and campaign performance (Figure 6.3), to a collection methodology that supports collecting granular, detailed data at an individual level (Figure 6.4). This format is well suited to predictive analytics because it summarizes all click activity across a customer's digital journey in one row.

Here is a review of what hotels should be looking out for in the technology sphere as you start down the path to personalization:

- **Single-line data collection insert.** Records all online behavior down to the millisecond against the session, visitor, and, most important, the individual guest, while reducing tag management challenges. In addition, the data is liberated to be used in any downstream application. This is in contrast to some digital data providers that only allow aggregated access to historical data.

- **Data normalization.** Is the process of converting raw event data into usable data with business context. This can be extremely challenging to accomplish because of the variety and complexity of digital data. Business rules are typically identified to capture the different permutations of paths to the same goal, resulting in digital data organized into business events that have meaning for your operation. A good digital intelligence solution will facilitate the creation and management of these rules in an operationalized manner.

- **Proprietary data management.** The biggest advantage of a digital intelligence platform over traditional web analytics is that you collect your own data, so you are not dependent on the third-party provider sharing (or not) what they collect. This means you have access to all of your data, you have the flexibility to configure your data model to suit your specific needs, and you can facilitate analysts' access to the data so they can spend more time analyzing and less time manipulating data.

- **Tying digital data to the guest.** Traditional web analytics aggregate data for business intelligence around the performance of the website. Digital intelligence solutions should capture this information for individual guests, at a level of detail and in a format that is appropriate for data mining, predictive analytics, forecasting, and optimization. We are interested in guest experiences, not just aggregated clicks.

The final crucial component in a digital platform is intelligent visualization. Your analysts should be able to access digital data through a highly flexible visual analytics platform, where they can not only see the trends and patterns, but can also apply analytics like forecasting or segmentation-centric decision trees, to visually predict opportunities (or threats). These visualizations will also help to facilitate conversations between analysts and business owners—making it easier for analysts to effectively communicate results.

Suneel Grover, Principle Solutions Architect at SAS, says the following about a company's journey from traditional web analytics to digital intelligence:

> The path to digital intelligence from traditional web analytics needs to cover the diversity of data, advanced analytic techniques, and injection of prescriptive insights to support decision-making and marketing orchestration. Digital intelligence is a transformation for web analytic teams—making it a competitive differentiator if executed well. It aims to transform brands to become:
>
> - **Customer-centric rather than channel-centric.** As customers and prospects weave across an ocean of marketing channels and connected devices, digital intelligence supports

the integrated analysis of interactions in concert, rather than with disconnected channel views. In addition to visibility across all channels, **analysis is highly granular** to identify, track, and prioritize next best actions for individuals. In other words, hyper-personalization to the segment of one!

- **Focused on enterprise goals as opposed to departmental.** To enable omnichannel analytics, digital intelligence is highly dependent on **customer data management capabilities** across all data types—structured, semistructured, and unstructured. This includes fusing interaction and behavioral data across all digital channels with first-party offline customer data, as well as second- and third-party data (if available). This enriched potpourri of data must be prepared to feed the analytical ninjas who sit within the marketing organization, line of business, or centralized customer intelligence team, because it is their job to exploit this stream of information and generate insights for the organization as a whole.
- **Enabled for audience activation and optimization.** The mission of digital intelligence is the direct application of analytics to generate data-driven evidence that helps business stakeholders make clearer decisions. The potential of data mining exponentially increases with richer customer data to support **segmentation, personalization, optimization,** and **targeting**—in other words, connecting data and analytics to the delivery of relevant content, offers, and awesome experiences.
- **Analytical workhorses.** The incredibly fast-moving world of digital interactions and campaigns means that marketers desperately need quicker analysis. Waiting days or weeks for reports and research equates to failure. Digital intelligence **delivers efficiency** at a pace that more nearly matches users' decision-making schedules.[3]

Attribution Modeling

A crucial component of digital intelligence is the ability to tie booking activity to the channel that generated it. As the path that consumers take through the Internet to a booking becomes more complex, it is both more difficult and more important to understand which of the many partners you are paying for reservations are actually helping you to generate those reservations. This is where attribution modeling comes in.

Attribution modeling is a set of rules that assign credit for sales and conversions across the online channels that the guest touched. There are several different methods for assigning this credit:

- **Last touch.** Assigns 100% of the credit to the last place the guest touched before the conversion.

- **First touch.** Assigns 100% of the credit to the first place the guest touched in the conversion path.

- **Linear attribution.** Splits the credit equally among all the channels that the guest touched in the conversion path.

- **Time decay.** Associates more weight to the channels more closely associated to the time of conversion. So, if a guest had clicked a banner add a week ago, visited the website three days ago, and clicked through the email right before purchasing a hotel room, the majority of the credit would go to the email, with diminishing credit to the other channels.

- **Position based.** More weight is assigned to the first and last interactions, and the remaining weight is split among the interactions in between. For example, you might give 40% each to first and last interactions, and split the remaining 20% among the remaining channels.

Analytical attribution uses science, usually proprietary algorithms, to assign conversion credit across all touchpoints preceding the conversion, using automated computation to decide where credit is due. Algorithmic attribution starts at the event level and analyzes both converting and non-converting paths across all channels. Weights are then combined by grouping such as placement, site, or channel as reporting granularity is decreased, allowing the data to point out the hidden correlations and insights within marketing efforts.

I reference at the end of the chapter an excellent blog from my former colleague, Suneel Grover at SAS, who is a digital marketing expert and evangelist, that will walk you through great examples of how the data and analytics need to be organized to effectively execute analytical attribution. This is a very complex and ever-changing domain. It is quite difficult to keep up with, even if you have a strong team in house. There is value in combining that bench strength in house with some expert consulting (I won't say this about everything). The experts, particularly if they are looking at trends across many customers, can more quickly identify things like the impact of changes to Google's algorithms or other trends in the digital ecosphere, and advise you how to adapt. Just make sure that you are smart about who you partner with.

BENCHMARKING MARKETING ANALYTICS CAPABILITIES

I often get asked what the "best" companies are doing in the area of marketing analytics, or what the "typical" company is doing in the area of marketing analytics. While I have not done a formal study on this, I can provide some high-level insights that can help you determine where your organization is on the journey to a strategic analytic marketing culture, and where to focus your future development and investment. I also called on my former colleague, Natalie Osborn, Principle Marketing Consultant, Hospitality and Gaming at SAS, to weigh in on what she sees in industry in terms of sophistication and opportunity, and to offer advice about the right technology and people investment to make a marketing program successful.

Beginners. For both hotels and casinos, the least analytically sophisticated organizations are operating in a very manual environment. They have little in the way of guest or patron information, and probably no formal guest database. Lists for marketing campaigns are pulled and deployed manually. They have a very difficult time pulling together any operating reports or tracking campaign metrics. They are probably doing some manual segmentation in Excel, and might be talking to a reputation management vendor about managing their online reviews and ratings. It is possible that someone is using or has thought of using Google Analytics to track their digital presence and website performance.

Average. The typical marketing organization in hospitality and gaming today probably has invested in some automated marketing execution technology. It is likely that they are doing some analytical modeling, and are considering investing more heavily in advanced marketing analytics technology. They have begun to think through building a guest data warehouse formally, and are collecting some relatively extensive metrics about their guests or patrons. They are very likely using a reputation management vendor to monitor and respond to guest reviews, and possibly to track sentiment as well. They are likely using Google Analytics extensively, and have begun to think about attribution modeling. When I was at SAS, I was having conversations with these companies about real-time marketing or location-based marketing, but they were not quite ready to adopt this kind of capability.

Most sophisticated. The most sophisticated hospitality and gaming companies have a large team of analytical modelers that are running advanced predictive modeling on their robust guest data warehouses. They are likely using some optimization to deploy marketing campaigns. These companies are probably in the early stages of location-based marketing initiatives, and likely have some real-time capabilities. Many of these companies have had marketing analytics and data warehousing for a while, so are likely considering some modernization options, like Hadoop, to manage their unstructured data, and changes to their processing infrastructure that will speed up execution of analytics on complex data sets (as I discussed in Chapter 2 and Chapter 4). If they are not conducting text mining and sentiment analysis themselves, they definitely are working with a vendor that provides this capability. These companies are extensive users of Google Analytics, but are also collecting and leveraging more detailed, guest-specific digital data, and have internal modelers building models with digital data.

CASE STUDY: HOSPITALITY MARKETING ANALYTICS, NATALIE OSBORN, SAS

CASE STUDY

I caught up with Natalie Osborn, Principle Marketing Consultant, Hospitality and Gaming, SAS, to get her perspective on the state of hospitality marketing and the opportunities available to hotels and casinos. Here is my interview with her.

1. What kind of marketing capabilities does the average hotel or casino have?

When it comes to marketing capabilities, I find that casinos are further along in their marketing analytics journey than hotels. Casinos are typically already collecting comprehensive data on the behaviors and preferences of their patrons, and using this data to perform segmentation analysis and predict likely response rates to campaigns. Some casinos are even using real-time marketing to present an appropriate offer to patrons while the patron is engaged in their casino experience.

However, for hotel companies, marketing analytics is more of an emerging area. Hotels may be collecting some data on guests, but often this data is limited by the systems that are currently in use. Hotels are starting to explore the possibilities of marketing analytics so that they can remain more competitive with third-party booking engines. I'm starting to see a focus on digital marketing analytics—particularly around pay-per-click and attribution; however, I would like to see hotels embrace customer analytics in the same way that casinos have done.

2. When you have conversations with your clients, what kinds of capabilities tend to be on their roadmaps?

While "personalization" is certainly a buzzword in the industry at the moment, it will take our industry some time to reach the goal of integrating data and marketing interactions across the entire guest journey. The typical conversations that I have with customers are aimed at more achievable goals, such as better understanding of where guests are spending, or the ability to react to customers with offers in real time.

3. What are the most sophisticated companies doing in the area of marketing?

In this chapter, you talk a lot about how hotel and casino companies trade for their guests' data. The hospitality and gaming companies that I admire most are those that have made the trade for data completely desirable for the guest. These companies are using the data that they collect on behaviors and preferences to drive a better experience for the guest, while at the same time ensuring that information will continue to be forthcoming. One great example is the MagicBands in use at Disney. When you have a MagicBand, your park experience improves, and some of the frictions in service are actually removed. Is Disney collecting data about every place you go in the park, everything you buy and eat? Probably. Is it worth sharing this data to be able to access a fast pass without holding on to a piece of paper, to collect photos to your guest account with ease, and to make purchases or open your hotel room without pulling out your wallet? Absolutely!

(continued)

194 ▶ THE ANALYTIC HOSPITALITY EXECUTIVE

(*continued*)

4. Where do you think the biggest opportunity for hotels and casinos is in the area of marketing?

Hospitality and gaming companies have access to a multitude of data from the guest experience. This is where the hotel and casino company has an advantage over third-party booking sites. However, in many cases this data asset is not being used to its fullest. The first opportunity is to know your customer through this data. The second opportunity is to use analytics on this data to anticipate your customers' needs and wants. I think that as an industry we need to stop thinking about marketing as something that we "do to" or "send to" a customer, and start thinking about marketing as a seamless part of the guest experience. Once you know your guests well, and start to anticipate what they want, delivering a great service experience becomes a whole lot easier.

5. How do you advise your clients to get started with marketing analytics?

If you are just getting started with marketing analytics, I would recommend that you do not try and resolve all of your challenges at once. Start with a narrow focus, and build up your confidence and expertise on a single project. It could be as simple as answering the question "Where do my guests come from?" or "Which guest segment is most profitable?" You could even explore which guests are most likely to respond to a certain type of campaign. Finding the answers to these questions can help the effectiveness of your campaigns, which means better conversions at a lower cost.

6. What kind of data should hotels and casinos focus on collecting for maximum impact?

Think about the data that you need to answer the questions that you have about your business. When we market, we market to a person, so as a starting point I need to collect the data that I have on my guests, integrate it, and clean it so that I am confident that I have a complete picture of my guest. Once you have achieved that with the data that is readily available in your existing systems, you can look to additional data that would enhance what you know about the guest. Clickstream data, social data, unstructured data in the form of profile comments, or call center logs—which of these sources can you tie back to your guest record? And if you can't easily tie it back to the guest record, how do you design a service program that helps you do so? For example, if you offer a loyalty reward for writing a review for a hotel, can you incent your customers to share their review site handles? How can you incent your guests to log in to the loyalty program before searching for your property, so that you can collect the clickstream data on the searches they perform in your guest database?

7. What kind of technology would you recommend for a typical hotel and casino to support their analytical efforts in marketing?

Starting with the data itself, I would recommend data integration and data quality so that you can build a complete and accurate picture of your guests. Data visualization can help you explore the characteristics of your guests, and begin to understand who they are. Once you are ready for building analytical models, you should invest in robust data mining tools. Marketing automation will help you deploy the results of your models into campaigns—I would suggest a solution that allows a seamless integration with your models so that you can easily incorporate scores into the campaign planning process.

Natalie uses the image in Figure 6.5 to describe a roadmap for hotels and casinos to achieve the vision of guest- or patron-centric marketing. It follows the reactive-to-proactive analytics roadmap, but in a marketing context. It may be useful to think about where your organization is on this journey, and the actions you need to take to get to the next level.

Figure 6.5 The Roadmap to Guest-Centric Marketing for Hotels and Casinos

TECHNOLOGY AND PEOPLE INVESTMENTS

I frequently get asked about the technology investments required to run an analytical marketing department. I am not going to provide any specific product recommendations, but I will outline the kinds of resources and technology you should plan for. Your specific choice of technology and vendor partner will depend on your goals, your budget, and your internal capabilities, of course.

Technology

The amount of technology investment depends, of course, on your budget, the type and size of the company, and the business strategy. Obviously, you need to consider the ROI, and you also need to make sure you have the resources that can effectively manage the investment. There is no point in buying a sophisticated analytical platform that requires extensive coding and configuration if you aren't willing to also invest in the right resources to manage that platform.

The Basics

The following list represents my suggestions for the set of technology that hotels and casinos should have for their marketing organizations to stay competitive.

- **Guest profile database.** It doesn't have to be a massive guest data warehouse, but you need some way to capture and access this information.
- **Reputation management** software is crucial as well. At a minimum, it should allow you to track and respond to reviews. If it provides some sentiment analysis and comparison to competitors, so much the better.
- **Data visualization.** You could use Excel, but ideally you'll want something a bit more robust and scalable than that to be able to visualize marketing results.
- **Google Analytics.** This software is free, so there isn't any excuse not to leverage it. Make sure someone on the team becomes an expert in this area.

- **Basic analytics.** This is a bit tricky, but still important. There are not really that many automated packages available for analyses like segmentation, and the "free" open-source software does require some specialized skills. Excel can provide some of these capabilities, but has limitations.

Next Steps

After gaining expertise in the areas listed previously, hotels and casinos should consider the following technologies as a next step.

- **Automated marketing execution.** This is very likely going to be a must-have very soon. The next step after building a guest or patron database is to implement an automated marketing solution. These solutions facilitate pulling contact lists for campaigns, tracking and monitoring campaign performance in real time, and consolidating campaign results. You probably want to look for one that allows you to infuse analytics like advanced segmentation or response likelihoods.

- **Advanced analytics tools for data mining**. Mining large databases of guest profile information, click stream data, or even text documents provides the opportunity to hone guest lifetime value calculations, apply advanced segmentation techniques, build acquisition and retention models, predict cross and upsell opportunities, and improve satisfaction. Of course, this will also require an investment in a resource that can effectively use such tools. There are very few, if any, "out of the box" capabilities in this area, and, given how proprietary the guest intelligence strategy should be, I would have trouble trusting them even if they did exist. More on that in Chapter 11.

Advanced

Marketing organizations who are ready for more advanced techniques should consider the following technologies.

- **Location-based data collection like beacons.** As organizations move toward location-based marketing, they will need to invest in a technology to identify a guest or patron's location, collect data, and deploy offers.

- **Real-time decisioning.** This allows for the deployment of offers and recommendations in real time. This can include anything from alerting the host that a high-valued patron has just carded into a slot machine to recommending the right offer when the guest logs into the website, based on a guest's likelihood to respond score.

- **Advanced analytics platform.** This means a robust, comprehensive analytics platform, including high-performance execution capabilities. This will allow organizations to conduct analyses like advanced digital marketing, sentiment analysis, text mining, and guest modeling in house. Building problem-specific analyses on your data, to answer your specific business questions, is the best way to build and sustain a competitive advantage.

- **Marketing optimization technology.** This technology also requires a specialized resource to execute. Even though there are some wizard-driven technology interfaces available, the resource really needs to understand optimization to effectively build and interpret the models.

People

Your best investment for a marketing analyst should be someone who is skilled in predictive modeling or data-mining techniques. This person should probably have some experience with guest profiles or using guest data. You'll want to look for someone who understands multivariate analysis, regression, segmentation, clustering, and logistic regression. Retail and banking use these kinds of techniques frequently, so someone with experience in either of those industries would be valuable to hospitality and gaming. Large gaming companies should consider investing in several of these analysts in house. Hotel companies should make this investment at the corporate level. An analyst with this skill set might be too expensive or even not required for an individual property or a smaller independent. It really depends on who collects your guest or patron data and how much the property is able to make decisions using it (i.e., if you are flagged with a Marriott brand, they may "own" the guest database, and control marketing to that database).

Hotels and casinos should also invest in a resource that has experience with campaign management. This is a different skill set to analytics, and this person will likely also be a consumer of the information created by the marketing analyst. The tasks here are to create campaigns, monitor and adjust during deployment, and report on results. Depending on how much flexibility the properties have to conduct campaigns, an individual hotel or independent will see value from having someone like this sit at the property. Again, this could be a corporate role if marketing is relatively centralized.

You will definitely want to bring someone in who has digital marketing experience. As fast as this area is changing, your best bet is probably a domain person who knows what to look out for in terms of technology, search trends, channel management, and web presence. They need to understand digital data, but you could have them collaborate with the predictive analytics person when it comes to applying advanced analytics to that data.

A market researcher has different experience to what I just described. Market researchers tend to be very skilled at new product analysis, brand research, and guest satisfaction work. They do survey design and analysis and conduct focus groups. It's a pretty specialized skill set that some corporate entities may find valuable, but it's also a role that can be easily outsourced if you don't conduct these kinds of activities regularly. Just be aware when you are reviewing resumes for an analyst position that someone who lists market research as their skill might not be the best fit for a marketing analyst job. As a practical example of the difference: the primary researchers on the Courtyard lobby redesign I referenced in Chapter 5 were market researchers, and Marriott worked with several market research consultancies as well.

CONCLUSION

Marketing is the area in hospitality that probably holds the most future potential for competitive advantage through analytics. It is also arguably the area that has been most impacted by the digital evolution.

Much has changed recently in the execution of marketing. Even more has changed in the available data for marketing. Opportunities are only limited by the imagination of the marketing organization (and their ability to back that up with data). Despite the reputation for creativity that marketing justifiably has, if hospitality and gaming companies want to gain an edge, they need advanced, predictive analytics.

The goal for hospitality marketing organizations is to move from reporting on guest behavior to predicting guest behavior to manipulating guest behavior. Each stage in that evolution requires data and technology investment and the resources to execute the analysis and interpret the results.

There are some very exciting advances in technology that will expand marketing's ability to promote the brand and reach new guests with creative and relevant offers. As of the publication of this book, many hospitality companies are launching virtual reality sites that allow prospects to experience the site without having to visit it. This is interesting for guests, but has a huge impact for meeting planners. Meeting planners typically visit the property to ensure the facilities will be sufficient to meet their clients' needs. This can get expensive, so between that and time constraints, the number of properties that they can consider is limited. Experiencing the property through virtual reality will allow meeting planners to do these evaluations without having to travel to the property, meaning they can evaluate a broader range of properties, and hotels that previously couldn't compete might be in the running for the business.

Leading Hotels of the World announced in early 2016 that they would be partnering with WayBlazer, a travel company powered by IBM's Watson technology. Watson employs semantic search in an innovative way, using natural dialogue with the user to power the search. WayBlazer will greatly expand the functionality of Leading's website, because guests will be able to search not just for location and dates, but for experiences or key descriptors. They can basically have a conversation with the website about what they are looking for in a travel experience, and the website can deliver personalized recommendations from the company's portfolio of luxury hotels.[4] Around the same time, Hilton Worldwide announced that they are partnering with IBM to test Watson and WayBlazer in a robot concierge, called Connie, to personalize and enhance the guest experience while they are on property (and the robot is pretty cute, too).[5]

The point is there is lots of activity in the marketing space. Companies that win will be those that are able to turn all of the complex data into meaningful marketing actions. Many companies have set developing a personalized, engaged relationship with guests or patrons as the goal of their marketing efforts. Simply leveraging business rules will not provide the right level of insight to differentiate from others attempting to achieve the same goal. This will depend on predictive, advanced analytics to support the creativity and guest-focus of your marketing team.

Now that we understand the analytic opportunities available to the marketing organization, let's move on to the other demand-generating area within hotels: sales.

ADDITIONAL RESOURCES

- Suneel Grover on Attribution, http://blogs.sas.com/content/customeranalytics/2015/12/08/making-case-algorithmic-digital-attribution.
- Suneel Grover on Digital Intelligence, http://blogs.sas.com/content/customer analytics/2016/03/22/web-analytics-vs-digital-intelligence-whats-difference.
- The SAS CI blog—on all kinds of issues in marketing, http://blogs.sas.com/content/customeranalytics.

NOTES

1. "British Airways Launches Customer Recognition Programme," PR Newswire, October 29, 2012, www.prnewswire.com/news-releases/british-airways-launches-customer-recognition-programme-176231211.html.
2. I would like to gratefully acknowledge the contributions of my former SAS colleague, Suneel Grover, who is an expert in this area. His work, particularly on the SAS CI blog, helped to inform much of this content.
3. Suneel Grover, "Web Analytics vs. Digital Intelligence: What's the Difference?" SAS, March 22, 2016, http://blogs.sas.com/content/customeranalytics/2016/03/22/web-analytics-vs-digital-intelligence-whats-difference/.
4. "The Leading Hotels of the World Taps IBM Watson to Launch Trip Discovery Tool on LHW.com," March 2, 2016, PRNewswire, www.prnewswire.com/news-releases/the-leading-hotels-of-the-world-taps-ibm-watson-to-launch-trip-discovery-tool-on-lhwcom-300229261.html.
5. "Hilton and IBM Pilot "Connie," The World's First Watson-Enabled Hotel Concierge," Hilton Worldwide, March 9, 2016, http://news.hiltonworldwide.com/index.cfm/news/hilton-and-ibm-pilot-connie-the-worlds-first-watsonenabled-hotel-concierge.

CHAPTER **7**

Analytics for Sales

There's a direct correlation between the amount of data you have at your fingertips and the odds that you'll come out on top during the negotiation phase.

—Christine Wilczek, agent

While marketing is responsible for attracting the individual, or transient, guest, the sales organization is responsible for generating group business. This can range from selling blocks of rooms, to selling functions like meetings, conventions, and weddings, to negotiating corporate contracts with global clients. Group business, for many hotels, is the core of their business mix. The groups and corporate contracts form the backbone of revenue, the base, that is filled around by other segments of business. Even in the casino industry, group business is an important revenue source, as was clearly demonstrated in 2008 and 2009 in Las Vegas, when the convention business dropped off so dramatically after the U.S. government put a spotlight on that kind of spending. Volume business can make the difference between a profitable year and a struggle to make budget. However, it is because of this volume that mistakes are amplified. The wrong pattern of stay, the wrong negotiated rate, or a poorly negotiated contract can be a huge missed revenue opportunity.

There are three factors that make the sales function at hotels both different from other functions and also a very interesting analytical problem—negotiations, relationships, and lead time. Sales is all about negotiations. Groups, events, and corporate contracts get special rates based on the type of business and value to the hotel, so every interaction with a potential piece of business becomes a negotiation. Negotiations require a slightly different application of analytics. Rather than providing a single best answer, analytics to support negotiations require ranges, best and worst case scenarios, and supporting details. The numbers need to be presented in such a way that they are flexible enough to account for all the possible permutations of terms and conditions, and also allow for a bit of "artful selling" based on what the salesperson knows about the client and the function. The analytics should give the negotiator a firm platform to stand on, but enough flexibility to do better, while maintaining the long-term sustainability of the relationship with the client.

Which brings me to the next important point about sales. Sales is very much about relationships. The amount of interaction between salespeople and their clients, at times over many years of successful events, creates relationships. The great salespeople have Rolodexes (such a cute, pre-digital term, isn't it? Google it, millennials) of people they've done business with in the past, who come to them every time they need to plan an event. That Rolodex is tied to the salesperson, not the company, which means that if a hotel company loses a salesperson to a competitor, they are likely to lose some clients as well.

The time scale of hotel and casino sales also creates an interesting challenge. While some business is booked during what could be considered a typical booking window for the hotel or casino, the larger dollar events are typically planned years in advance (sometimes up to 10 years). This is before any demand has materialized, and certainly beyond any window of certainty about the economy, industry trends, or regional conditions. This means that sales needs to be able to access some kind of expectation of conditions and performance in the face of this uncertainty and make a good estimate of the rates the hotel will be able to command.

While salespeople do use a lot of data in their jobs, I believe that these three factors contribute to the reasons that advanced analytics have not taken off for this function. The key for reaching sales with advanced analytics is to present those analytical results in such a way that they facilitate a successful negotiation, assist in the tradeoffs necessary for relationship building, and make an uncertain future more certain, but they can't get in the way of the salesperson's ability to achieve the desired outcome. This makes the problem very interesting from an operationalizing analytics perspective. (Think opportunity, not challenge.)

SALES DATA

There's an old saying in sales that each piece of business is about "rates, dates, and space." An organization's ability to measure and manipulate these three factors determines whether the business will be profitable for the property or not. Sales management generally considers the following five factors when evaluating a lead:

1. **Dates.** Does the group have a good arrival and departure pattern? Considering the day of the week and seasonal patterns, will the group fill rooms and space during a need period, or are they asking for space during a peak period? Are they willing to shift dates in exchange for a better rate?

2. **Rooms.** How many rooms does the group want to book? Is there sufficient capacity? What is the group's budget? Will they be displacing any transient business or are they filling rooms when the hotel would otherwise be empty? Generally, groups expect that they will get a preferred rate for booking volume. Hotels need to be careful to understand what the prevailing rate will be when the group arrives. During the 2008–2009 economic downturn, prevailing public rates dropped below group rates, so groups started booking outside the group block to save money. This was damaging to the hotels' budgets and cash flows.

3. **Meeting space.** Most sales teams look at the ratio of space to guest rooms booked and try to establish a reasonable balance. If the group is a "space hog," requesting a lot of space with relatively few rooms, that might not be as valuable to the hotel, because they lose the opportunity to use the meeting space to fill hotel rooms. Meeting space rental fees are all flow through. They are highly profitable, but because there are no costs to cover, sales do tend to use waiving or reducing rental fees as a lever in the negotiation.

4. **Food and beverage minimums.** Generally, hotels have a standard formula for how much catering spend they would expect depending on the amount of space requested and the time of day the function is booked.

5. **Concessions.** Sales teams can offer certain incentives to the groups to book, including free room upgrades for VIPs or free rooms for organizers, food and beverage packages, amenities— basically any of the products or services offered at the hotel can be included to make the hotel's or casino's offering look more attractive.

The other tricky part of the sales negotiating process is that each of these revenue streams has a different profit margin, so the sales teams need to consider that when putting together the deal. In order of profitability, this is: meeting space, hotel rooms, beverage (particularly alcohol), and food.

Generally speaking, given the complexity of group business, many sales organizations have established rules of thumb or standard operating procedures to guide negotiations. These tend to be based on best practices or the judgment of experienced sales managers, but they also tend to be relatively fixed and inflexible. There is an expected function space to rooms ratio, which may vary by season. Function space tends to be held for business with rooms associated for functions starting before 5 p.m. until 30 or so days in advance, and catering is able to book local events with no rooms associated weekday evenings and weekends. Certain dates are set aside as free sell, meaning set restrictions are released. Food and beverage minimums are calculated according to a fixed formula. In the case study at the end of this chapter, Kate Kiesling, Product Manager for IDeaS—A SAS Company, describes the opportunity to generate additional profits from putting a bit more analytical discipline around the function space.

Sales tracks data from their leads and materialized business. They track the rates that are offered, the number of rooms that were contracted, and the number of rooms that actually materialized. If it's a function, they can store the details of the function, including how much space was booked, for how long, the food and beverage spend, and any other ancillaries associated with the group. The percentage of leads that materialize into business is also important. Many groups will rebook with some frequency, so understanding the history of the group is important to knowing how you should treat them in the future. This is where comparing the number of rooms or revenue they contracted for versus what actually materialized is important. The group may not have ended up being as good as they looked at the beginning of the negotiation. This is important to know if they return, or if a group like them wants to book a function or block of rooms.

Groups contract for a block of rooms for a certain date. Corporate contracts, on the other hand, contract for favorable rates for a certain volume of rooms across the entire hotel system, over the course of the contract. This means you need to understand not just the volume of rooms that will be generated, but also where they will be generated and the typical pattern of bookings. For example, do they generally check in on a Sunday night, which is very slow for a business hotel, or do they check in midweek, which is a much busier time? What cities do they book most frequently? The characteristics of the client and whether they fill in need periods or need cities, determines how favorable of a rate or other terms they should be given. Accessing as much history about the client as possible is very important to understanding how to structure the contract when it is up for renewal. This is also useful if you are evaluating a client that hasn't contracted with you before but has a similar profile to existing clients.

Since sales deals with both new and existing clients, it is important to be able to segment leads, and understand booking patterns by these segments. This helps to evaluate a new group, because you can use the behavior of members of the same segment to predict how the new group will behave. Sales teams are frequently organized around segments, with all of the segment sales managers trying to book the same space. When you understand booking patterns you can release function space being held for conventions when the booking window has passed, or know when to open up dates to sell to local groups with no rooms attached. I did an internship in function space revenue management in Singapore while earning my master's degree (Kimes and McGuire 2001). One of the more impactful analyses we did was on exactly this. The team was broken up into conventions, weddings, meetings, and leisure business. When we did a booking curve analysis, it became very obvious how far in advance weddings and conventions booked. The team was holding space for these segments long past this window, hoping for a booking, because these groups were so profitable. However, other events were potentially being turned away during this period. The first thing the team did after I presented the results was to rethink the way they held space by segments.

Sales should also be looking at external data when evaluating their potential performance. Since the lead times are so long for sales, having a picture of economic conditions is quite helpful. This will help to forecast whether and how much rates are likely to increase over the few years until the group's actual arrival dates. This involves understanding both macro- and microeconomic factors, including both regional and local performance as well as industry dynamics. This was one of the problems that occurred in 2008–2009 for the hotel industry (not that anyone should have foreseen that coming). When the bottom fell out of the industry, group rates were so much higher than the prevailing rates, for those groups that didn't cancel, that the attendees were booking outside of the group block or the hotels risked turning away a lot of transient business in an effort to keep their rates as high as the in-house group's negotiated rate.

The concept of customer relationship management in sales is very interesting. Group business tends to be organized by a meeting planner. For certain corporate clients, this one meeting planner can be responsible for hundreds of thousands of dollars or more for a hotel. Understanding the clients' needs and preferences, and cultivating a relationship with the meeting planner, is critical to long-term revenue and profits for the sales teams. This is further support for the importance of that sales Rolodex that I mentioned earlier.

Emerging Data Sources

Emerging data for sales include some of the same elements that are of interest to other functional areas. Reputation is important to sales, as it is something that the meeting planners and corporate negotiators also look at these days. Sales teams now have access to forward-looking demand data, which can help them to benchmark their production against the performance of the market. Many meeting planners have become interested in sustainability metrics as well, so hotels need to be thinking about tracking and reporting on the metrics associated with their green initiatives. Location data from mobile tracking could also be of large value to sales organizations. Understanding the ancillary spend associated with certain groups is a measure of their potential profitability. This includes knowing whether the attendees will use other services the hotel offers, like spa or restaurants, separately from their booked functions. Tracking their movements in the hotel, and possibly the local area, will help sales managers understand the potential for ancillary revenue associated with each group or each segment.

ADVANCED ANALYTICS FOR SALES

Despite the art that goes along with the sales function, there is still ample room for applying advanced analytics. Sales negotiations can be quite time consuming. Clients value responsiveness. Any analytics that streamline the process, provide support for decision making, and help sales to make more profitable decisions faster would be highly valuable to this function.

STATISTICAL ANALYSIS

Statistical analysis can be used to predict the materialization of a group (how many rooms will actually book versus the contracted amount), which will improve planning at the property level. Statistical analysis can assess the most profitable patterns of stay for groups and the components of a function that are highly associated with profits.

Statistical analysis is also useful for evaluating contract business. Using statistical models, the sales team can analyze the past performance of the client and match that with current and forecast operating conditions to determine whether that client was profitable for the hotel. It can identify need cities and seasonal patterns and compare them to the behavior of a specific corporate contract. During the term of the contract, statistical analysis can use booking trends to identify whether the contracted business is behaving as expected, according to contracted terms, or if they are failing to produce. The sales teams can then take appropriate steps to work with client contacts, or use that information during the next negotiation.

Forecasting

Sales always keeps an eye on forecasts. Since they are incentivized to produce a certain amount of demand, sales keeps careful track of the forecast of business they expect to bring in. This forecast is rolled up to the corporate level. Given the long lead times involved with sales, a robust forecast with a longer term view is pretty important to present the right picture of demand. The forecast will always be a combination of predictive modeling and expert opinion, but it needs to be anchored on performance.

As I alluded to earlier, sales needs to keep an eye on the long-term economic conditions that could impact groups that have booked with a longer lead time. They need to negotiate rates that should be a good deal for the client, but that are also aligned with market potential. Forecasts can also help sales understand where softer periods or locations are in the portfolio, as well as where they can be more aggressive with rate setting.

Demand for group business, including both rooms and function space, needs to be forecasted at the hotel level. Forecasting demand for function space is tricky, given the dependency between rooms and space, but it is an important factor in understanding the value of the space, as well as when it needs to be held or released for free sale. Segment-level forecasts are useful to help identify the most profitable mix of business to attract to the hotel.

Forecasting can be used during contract negotiations as well. Based on previous performance, the future expected performance of that contracted client can be evaluated. This can be compared to the hotel's expected overall performance to see if the client will add to profitability overall, or displace other demand. The client will also have a forecast, so it can be useful to compare their performance expectations with that of the hotel's.

Predictive Modeling

Predictive modeling would be useful for mining characteristics of groups in the same way it can be used for evaluating customers. Based on the past performance of similar groups, a predictive model can provide insight into the likelihood that a certain group would book, or give some guidance as to the minimum, maximum, and most likely rates they would accept. Looking across the tentative groups on the books, predictive modeling will provide a materialization or cancellation rate.

Optimization

An optimization for the sales function is probably best associated with the revenue management system. Sales should be able to enter the details of the group, the number of rooms, dates, rates, and ancillary revenue. The system should allow them to indicate which factors are flexible, and the algorithm can return either the best placement or rate that will ensure they are profitable, based on other predicted and actual streams of revenue. Ideally, the system would provide a floor and ceiling rate (confidence interval around the most likely rate), or some other similar tools to facilitate the negotiation. A strict recommendation does not really give the sales team the power to use what they know about the group plus their experience, to drive the best combination of revenue and terms. Still, if the group is not profitable, they just aren't. It's best to know that before you spend too much time and effort on that group. Optimization can definitely help with that.

THE CHANGING LANDSCAPE OF SALES[1]

As I prepared this chapter, I had several conversations with sales executives about the current challenges and opportunities the function is facing. We talked about evolutions in two main areas: leadership and technology.

From a sales leadership perspective, there are a couple of emerging trends. First, many brands are consolidating sales functions either into a leader who is responsible for general commercial functions, or, specifically, into a leader who also has responsibility for revenue management. This consolidation helps organizations to look more holistically at their business and make decisions that benefit the enterprise as a whole. Many think of the three-legged stool of sales—revenue, management, and marketing—as the ideal to properly manage demand, either through controlling it by pricing, generating group business, or generating individual demand. Having all of the functions report to a single leader helps to balance these critical but frequently conflicting activities.

Organizations are starting to consolidate sales functions across brands or management companies as well, attempting to centralize where it makes sense. The technology automation that I will describe next is contributing to this trend, but there are certainly complications to this strategy due to the organization of the industry, particularly on the hotel side. A management company may manage several brands.

If a lead comes to them from the brand, they have to consider just the hotels in their portfolio from that brand, even if the group would be better for the management company if it were hosted at a differently flagged property. It's also possible that two different hotels under the same management company portfolio could be competing for the same piece of business, which came through each brand's corporate sales function.

The sales function is also moving toward digital, automated, or third-party bookings in a major way. Many brands have developed a small group booking tool online. Groups that are less than, say, 50 people in a meeting room or 25 guest rooms can use this tool to request rooms and get an instant confirmation. Only a small amount of demand is driven through this channel. It is managed centrally by the brand.

Third-party vendors are starting to digitize the process of submitting an RFP (request for proposals—a meeting planner's request for an estimate of what the hotel could offer their group). Instead of sending these RFPs to hotels individually, the meeting planner creates them in one of these technology solutions and selects which hotels they would like to send them to. This streamlines the process for the meeting planner, but it can be challenging for hotels to manage. Naturally, the hotels are charged a fee to participate, and they can pay more to market themselves in a deeper way on this channel.

The final trend in booking group business is a growing number of third-party intermediaries that are starting to insert themselves between the hotel and the companies that book group business. These tend to be experienced hotel salespeople with extensive industry contacts. They are beginning to represent the corporate entities as meeting planners in contract negotiations. They approach a corporation to offer to act as their agent, so that instead of having to employ a meeting planner, the corporation can use this service. This is free to the corporation, but the hotels pay a commission to the third party for any booked business. They pay an extra commission if the piece of business comes through the brand's global sales team, since they must pay the intermediary and also the global sales team. This also means that the hotel does not get to interact directly with the client until they are on the property at the function. It is much more expensive for the hotels when events are booked through these services. Yet, this is where a large portion of group business is now coming from.

The sales leaders whom I talked to were concerned that they were losing control of their inventory for group business in the same way that is happening on the transient side with the growing power of third-party distribution channels. The proliferation of bookings through these digital and third-party channels is making the selling process much more transactional and less relationship driven. It is also becoming much more expensive for hotels.

All of this activity is making it more important that sales teams are able to evaluate each piece of business in light of a decision that is most profitable for the hotel or casino as a whole, considering all of the factors just described, as well as the channel. This is an additional layer of complexity in an already complex process. Applying advanced analytics, as I described, can help hotels and casinos make more profitable decisions in the face of these changes.

BENCHMARKING SALES ANALYTICS

Sales teams are used to evaluating all kinds of data about groups and functions, and the most experienced salespeople have good instincts about the attractiveness of certain types of groups and how they will materialize. While they may be extensive users of business intelligence, many sales departments in general have yet to fully embrace advanced analytics.

Technology and Resources

It would be typical for a sales organization to have a lot of reports of production and past performance. Most of this is likely in Excel, although some companies do use an automated sales and catering system that might also be delivering some reports. Corporate might have a sales analyst who runs reports and maybe manages the forecasting process. The process of evaluating an RFP is highly manual, driven by rules of thumb, and it can be very time consuming.

At the risk of sounding like a broken record, I'll say again that the sales department could see tremendous benefit from a visualization platform that allows them to see their data in a flexible and immediate format. Given the amount of information that needs to be pulled together to successfully negotiate some of the larger and more complex deals that sales manages, a consolidated view that can be sliced and diced according to the conditions of the current project would be very valuable.

Most revenue management solutions have some functionality that evaluates the displacement associated with group functions and recommends a rate to account for displaced revenue. This is very useful to ensure that the sales department is keeping focused on booking profitable groups. Some of the revenue management vendors are working on analytical solutions to support the function space sales process. There is going to be tremendous benefit to those organizations that are able to apply revenue management to this important revenue source, but it is pretty complicated. Hotels and casinos should definitely consider investments in this area, if they fit within the sales process, of course.

I have seen some consulting services offered around corporate contracting, which is also valuable. An advanced analytics platform operated by an analyst that understands statistical modeling or data mining would benefit hotels large enough to support the investment.

CASE STUDY: MEETINGS AND EVENTS REVENUE MANAGEMENT, KATE KEISLING, IDEAS—A SAS COMPANY

Kate Keisling is a product manager in new business development for IDeaS and has been working on meetings and events revenue management. The key points of her case study are summarized here; the full article, a great example of operationalizing analytics, is in Appendix 2.

Industry experts have been talking about optimizing function space for years. In rooms, we settled on a core set of metrics that we all agree are the best tools for measuring success, and these are widely reported. Basic metrics like occupancy, RevPAR and ADR are widely accepted across the hotel industry. Somehow, we haven't done the same with function space. Room metrics provide the base for so much of our decision making. Other sources of income, specifically food and beverage, can make up nearly equal portions of a hotel's revenue budget and are not represented in these metrics.

(continued)

(*continued*)

Function space is a bit like a jigsaw puzzle, both in reality and metaphorically. You have pieces for the various team members involved. The meetings and events business touches almost every department in the hotel, and they all have a potential impact, some more than others.

Then there are the pieces that represent the systems that meetings and events touch. These include the sales and catering system in which the meeting or event gets booked, all the way through the point of sale system where the banquet check for each event is created. Each system has unique data elements necessary to understand demand, revenue, and profit conditions.

And, of course there's the fact that you don't have a single price for function space. There are a lot of interdependent revenue streams involved. What impacts one revenue stream will likely impact another, sometimes in ways that might not be obvious without some data. You need to understand how the data fit together to predict whether those impacts will combine together in a positive or negative result.

If you take a simple but strategic approach and work your way through each element, you can fit all the data together and find ways to generate more positive results. Before you jump into collecting data and compiling spreadsheets, take a step back and look at current processes. Take into consideration all of the pieces involved in delivering meetings and events. Talk to each of the departments or team members involved from initial contact through reporting on actuals. Do a basic inventory of your current reports and methods for forecasting, evaluating business, and measuring results. Look at each of the systems involved in those processes. You might be surprised at what you find. As you do this, the adjustments needed will reveal themselves.

Group business evaluation in the absence of a revenue management system often consists of a first-come, first-served approach. It is tempting to take the first group that wants the rooms or space if you don't have empirical data to show you that a better and more profitable group may be on the way. It is possible to do some basic evaluation without a system, but evaluating groups effectively requires comparison to established baselines and/or thresholds. Establishing those baselines and thresholds will depend on clean meetings and events data.

There are several baselines that can be established to help give a quick guideline on which to base a decision. These include identifying demand patterns by season, day of week, and segment and historical averages of revenue and profit. However, they all depend on clean data.

Appendix 2 contains some suggestions for improving data quality for accounts, bookings, guest rooms, and events.

Once you've gotten your data cleaned up, you can have more confidence in what it is telling you. The cleanup is the tough part. The payoff is in finding the patterns that will help you to fill gaps in low-demand periods and drive profits in high-demand times. In many sales organizations, knowledge of demand patterns is the biggest opportunity for improvement. With it, you can price dynamically and release function space to event-only business when group room demand wans, preventing unsold or undersold space. You can also better target profitable business that is still within their lead times that matches the openings in your inventory. Without knowledge of demand patterns, you are basically playing the odds.

In Appendix 2, I provide some suggestions for tracking demand patterns, including evaluating lead time, seasonality and day of week, demand calendars, and spend patterns.

No matter what your vision, it will require a set of performance metrics. This is where your work to clean up the data is really important. These metrics can be used not only to evaluate past performance but also to manage the business on an ongoing basis. Making them a regular part of your weekly revenue meetings will give them the emphasis they deserve and get the team to think more about the overall impact of their meetings and events.

Appendix 2 also contains a methodology for calculating some key metrics like utilization, profit per occupied space/time, and profit per available space/time.

You have many team members involved in selling, planning, and executing events. At each step in the cycle, your team members have the ability to impact the profitability of a group or even a single event. This is also an area of the business where there are habits and processes that have been in place for ages. Intuition plays a key role in meetings and events decision making because there have been so few tools to analyze

(continued)

(*continued*)

the data and prove that intuition right or wrong. This is changing, but there is still a strong pull toward those old habits. Here are a couple of areas to include in your assessment:

- When evaluating your meetings and events program, be sure to also think through incentive alignment, training, and organizational structure.

- Knowledge really is power. Your systems and standard processes need to support the efficient collection of the data you need to understand the demand patterns and spending habits of your business. The entire selling and servicing team needs to be invested, both financially and emotionally, in success. Revenue management principles and concepts should be applied to all the revenue streams and should be a part of each person's job.

Building a strong revenue management culture doesn't happen overnight, but the more knowledge your team gains and the more success they see from its application, the faster it will build toward revenue breakthroughs in your meetings and events business.

CONCLUSION

The sales department in a hotel generates a lot of revenue, but they are competing for the same inventory that is leveraged by transient guests who may be paying higher rates. Making the right decisions about what group business to take and what rate to offer the corporate negotiated deals involves understanding all demand patterns, forecasting economic conditions into the future, and predicting the behavior of that group when they eventually do start booking.

To me, the most interesting opportunity when it comes to the sales function is figuring out how to operationalize the analytics. Determining what information is most useful to the salesperson when they approach these complicated negotiations, and how that information should be delivered to the salespeople, is an interesting problem that has yet to be widely solved. If the data were available in an integrated, flexible, data visualization platform, the sales teams probably could get to it faster, which would be a benefit. Giving an experienced sales resource guidance that is too restrictive, for example, enforcing a rate plan or requiring them to check with revenue management, limits their ability to close a deal. However, some guidance, like a floor rate, could be very useful information to ensure that the group deal is profitable for the hotel.

I've alluded to the revenue management function several times in this chapter. Clearly, marketing, sales, and revenue management are closely related functions that must remain in close communication. In the next chapter, I'll talk about the data and analytics that revenue management can utilize, and in Chapter 11, I'll describe how these departments can work better together.

NOTE

1. The author would like to gratefully acknowledge Michael Smith, Vice President of Sales and Marketing for JHM Hotels, for providing the background for this section and for spending time talking through the sales function in general.

8

Analytics
for Revenue
Management

The goal is to sell the right product, to the right customer, at the right time, for the right price.

—Bob Crandall, former CEO of American Airlines

Revenue management, or yield management, was first applied in the airline industry after deregulation in the 1980s. After witnessing the successful implementation by the airline programs, hotels adopted revenue management beginning in the early 1990s. Revenue management is a specialized pricing discipline applied to industries that have the following characteristics (Kimes 1989):

- **Relatively fixed capacity.** For example, there are only 350 rooms in the hotel.
- **Time-perishable inventory.** If a room is not sold for this evening, you lose the opportunity to sell it.
- **Time-variable demand.** There are peak periods and off-peak periods, like for a business hotel that is busy during the week and slow on the weekends.
- **Low cost of sale as compared to fixed costs.** It costs relatively little to sell one more room as compared to the operating costs of the hotel.

Revenue management is important to capacity-constrained firms, like hotels and casinos, because they need be smart about how they sell their inventory. During busy times, they want to sell the inventory only to customers who are willing to pay the most, but during off-peak periods, because it doesn't cost that much more to sell one more unit, they are willing to discount to drive revenue through volume, or occupancy. The first revenue management applications were based on the ability to forecast demand for the highest fares (or rates) and "save" (protect) sufficient inventory to serve that high-valued demand. Market dynamics have changed the problem a bit since revenue management's earliest application in the airline industry, but it is still based on these same principles. I will discuss this more later in the chapter.

Revenue management has always been a data and analytics heavy discipline, and was arguably the first extensive application of advanced analytics in the hotel industry. Today, most hotels have an extensive revenue management organization, including corporate revenue management, regional resources, and property-level revenue managers who are responsible for setting rates and executing strategy. Many hotels are using an automated, analytical revenue management system.

The core function of revenue management is to set prices for each product (rate, room type, length of stay) over the booking horizon. Recently, revenue managers have begun to explore applying revenue management to other revenue-generating assets within the hotel like function space or food and beverage outlets. They are also called upon to take a more strategic role, requiring an understanding of market dynamics, guest lifetime value, digital marketing, and brand strategy.

Gaming companies have been slower to adopt revenue management, and for good reason. Their problem is slightly different than a traditional hotel problem because their primary source of revenue comes from the casino floor. Generally speaking, knowing that guests play where they stay, casinos thought of the hotel rooms as amenities for their highest-valued casino customers, so they were willing to give away or deeply discount rooms to encourage this segment to stay with them. Then they filled the rest of the rooms with whatever demand happened along. However, the gaming market has been changing dramatically in the last couple of decades. In 2000, nongaming revenue actually surpassed gaming revenue in Las Vegas, and many casino-focused markets are morphing into destination markets focused on entertainment, shopping and restaurants. Casino companies have realized that rooms can represent a profitable secondary source of revenue, and are now trying to balance nongaming, or retail, patrons with their more traditional casino base. This means that the casino revenue management solution must consider the gaming value of the patron along with retail demand for the hotel rooms and that guest's willingness to pay. I address this unique characteristic in this chapter and in the chapter on gaming analytics (Chapter 10).

REVENUE MANAGEMENT: A HISTORY LESSON

Because revenue management is a complex and very specialized discipline, it is worth providing a bit more background on this topic than I have for others. This will give you context not only to understand revenue management, but also to appreciate how it has evolved due to recent market conditions. The fact that I have a background in this area and a particular affection for its application in hotels has only a little bit to do with why I am subjecting you to this history lesson.

Revenue management, or yield management, as it was originally known when it was first applied in the airline industry, started as a method for airlines to control the number of discounted fares they sold. The idea was to move away from first-come, first-served selling and start preserving the right number of full-fare seats for more valuable demand (Figure 8.1a). Airlines started by forecasting demand by fare

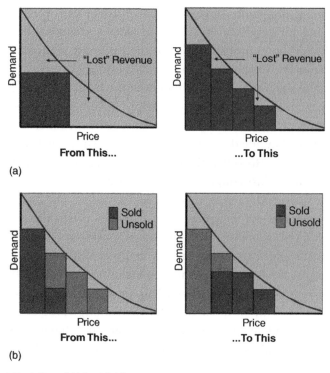

Figure 8.1 Evolution of Airline Yielding

(a) In this graph, the gray area represents lost revenue opportunity. If you only offer one price, you lose revenue opportunity from consumers who would have paid more. Increasing the number of prices offered means you can capture more of the revenue opportunity, while still preserving seats for those that would pay higher prices. (b) The area under the curve represents all demand for a flight by price. There is more demand for the flight than available seats. For flights, leisure travelers tend to book further in advance, and they are more price sensitive. If the airline uses first-come, first-served booking, as on the left, the plane will fill with lower-value demand. If they save seats for higher-paying customers who book later, as on the right, more revenue is generated through higher prices charged for the same limited number of seats. This is the basis for the first yield management systems, preserving inventory for higher-rated demand.

class and protecting a certain number of seats for higher paying fares. *Fences*, which are rules to qualify for purchase, were created around the discounted fares, such as advanced purchase or a Saturday-night stay. This was designed to discourage those who would pay a higher fare from booking the lower fares.

As this business process evolved, airlines saw the opportunity to add more discount levels to drive even more incremental revenue (Figure 8.1b). As the number of fares increased, the problem started to get more complicated, so mathematicians got involved, to find the mathematically optimal protection levels that would maximize revenue. The output was the number of full fare seats to protect and the number of each of the many discounted products to sell in order to maximize revenue. The early systems developed for this purpose were known as yield management systems (Smith et al 1992).

After the carriers began to move toward the *hub-and-spoke* model, where a significant percentage of passenger itineraries involved a stop at the carrier's hub, yield management systems needed to account for large numbers of connecting passengers. This involved managing demand for a specific segment, known as a *leg*, of an itinerary when many different kinds of itineraries, all with different values to the airline, also flowed over it, and optimizing the availability of different fares on these connecting itineraries.

For a simple example, think about a flight from Raleigh, North Carolina, to Newark, New Jersey, a hub for United Airlines. This is considered a *leg*. There are passengers on that flight who are going to Newark, but there are also passengers connecting to flights around the world. Many of these international connecting flights will have much higher fares than the Raleigh to Newark fare. If the airline does not balance passengers who will stop in Newark with those continuing on, they may end up with many empty seats on connecting flights. It might be better for the revenue over the entire system to raise the local Newark fare, thus restricting this local demand and leaving seats available to customers who wish to travel beyond to, say, Tampa, San Francisco, or even Milan. Raising this one fare may lower the revenue return from Raleigh-Newark customers but raise the overall revenue across the flight system by freeing up those seats for connecting flyers. This is called the *network effect*.

Modeling after the success of airlines, hotel companies began to adapt the airline methodologies to their business problem. The first revenue lift hotels gained from revenue management came from two areas: length of stay controls and overbooking.

Length of stay controls. For hotels, length of stay creates a similar issue to the hub-and-spoke problem in airlines. Think about a hotel that is popular on weekends. The decision of what demand by length of stay you accept on a Saturday night has an impact on the surrounding nights. If you sell too many one-night stays on a Saturday night, you block out demand that would have stayed Friday and Saturday or Friday, Saturday, and Sunday. This can have a significant revenue impact for hotels, particularly if the majority of demand for Friday night is for two-night lengths of stay. If you fill the hotel on Saturday for a one-night length of say, you leave rooms empty on Friday. If you instead only accepted reservations that wanted to arrive on Friday and stay for two nights, you'd fill the hotel on Friday night and Saturday night. Obviously, this is quite simplistic, but it does illustrate the problem. It is important to consider the peak night along with the surrounding nights, known as *shoulder periods*, to truly optimize revenue. Some of the first revenue management practices in hotels involved manually analyzing demand by length of stay for busy periods and putting availability restrictions, in the form of length of stay controls, in place to increase occupancy and revenue on the "shoulder" nights around the busy period.

Overbooking. Hotels take reservations in advance, frequently without a guarantee. When this happens, there is a chance of no shows or last-minute cancellations, meaning the hotel is left with empty rooms that could have been sold ahead of time—a potentially significant loss of revenue. Overbooking the hotel protects against this, but also creates the risk that all of the booked rooms will show up and the hotel will have to "walk" guests with reservations (send them to another hotel at the hotel's expense) because there are no available rooms at the hotel. Many hotels were reluctant to risk overbooking due to potential loss of goodwill from walking too many guests. Initial applications of revenue management applied basic analytical techniques to analyze and predict no-show rates so that the hotels could overbook with more confidence. This resulted in fewer empty rooms and more revenue, usually without incurring any additional walks.

These initial improvements were gained through relatively manual processes, but based on the success of these initiatives, they quickly moved on to more analytically based processes, using optimal pricing recommendations derived from an automated revenue management system.

THEN THINGS CHANGED . . .

The original revenue management algorithms in these automated systems were based on the use of fences to ensure that consumers who would be willing to pay a higher price could not access lower priced inventory. In other words, demand could be perfectly segmented according to the value they placed on access to the inventory. Following that, the models then assumed that even though different fare products used the same inventory unit (an airline seat), each different fare type could be treated as a separate product, with each servicing a distinct and separate market of customers. This last assumption meant that demand for these different products could be treated as independent— a key assumption that underpins traditional revenue management forecasting and optimization.

Several important trends, driven by evolving market conditions, have emerged since these original algorithms were developed. These are:

- Low-cost airlines introduced simplified fare structures with fewer fares and significantly reduced fencing, meaning everyone "qualifies" for all of the fares. Today, these simplified fare structures dominate most air travel markets—effectively invalidating the assumption of demand independence made in revenue management models. Figure 8.2 represents a typical online airline purchase. In this case, a consumer could purchase any of the available fares, instead of being fenced into one option according to their travel pattern (looks pretty similar to how hotels are booked today, right?).

- Revenue management has been introduced into markets where strict fences on rates or fares don't really exist. Hotels, rental cars, and cruise lines have rate or fare structures that do not contain strict fences. Prices are tiered based on product characteristics (room type, car type) as opposed to consumer characteristics (business traveler who won't stay over the weekend)— thus, demand independence cannot be assumed, since the same consumer can qualify for multiple rates or fares.

■ The advent of e-commerce and OTA (online travel agencies) ushered in an era of price transparency, where consumers have easy access to all the prices in the market. This means that hotels had to compete more directly on price and consider the price sensitivity of their demand both to their rate changes and that of their competitors. OTAs began to enforce rate parity in their hotel contracts, such that hotels must offer the OTAs the same price for the same product (room type, date) that is offered everywhere else in the market for *unqualified transient demand*, guests who are not part of a group and do not have an arrangement for a special rate.

All fares are rounded up to the nearest dollar.

Depart	Arrive	Flight #	Routing	Travel Time	Business Select $629 - $641	Anytime $601 - $613	Wanna Get Away $278 - $388
6:00 AM	10:50 AM	414 1694	1 stop Change Planes MDW	7h 50m	$637	$609	$326
6:50 AM	9:10 AM	4480	Nonstop	5h 20m	$629	$601	$278
8:20 AM	12:15 PM	491 1027	1 stop Change Planes STL	6h 55m	$637	$609	$326
8:20 AM	1:00 PM	491 3226	2 stops Change Planes STL	7h 40m	$641	$613	Unavailable
9:10 AM	1:50 PM	752 4026	1 stop Change Planes DEN	7h 40m	$637	$609	$388
10:40 AM	3:25 PM	490 611	1 stop Change Planes MDW	7h 45m	$637	$609	$326
12:10 PM	4:20 PM	482 747	1 stop Change Planes PHX	7h 10m	$637	$609	$326
3:00 PM	8:15 PM	4969 3673	1 stop Change Planes TPA	8h 15m	$637	$609	$326
5:15 PM	9:20 PM	315 134	1 stop Change Planes MDW	7h 05m	$637	$609	$286
7:10 PM	10:50 PM	2774 1282	1 stop Change Planes DEN	6h 40m	$637	$609	$326

Figure 8.2 Airline Fare Screen

Note that there are multiple products available with different characteristics. Every consumer is eligible to purchase any of them, depending on what is most important to them.

These recent trends have moved hospitality revenue management away from the assumptions made by the original hotel revenue management scientists, who modeled according to the airline revenue management problem. No demand independence, limited rate fences, simplified rate structures, rate parity, and price transparency have made "traditional" revenue management algorithms relatively ineffective to price transient demand. It is these factors that have created an environment better suited to *price optimization*. I covered optimization as a broader analytic technique in Chapter 4, and I will talk about price optimization specifically later in this chapter.

In order to understand the current state of revenue management in hotels and casinos, and to identify future opportunities, let's take a look at the data and analytics that drive revenue management.

REVENUE MANAGEMENT DATA

As in previous chapters, let's start by understanding current and emerging data for revenue management. To a certain extent, revenue management, among the most data-intensive applications in hospitality, has always been a big data problem. Revenue management systems require at least a year of historical demand data to develop detailed forecasts at the rate, length of stay, and arrival day levels across the booking horizon, which can be up to a year.

A typical hotel has the following input data:

- Detailed customer or market type segments (optimal for revenue management analytics): 60
- Room types: 12
- Historical dates (two years of history): 730
- Future dates (one year): 365
- Length of stay types: 8
- Snapshots stored for each occupancy date: 40

The combination of all of this input data for just one property is 252 million observations. If you generate and store decisions based on this data, you will need to store 10 to 20 gigabytes per property. For a hotel chain with 2,000 to 4,000 properties, that would equal 20 to 80 terabytes of data. This may be only a fraction of the data generated by a large credit card company or a major online retailer, but if the internal infrastructure is not set up to manage this amount of data, you have a big data challenge. This is even before the hotel explores adding additional detailed data from other revenue-generating assets.

With the advent of price transparency, revenue managers had to start paying attention to competitor rates. Vendors have emerged that will provide data feeds containing the prices that a predefined set of competitors are offering across the booking horizon. These prices are incorporated into the revenue management system so that the competitive dynamics can be factored into price recommendations.

Emerging Data Sources

Market dynamics influence consumers' value perceptions and ultimately the price that a hotel is able to charge. As the market evolves, revenue managers have begun to investigate a myriad of other data sources that could inform pricing decisions. These include:

- **Forward-looking demand data.** Vendors have started collecting information on booking pace into key markets. Hotels can have access to aggregated market demand data so that they can understand the market potential versus what they have on books already.

- **Net rates/distribution costs.** Studies have shown that distribution costs are outpacing revenue growth, and if hoteliers aren't careful, these rising costs will eat away all of their profits. These studies seem to indicate that hotels should be carefully tracking distribution costs. The challenge is that for some distribution partners, the hotel only ever sees the net rate minus the commission, so the costs are not accounted for on the P&L. True cost of distribution is, therefore, masked to a certain extent.

- **Reputation.** There is strong evidence (including from my own research with Dr. Breffni Noone; see the links at the end of the chapter) that a hotel's reputation, particularly as expressed in reviews, has a relationship with a hotel's pricing power. Of course, all things being equal, consumers still prefer to pay the lowest price possible.

- **Airline lift.** Some argue that airline capacity into a market is a marker of how much demand a hotel can expect, and should be accounted for in forecasting. Further, many say that consumers will generally book an airline ticket before they book a hotel, so the number of airline bookings for future dates might be a directional indication of demand. This could be more impactful in certain markets than others.

- **Customer lifetime value.** Casinos have been considering patron value in the revenue management algorithms and decisions for a while now. Hotels are now starting to consider how guest lifetime value should fit into revenue management tactics and strategies.

- **Search data.** Some believe that search data is a leading indicator of demand into a market, even before any bookings are made. If a hotel notices that search figures are higher or lower than normal during a particular period, it could indicate that demand will be higher or lower as well.

With any new source of data, the important decisions that revenue managers need to make are exactly how and where to use this data. Some may belong in the algorithms that calculate a day-to-day pricing decision, whereas others should be used for a more strategic analysis. Revenue management modelers are still investigating some of the newer data sources, so it remains to be seen whether they would improve the algorithm's output or if they are best utilized in analyses outside of the core revenue management system. Keep in mind that simply cramming all the data into the revenue management system and trying to get the algorithms to produce a rational price is not the right way to approach this complex problem (see my discussion in Chapter 2 about the issues associated with adding more data sources to an algorithm).

REVENUE MANAGEMENT ANALYTICS

Unlike many of the analytic applications that I describe in this book, revenue management involves an interrelated series of analytics, with the outputs of one process becoming the inputs of the next. This means that the inputs and outputs need to be stable and in the right format to feed the next step. Note that in the following section,

I am using the term "revenue management analytics" as a blanket term for any type of analytics used to set a price that optimizes hotel revenue. Some might use the term "revenue optimization" or "price optimization," but since the broader function in hospitality tends to be called revenue management, I'm going to use that term here.

In Figure 8.3, the elements inside the circle represent the interrelated processes in revenue management analytics that result in a pricing recommendation. The process loosely follows the steps in our advanced analytics capabilities. The areas around the circle also leverage the analytic capabilities, but are separate from the interrelated processes that result in a daily price recommendation. In the following section, I will cover the analytics in a revenue management system

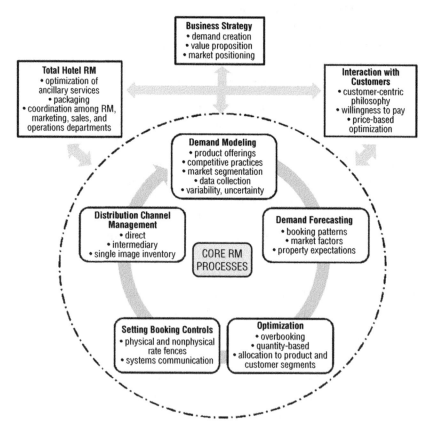

Figure 8.3 Evolving Scope of Revenue Management Activities
Source: Noone et al. 2011.

under the headings we've been using in previous chapters, but will also describe how they relate to each other.

Statistical Analysis

In the revenue management process, statistical analysis supports the demand modeling step. In this setup, the statistics provide a profile of demand behavior, which then becomes an input into the forecasting models and the optimization. Regression modeling detects market segments with similar booking patterns and rate behavior. Similarly, the algorithms can detect seasonal patterns and special events by comparing patterns in the data. No-show and cancellation rates are determined and competitive impacts are calculated. Price-sensitivity parameters are calculated. This set of parameters then form the inputs for the demand forecasting step.

Remember, the goal of revenue management is to set a price to attract the most valuable demand, because hotels have a limited capacity of rooms to sell on any given night. Hotels may fill before all of the demand in the market is satisfied. Hotels may also offer a price that is higher than the market will bear, and turn away demand that would have booked at a lower price. In order to maximize revenue, it is important to understand the value of all demand for the rooms, even the demand that was not captured because there were no rooms left (also known as a denial), or because the price was higher than some consumers wanted to pay (also known as a regret). Therefore, the revenue management forecast requires an estimate of *unconstrained* demand, or a prediction of all available demand, regardless of price or availability constraints. There are several mathematical methodologies available that can provide a good approximation of unconstrained demand.[1] Unconstrained demand modeling, which uses patterns in the data to project what demand would have been if there were unlimited capacity or lower prices, is also an input into the forecast.

Generally, there is an extensive demand modeling effort when a hotel or casino first starts implementing revenue management. These algorithms either only need to be run once, or can learn over time, so after this initial modeling effort, generally the parameters established here are only recalibrated every so often to make sure they are still accurate.

Forecasting

Demand forecasting tends to be an important and very extensive component of revenue management analytics. Some might argue that revenue management tends to obsess a bit too much over this step, since it doesn't actually produce a recommendation. Others think of this as the core function of the entire process. For the purposes of this discussion, I am going to remain neutral.

In the demand forecasting step, a detailed prediction of demand by market segment, product type, and time period (date and length of stay) is calculated. There are several key differences between revenue management forecasting and the general forecasting I explained in Chapter 4. First, as I described previously, it is important to account for unconstrained demand, so the models need to be allowed to forecast beyond what demand actually materialized in history. The optimization algorithm will constrain the demand to what will fit in the hotel, picking the demand willing to pay the highest prices first.

The second difference is the need to consider booking pace or reservations on hand when building a demand forecast. Unlike many businesses, hotels take reservations, so the pace at which these reservations materialize can be predictive of the eventual occupancy the hotel will reach. Hotels track the current booking pace against typical patterns to evaluate whether the hotel is performing according to expectations. Therefore, the revenue management system generally takes pace, in terms of reservations on hand at certain days before arrival, into account during forecasting.

For the typical hotel, if you consider all of the market segments, room types, and lengths of stay across the booking horizon, the revenue management system can produce literally hundreds of thousands of forecasts. This raises two issues. The first is that one forecasting method is definitely not going to fit all of these forecasting problems. Recall from the discussion in Chapter 4 that the most accurate forecasting method to use depends on the characteristics of the data. With so many different forecasts, there are bound to be many different data patterns. There is an advantage to being able to employ multiple forecasting methods, and have the system automatically determine the most accurate method for each individual forecast. Second, some of the forecast combinations might have very sparse data. For example, a hotel might only have one or two presidential suites, so the amount of historical booking data associated with each length of stay for these suites is quite small. The more sparse the data, the less accurate the forecast. Ideally, the revenue management system should be able to do pattern matching or aggregation to account for this sparse data.

The forecasts are an input into the final step of the revenue management analytical process, optimization.

Optimization

Revenue management was arguably the first hotel function to take analytics capabilities all the way up the continuum I presented in Figure 4.1 to the optimization bubble. As I described in Chapter 4, the goal of the revenue management optimization is to maximize revenue. The constraints can include hotel capacity, reservations on hand, and demand by market segment and room type. The typical output is the rate to offer through the public channels and availability controls for the qualified demand, for each date and length of stay across the booking horizon.

As I described previously, traditional forecasting and optimization algorithms used the airline approach of preserving inventory for higher valued demand, which optimizes the use of the inventory to generate revenue. Price transparency has changed the way that consumers book, so traditional revenue management inventory optimization methodologies have become inadequate because they don't account for price sensitivity of demand. Since price optimization represents such a dramatic shift from traditional revenue management analytical processes, I cover it in detail in a later section.

Revenue managers are primarily responsible for interpreting, managing and implementing the recommendations that result from the core revenue management processes described earlier. However, there are many ad hoc analyses that they are also responsible for, including long-term forecasting for budgeting or planning and predictive modeling to understand rate spectrum opportunities. Revenue management has begun to think through more strategic pricing opportunities like supporting brand promise, incorporating reputation, or managing distribution channels. The following sections describe some special areas of analysis that revenue management participates in, both around and within the core revenue management processes. These areas and more are covered extensively in my first book, *Hotel Pricing in a Social World*.

Price Optimization and Hotels

As airlines evolved their revenue management practices, other industries that did not meet all of the necessary conditions for revenue management were also attempting to maximize revenue and profits through analytic pricing. In industries like retail, products are made available at a single price to a broad market. Each customer has a different ability or willingness to pay, and the retailer can change the price of the product over time. As in economic theory, if the price of the product is increased, the price will exceed the willingness-to-pay level of some customers and demand decreases. If the price is decreased, the product price drops below the willingness-to-pay level of more customers, and demand increases.

This theory is the basis for *price optimization*. In price optimization, demand for a product is estimated as a function of price, and the price becomes the decision variable that is used in maximizing revenues or margin. So, as opposed to protecting rooms for higher paying guests, like classic revenue management models would, price optimization determines the optimal single price to charge the broader market (*unqualified demand*), considering that demand changes as the price changes (Phillips 2005).

Let's think about why this approach is well suited to hotels. Think about a roadside hotel. It may meet many of the necessary conditions of revenue management, such as fixed capacity, perishable product, and advance reservations. However, it very likely does not have clearly delineated segments, so there is no need to protect inventory for higher valued segments. Generally, the hotelier chooses one of several possible rates to charge on any given date for any customer who wants a room. Once again, there is no independence of demand between these rates. They all have the same set of characteristics. Therefore, the prospective consumer will always select the least expensive one. This is an extreme example of *price-able demand*—demand that can be offered an optimized price, based on the price sensitivity of demand.

The unqualified guest in limited or full-service hotels also could be considered to be priceable. Based on distribution agreements, hotels need to offer one publically available price for a room type in the market through all channels, like OTAs and brand.com, creating a price-sensitive demand environment.[2]

Table 8.1 provides a very basic example of the importance of accounting for price sensitivity. The hotel in this example has 50 rooms, but is not forecasted to sell out this particular day. A revenue management system that used strictly yield-based controls (set by a threshold rate or hurdle rate, for example) would recommend the lowest price point, in this case, $80. This is because, without a sellout, inventory-based optimization models calculate the hurdle rate at zero, and the selling system offers the lowest rate.

However, if the pricing system has access to the information in Table 8.1, according to the price sensitivity of demand illustrated in this table, pricing at $160 actually results in higher revenue. While the $80 price results in the highest occupancy, if the hotel had chased the occupancy strategy, they would have missed out on a significant amount of revenue. This is a very simplified example, clearly, but it does illustrate a case where optimizing considering the price sensitivity of demand can result in higher revenue.

Table 8.1 Price Sensitivity of Demand Example

Price Point	Demand	Revenue
$200	10	$2,000
$180	12	$2,160
$160	15	$2,400
$140	17	$2,380
$120	19	$2,280
$100	21	$2,100
$80	23	$1,840

Priceable hotel products represent a large portion of demand in today's market. Basically, any product for sale in the broader market place, without any restrictions, is priceable. In highly competitive markets, there is a significant advantage to using price sensitivity of demand, or price elasticity, in revenue management modeling. The analytics account for the price sensitivity of demand for your hotel, and can also account for the impact of your competitor's pricing moves on your own demand, to recommend a price that analytically accounts for competitor impacts and also how many rooms you have left to sell.

Many consultants and vendors claim that they provide price optimization capabilities. In fact, optimization is as pervasively misused in this context as it is everywhere. To understand whether a specific solution will meet your price optimization needs, it is important to be able to identify not only what actual optimization is (a mathematical algorithm) but also to understand the specific application of price optimization. Remember, price optimization is a mathematical algorithm that uses the relationship between demand and price for each of your products, hopefully considering competitors' pricing actions, to provide a revenue-optimizing single price that is deployed through all public channels.

Complicating this issue of price optimization is that many hotels still serve significant portions of demand that fall under the more traditional revenue management approach. Demand streams like some corporate agreements, groups, and wholesalers have prearranged pricing and the hotel can only decide to offer the rate or not. These groups are managed through availability, or yielding, rather than pricing. The number of rooms allocated to these segments impacts the number of rooms available to sell to priceable demand. As you have more or fewer rooms to sell, the optimal price to sell out those rooms changes. This means that in order to maximize revenue, you cannot make these two decisions (demand controls and optimal price) in isolation. The optimization must simultaneously solve both problems. If you'd like more detail on advances in revenue management analytics, as well as the practice of revenue management in general, I would encourage you to read my first book, *Hotel Pricing in a Social World* (have I mentioned my first book yet?).

Revenue Management Outside of Rooms

As revenue management gained success in maximizing revenue from hotel rooms, they naturally started to extend the application beyond hotel rooms to the other revenue-generating assets in the hotel such as:

- Function space (Kimes and McGuire 2001)
- Restaurants (Kimes et al 1998)
- Golf courses (Kimes and Schruben 2002)
- Spas (Kimes and Singh 2009)

Hotel room revenue management is a fairly well-established discipline with researched and tested technology, analytics, and business processes. While some opportunity for innovation remains, most hotels have some systems and processes in place to manage rooms revenue, which are based on research and experience. Outside of rooms revenue management, however, there is little infrastructure, practically no business process, and few technology options. There has been some preliminary research into the opportunities (as previously mentioned). There are also some vendors building preliminary solutions to address opportunities outside of rooms (for example, Avero is pulling together food and beverage data and IDeaS has released a function space revenue management solution). Applying revenue management to new areas is ripe for innovation (and analytics), but there are a few things that analytic hospitality executives must consider as they embark on this effort.

Measuring (and Manipulating) Performance

The performance metric that is used for all revenue management programs is an efficiency metric that measures how well the capacity-constrained, time-based inventory is generating revenue (revenue per available time-based inventory unit or RevPATI) (Kimes 1989). Revenue per available room (RevPAR) is the ubiquitous metric used for measuring the efficiency of hotel operations, and the success of hotel room revenue management (equation follows). RevPAR is calculated by multiplying average daily rate by occupancy. In this way, revenue (ADR) is adjusted for how many of the capacity-constrained inventory units (room nights) are sold.

If you think about how this measure is calculated, revenue divided by room nights sold multiplied by room nights sold divided by room nights available, it accounts for all of the strategic levers: price (room rate), duration (a night), and space (a room).

$$\text{RevPAR} = \text{ADR} \times \text{Occupancy}$$

or

$$\left(\frac{\text{Revenue}}{\text{Room Nights Sold}} \right) \times \left(\frac{\text{Room Nights Sold}}{\text{Room Nights Available}} \right)$$

or

$$\frac{\text{Revenue}}{\text{Room Nights Available}}$$

In the case of hotel rooms, the space is fixed (it's a hotel room), but hotels have opportunities to make price more variable and duration more predictable (forecasting and optimizing by length of stay considering price sensitivity of demand). Measuring RevPAR helps to define and manage the goal of the hotel room revenue management program, identifying and rewarding the successful manipulation of the levers that can be pulled to increase revenue. For example, hotels could raise prices, increasing ADR, or lower prices, increasing occupancy. They could deploy an overbooking strategy to hedge against no-shows, which will increase occupancy, or they can price by length of stay, which may lower ADR on one peak night, but generate more revenue by selling more rooms on the adjacent days, or shoulder periods. Each of these revenue management strategies have been proven successful in generating incremental revenue from hotel rooms. Each of them is reflected in a higher RevPAR.

When bringing revenue management to another revenue generating outlet, the first step is to understand whether that outlet meets the necessary conditions (see earlier). Next, you need to define the revenue metric (usually easy), capacity-constrained inventory unit/ space (can be challenging), and time (can also be challenging). These three factors represent your opportunity, the levers, to apply revenue management. I give two examples that describe how to derive these metrics using two assets that tend to represent a large portion of hotel revenue outside of rooms: restaurants and function space.

A Restaurant Revenue Management Performance Metric

For restaurants, the typical revenue metric is the average check per person (total nightly revenue divided by the number of people served). The capacity-constrained inventory unit is the number of seats in the restaurant—you can't easily add more space for seats, so you can only serve as many customers as there are seats. Next, consider how long people use the seats (time). Generally, you can use a seat more than once per day, so a daily measure is not going to uncover the full extent of your opportunities. The same goes for a meal period; likely, you could turn the tables more than once during a meal period. Most applications of restaurant revenue management use hour as the time measure, which represents the dining duration (how long a particular party uses the table), as well as the time variability of demand (at 5 p.m., there are fewer diners than at 7 p.m.). The metric that is commonly used for revenue management is RevPASH—revenue per available seat-hour (Kimes et al 1998).

Function Space Revenue Management Performance Metric

Some RevPATI definitions are very straightforward, but others are a bit tricky. When we first tried to apply revenue management theory to function space (Kimes and McGuire 2001), we ran into some problems. Function space met the necessary conditions—fixed capacity (only so much function space to sell), time variable demand (peak and off-peak periods for function demand), high fixed costs and low variable costs (compared to the cost of operating a hotel, the cost of booking an additional function was small), and segmentable demand (different groups want to use the space for different purposes). The next step was to understand how to evaluate the effectiveness of the pricing and use of the space, and determine which of the strategic levers would be most effective in increasing function space revenue.

Starting with the price lever, revenue in function space is a combination of room rental, per-person food and beverage charges, and AV/equipment rental. Each of these revenue sources has a different profit margin. Additionally, the different types of events (weddings versus conventions, for example) had different profit margins based on the number of staff and required setup time. Since these revenue streams didn't have the same value, we determined we needed to use "contribution" not "revenue." This means that we needed to have a contribution margin percentage that could be applied to each of the revenue streams. As you probably know, determining contribution margin isn't always a straightforward activity. However, we were able to determine at least an estimate of contribution margin by revenue stream and function type that the entire team could agree on.

Defining capacity was also tricky. The number of customers that each function room could hold depended on the configuration and setup of the space. This meant a "per-person" measure—like number of seats or a maximum occupancy (as for restaurants)—would not work. Since some rooms could be divided, and portions of events could be held in the foyers, hallways, or patios of the function space, a "per-room" metric (as with hotel rooms) also did not really work well. We realized that in this problem, given the configuration flexibility, the hotel was really selling the "space" itself, to be used as dictated by the function, so a square foot or square meter as the "inventory unit for sale" would work to measure how efficiently the hotel was using the function area.

Finally, we needed a time definition. Function space is typically sold by "chunks of time" (as opposed to an entire day at a time, or by hour). One determining factor for how often the space can be resold in a day is the setup time for the next function. For example, if you have a complicated wedding setup on a Friday night, it might not be possible to sell the room for a breakfast meeting on Friday, because there will not be enough time to flip the room. However, a break area could be sold multiple times per day because all that needs to be done is to clean the high-top tables and pull in a refreshed snack and beverage cart.

The first thought was to use hours, as in the restaurant problem. I argued that this definition was not actually the way that time was "sold" in the function space problem. Most of the salespeople I talked to said that they sold by day part, so perhaps that time frame would be a more accessible metric for the sales team. Sherri Kimes, my coauthor, argued that an hourly measure would help the hotel team account for the revenue impact of operational improvements like shrinking setup time. In the end, I'm not sure that we ever really agreed on whether the function space metric should be ConPASf(m)H (contribution per available square foot/meter hour) or ConPASf(m)DP (contribution per available square foot/meter day part). (Either way, it does not seem to roll off the tongue like RevPAR or RevPASH.*)

The Analysis

Establishing this core performance metric forms the foundation of the revenue management strategy, and, by extension, the analysis process. Walking through the process of defining performance measures identifies the levers that can be pulled, and the degree to which they could be impactful. Statistical analysis and predictive analytics can provide insight into the application and success of the strategy. Much of this initial phase will be manual application of strategies (such as broadly offering discounts during off peak periods, setting up time restrictions for usage, or requiring guarantees to reduce cancellations and no-shows), but the analytics will evaluate whether these manual interventions are successful in improving the core metrics.

As you can tell from this discussion, the application of revenue management outside of hotel rooms requires a good understanding of the operation, and the ability to adapt the core theory to a new problem with a slightly different operational condition. In order to be successful, you will need to spend time with the operators, fully understand how the operation works, and then socialize the revenue management theory with them. Revenue management at its best is a new way of thinking about an existing problem, but it should also be intuitively in tune with operations such that a savvy manager can easily understand and implement it.

---

* See the discussion in Appendix 2 for further information about calculating performance metrics in function space revenue management.

CASE STUDY

CASE STUDY: PARTNERING WITH THE OPERATIONS TEAM

Early in my career, I had the opportunity to do a consulting project with a 400-seat seafood-focused buffet restaurant. During certain meal periods, there was significantly more demand than supply, so there were long waits for tables. Customers were (understandably) upset about the long waits. We were called in to apply revenue management techniques to increase throughput and revenue. In our discovery and planning meetings, as we asked questions and observed the operations, we started to brainstorm techniques we might eventually apply. One option we brought up was to conduct an *optimal table mix analysis* (Kimes and Thompson 2004).

As I discussed earlier, seats are the constrained inventory unit in restaurants, but the seats are typically arranged around a table—and only one party at a time will use that table. This means that if the mix of party sizes does not well match the mix of table sizes, there will be empty seats—representing a lost revenue opportunity. In an extreme example, if a restaurant has 100 seats, arranged in 25 tables of four, but they have demand only for tables of two, at any given point, every table might be full, but only 50% of the seats will be occupied. If the restaurant instead configured their seats into 50 tables of two, they would have the opportunity to serve 50 additional customers per turn (assuming the demand exists, of course).

Optimal table mix is generally calculated using an optimization algorithm, which mathematically matches the typical mix of party sizes to a table mix configuration, accounting for uncertainty, configuration issues, and demand patterns. The output of the optimization algorithm is the best possible table mix, which maximizes the number of guests served, considering all operational constraints. When we left the meeting, we had decided that our next step would be to see if the data the restaurant had provided us was sufficient to conduct this analysis, and, if so, we would start developing the model.

About a month later, when we were back, the buffet manager pulled me aside. "Kelly," he said, "I heard what you said last time about the table mix, and it made sense to me, so I went ahead and switched out a bunch of four tops for deuces in the dining room." "That's great, Bob!" I said.

"What happened?" "Well, we're getting about 36 additional covers per hour during our peak periods. That reduced wait time, satisfaction is up slightly, and we're making more money. This revenue management is really great stuff!"

It turned out that the optimal mix as calculated by the optimization recommended a few more tables for two than Bob initially added. However, the technique, while not something that Bob had considered previously, was intuitively logical to him enough that he was willing to experiment on his own. Although he did not come up with the exact right answer, he still was able to make an improvement in the short term, and became a strong internal advocate for our future recommendations.

Patron Value Optimization: The Casino Problem

For casinos, the largest and most profitable revenue source is the revenue from the gaming floor. Casino managers use the other outlets, including the rooms, to drive revenue on the casino floor, through discounting and other special promotions. Player loyalty cards help casinos track patron play behavior and this information is used to calculate theoretical player value—the patrons' expected spend per visit. Casino managers use that player value to assess how the patron qualifies for promotions and offers. The goal is to profitably incentivize patrons to come and spend more at the casino. More on this in Chapter 10.

> *We make the most money when no one is paying for a room. If we've done it right, the casino is full of our highest value gamers, spending on the casino floor, all staying in comped rooms.*
>
> —A vice president of revenue management for a major U.S. casino company

Casino revenue management follows a slightly different process than hotel revenue management. Casinos segment their known gamers based on their predicted value, and forecast demand by these gaming segments along with the other segments of "unknown" patrons, which include retail and group demand. This forecast by segment is then used for two purposes: determining what level of discount to offer each known patron segment, and setting the retail rate for the rooms.

There are a couple of different ways that current casino revenue management systems handle this in the forecast and optimization. As you could imagine, some segments get huge discounts or even complimentary rooms. The average room rate for these segments is artificially low, so using those rates as a value or rate segment would discriminate against rather than reward that segment. To account for this, the revenue management system supplements the gaming segments with their player value, using this as a proxy for the rate that would ordinarily be an input to the optimization.

Following the optimization, either the optimization outputs are matched to a rate plan that provides the appropriate discounts by gaming segment, or the selling system uses the threshold price from the RM system output to derive the per-patron rate (Metters et al 2008). The threshold price, or hurdle rate, is an output from the optimization. It represents the value of the hotel having one additional room to sell, and therefore, is the minimum that the hotel should accept for a room. When a patron calls to reserve a room, if they are a known player, the system subtracts the hurdle rate from their individual forecasted player value. The amount remaining is the rate they pay. If their player value is higher than the threshold rate, the room is free. Unknown patrons are quoted the best available rate or retail rate derived by the revenue management system. This pricing method works because known gamers book through private channels, like behind a log-in on the website, through the call center, or with their host, so no rate parity or fairness perceptions are violated.

Most recently, casinos are attempting to build a 360-degree view of patron value. They are aggregating patron spend across the organization and augmenting the patron's gaming value with their non-gaming spend. Obviously, the revenue streams have to be adjusted for contribution, as not all revenue streams have the same profit margin. This value is then incorporated into the forecast and optimization the same way that the gaming value is used.

One of the downsides to rewarding patron spend this way is that casino patrons become trained to expect discounted or free rooms. This became particularly problematic during the recent economic downturn, when casinos were struggling to attract any demand by deep discounting rooms, or offering other services at drastically reduced rates. The deep discount offered over time became the patron's anchor, or reference, price (the price they felt the room was worth), and it was difficult to recover price when demand recovered. Hotels also had this same problem during the recent recovery. A better understanding of price sensitivity by casino segment will help casinos generate additional incremental revenue, while reducing the negative impact of consistent deep discounting.

BENCHMARKING REVENUE MANAGEMENT ANALYTICS CAPABILITIES

Revenue management was probably the first analytic discipline that hotels adopted. Even so, adoption of analytical technology to manage prices and drive revenue is still not exactly widespread in the hotel industry. While most hotel companies, and even independents, have a revenue management function, many are still operating in a manual, Excel-driven, environment.

There are several reasons for this. Obviously, for independents, there are cost considerations. If they invest in a system and the personnel to manage it, they want to know that they will see a return. If the hotel is small and only a single location, the incremental revenue the system drives needs to balance against the cost of the technology and people investment. The origin of revenue management was in a full-service hotel environment, where hotels need to not only optimize price, but also balance many different demand streams like groups, corporate contracts, and wholesaler arrangements. Solutions built to fit in the full-service environment ended up not being a great fit in other environments like extended stay, limited service, or economy. Only recently have revenue management vendors begun to address these other industry segments. On the casino side, because rooms are considered an amenity to support revenue on the casino floor, rooms revenue is a relatively smaller component of overall revenue when compared to the gaming floor, and so casinos did not tend to see value in the investment in people and technology to support revenue management. As the casino market is morphing to a much larger focus on nongaming revenue, this is changing of course.

Beginners. Hotel and casino companies that are on the lower end of analytical revenue management capabilities are tactically managing price through Excel. They may have some basic forecasting models built in Excel. They are probably looking at competitor rates through a service like TravelClick. There is a lot of painful data manipulation to get information to help revenue managers make the right decision, as well as a lot of flipping through reports.

Average. At the average revenue management capability, the hotel has invested in a commercially available revenue management system that forecasts demand and optimizes to provide pricing decisions. Many of these revenue management systems have feeds that incorporate competitor rates, so the process of pricing considering competition is automated to some degree as well. Generally, they also work with sales to manage the process of pricing group rooms as well, using the analytics in the revenue management system to ensure that displacement is minimized. These hotels are starting to think about reputation's influence on price, and the possibility of extending revenue management to other revenue-generating assets. The pricing function for these companies can still be quite tactical, with a lot of attention paid to competitor impacts.

Most sophisticated. The most sophisticated hotel companies are using the revenue management function as a strategic asset. The discipline gets support and investment at the very highest levels of the organization. These companies might be using a proprietary revenue management system built by an in-house science team; however, they could also be using a commercially available solution with some custom configured elements to suit their specific business problem. They have incorporated price optimization methodologies with traditional inventory optimization for yieldable demand. Revenue management departments contribute to business strategy discussions, and have a longer term view. These companies are actively working toward establishing a revenue culture at their properties, and have applied revenue management to one or more revenue generating outlets beyond hotel rooms. Some companies are actively leveraging data visualization technology to provide key revenue management metrics to stakeholders across the organization. There is generally some active integration with marketing departments in terms of planning promotions, and consideration of how to incorporate guest value into pricing and allocation strategies. They are also looking closely at reputation impacts on the revenue management system, as well as considering some of the emerging data sources as described previously.

TECHNOLOGY AND PEOPLE INVESTMENTS

In the following sections, I outline some options for technology and people investments for revenue management, both for hotels and casinos that are just getting started, as well as those that are ready to advance their practice.

Technology

For a generally relatively mature analytic discipline, a revenue management system has become a must-have rather than a competitive advantage. Of course, the advantage comes from how the recommendations from the system are incorporated into an overall strategy. I recommend that revenue management departments consider the following technology investments as a good starting point to keep them competitive.

- **Automated revenue management system.** A revenue management system that provides forecasting and optimization for a daily pricing decision is a requirement for today's hotel and casino companies. The system should consider competitor rates, and provide true price optimization along with inventory allocation decisions across the hotels booking horizon. The good news for hoteliers is that this technology can be quite accessible even down to smaller independents, as most revenue management vendors today are providing this technology via software as a service (SaaS), reducing the cost and infrastructure burden.

- **Business intelligence.** Perhaps more so than most hotel departments, revenue management is required to perform ad hoc analyses and generate reports for personas across the organization. Even though revenue management systems do provide some reporting capabilities, they are not designed to support every data and reporting need in revenue management, so revenue managers can find themselves exporting data and working in Excel. A business intelligence or data visualization platform facilitates this activity.

- ▪ **Reputation management.** While managing reputation is not in the provenance of revenue management, research and experience has shown that a hotel's reputation greatly impacts their ability to generate demand and drive price, so revenue managers need to be able to access information about their hotel's reputation, as well as that of the competitors. Some revenue management vendors provide an automated feed of reputation data from certain reputation management vendors into the revenue management system. This can be either incorporated into the algorithm, or simply available to view next to the pricing data to identify opportunities, validate behavior, or set a strategic direction.

People

Revenue management departments need a core set of personas to manage the system and the process. Remember that the job of the revenue management system and the job of the revenue manager are not the same. The system does automate the process of calculating rates and availability controls, but the revenue manager must determine how to implement them in practice, tactically and strategically. Therefore, the revenue manager must have a good tactical understanding of system performance, and a great business acumen to implement and track the results.

The director of revenue management is the key persona at the site level responsible for making the pricing decisions for the hotel or set of hotels. They set and drive the strategy. They may or may not have a team of revenue analysts, depending on the size of the property. The role of the analyst is to generate reports and analyses not available in the revenue management system to support departmental activities.

This is sometimes a controversial opinion, but I believe the days of hiring a highly analytical (read: forecasting and optimization proficient) revenue manager at the site or corporate are going away. Unless the company plans to build their own revenue management and price optimization solution (and there's nothing wrong with that), the vendor can take care of the deep advanced analytics for you. After the solution has been vetted, you are much better off with an internal team that has the strategic vision and business acumen to determine how the outputs of the system will support a holistic revenue management strategy, rather than investing in expensive data science resources to replicate what a commercial system could do for you.

If you do intend to build your own revenue management system, you will need demand modeling (statistical and predictive modeling), forecasting, and optimization experts. My team at Wyndham Destination Network has five of these data scientists (all with advanced degrees in analytics) and six application developers to build the analytical pricing solutions we deploy across our rental companies. When we first started working with IDeaS, the team at SAS had 15 scientists, mostly PhDs, who built the analytics behind IDeaS revenue management solution, G3, and they were able to leverage existing SAS analytical tools (this did not count the army of application developers, testers, and report builders who supported the delivery of the application). I think the team has grown since then.

The point I am trying to make here is that it is a serious decision, requiring serious investment, to build your own system. It's not a matter of getting a few folks together to play around in Excel or Tableau. However, as I discuss in Chapter 11, once you have this team in place, and they've solved your revenue management problem, you can leverage their skills across all the analytical problems the organization may come across.

CASE STUDY: REVENUE MANAGEMENT MATURITY, PAUL VAN MEERKENDONK, IDEAS—A SAS COMPANY

CASE STUDY

I spoke with Paul Van Meerkendonk, Director, Advisory Services, at IDeaS—A SAS Company. He and his team are responsible for assessing the maturity of IDeaS clients and recommending a revenue management roadmap to help them grow their capabilities. This was his assessment of the state of the current market:

(continued)

(*continued*)

When I consider revenue and pricing maturity, there are, of course, degrees. The ideal is a company that has an extensive organization of revenue managers, with corporate support for making pricing and inventory decisions at the individual hotels. These teams are involved in more strategic decision making, and you might even see a chief revenue officer at the helm, if not a senior vice president who has broad responsibilities across revenue management, distribution, e-commerce, marketing, and even sales. The company is definitely using an automated revenue management system, with robust analytics, but understands that they need people with business acumen to support that system. These companies are definitely talking about extending revenue management to other areas of the hotel, if they have not already made significant strides in one or more outlets. You see some companies that have portions of this ideal vision, maybe a great system, but no executive support, or a great business infrastructure, but haven't yet fully rolled out an automated system, for example.

If you consider the landscape, the degree of maturity in revenue management varies from region to region, as well as across industry segments. For example, companies in the United States tend to have developed faster in revenue and pricing analytics than, for example, Eastern Europe or certain parts of Asia. The large brands tend to be more mature than the independents, and full-scale brands are more mature than, say, economy or limited service. What I have definitely seen in the last decade or so is a huge interest in developing revenue management capabilities. Even the most advanced companies are modernizing their systems and processes. The less mature are developing strategies and building roadmaps. More recently, owners and asset managers are becoming increasingly aware of the role of revenue management in driving top-line and bottom-line performance. The industry understands how critically important this function is, both as a day-to-day revenue generating function and also as a strategic asset.

CONCLUSION

Of all of the data and analytics opportunities in the hospitality and gaming industries, revenue management is the one that most directly impacts the top and bottom line. If analytic hospitality executives are looking to make a big impact fast, revenue management is, generally speaking, the way to do it. Despite relatively widespread use of revenue management in both hospitality and gaming, there still remain many opportunities for improvement, even for firms that are relatively mature in their use of revenue management. As the market has evolved and consumer behavior has changed, the discipline needs to adapt as well. This leaves opportunity for innovation and continued revenue generation. Just as with every analytical endeavor, however, implementing a revenue management system is not a guarantee of success. The system needs to be part of a broader strategy, and all new data sources and changes in process need to be carefully considered and thoroughly tested.

Speaking of strategy, as of the publication of this book, the biggest topic of conversation in revenue management and beyond is the alarming trend of rising distribution costs. I spoke with Cindy Estis Green, founder of Kalabri Labs, and Mark Lomanno, partner and senior advisor at Kalabri Labs, about this issue early in 2016, just before their second book on the topic, *Demystifying Distribution: Distribution Channel Analysis for Hotels*, was published. Kalabri Labs is collecting data about distribution trends, and as of the end of the first quarter of 2016, Kalabri Lab's Hotel Industry Database has guest stay and cost of sales information from over 25,000 (and growing) hotels primarily in North America, representing 100-plus brands, over 3 million rooms, and over 3 billion transactions.

In 2011, their research showed that the median U.S. transient direct-to-indirect booking ratio was 4.3 to 1. Just four years later, in 2015, the ratio had fallen to 2.7 to 1. OTA share of bookings is growing across all segments, but particularly in the economy segment, where OTA share grew from 5.6% in 2011 to 16.5% in 2015. Their research also shows that around 26% of bookings into New York City in 2015 were from OTAs or other third-party distribution channels.

Cindy and Mark have been advocating for new benchmarking metrics for the hospitality industry, specifically, Net ADR and Net RevPAR, or revenue per available room net of all commissions. This metric has been surprisingly difficult to define, because distribution costs are not always accounted for on the P&L, or in the ADR metric. The OTAs frequently send revenue net of their commission, so the cost is not visible, or accounted for anywhere. The point is that simply tracking (and incentivizing) RevPAR or RevPAR index, as we traditionally have done, masks some very real acquisition costs. "RevPAR was a very useful performance calculation 15 or 20 years ago, when revenue was the primary measure of effectiveness," says Mark. "These intermediaries did not exist then, so the cost of acquisition wasn't an issue. The shift to digital has changed the landscape, and the metrics we use to measure effectiveness need to evolve along with the way we do business today."[3]

Cindy and Mark use the term "revenue capture" to refer to the amount of revenue that hotels receive net of acquisition costs, which is then divided by the hotel capacity to derive the NetRevPAR metric.

Mark explained to me that the Kalabri data shows that revenue capture in the United States in 2015 was three-tenths of a percent less than in 2014 because of the shift toward higher commissioned business. This does not seem like a lot on the surface, and revenue did grow 6.8% during this time. However, if you calculate that –0.3% in dollars of lost opportunity, it represents about $406 million that shifted from the hotels to the third party distributors. Mark calculated that at a cap rate of 8%, this shift in revenue capture resulted in about a $5 billion loss in asset value to the hotel industry as a whole (and a gain for the third-party distributors).

This staggering statistic is illustrative of the need to pay close attention not only to pricing strategy, but also to the hotel's distribution strategy. The metrics we have been using to measure performance mask what might potentially be a less profitable distribution strategy. The landscape is getting extremely complex between the existing OTAs and the emerging electronic travel agents like Google or Facebook. Owners, asset managers, general managers, and revenue managers need to start tracking distribution costs, and understanding the implications of their distribution strategies.

I always say the job of the revenue manager isn't getting any easier. The challenges I lay out here are larger than the role. It is crucial that revenue management collaborate with counterparts in marketing, operations, and finance, as well as with owners and asset managers, to find the most profitable operating model for the hotel. I describe collaboration opportunities in the final chapter of the book, but first, I talk about the department within the hotel that is responsible for evaluating performance, and then I describe the opportunities in gaming-specific analytics.

ADDITIONAL RESOURCES

- Kelly McGuire and Jeannette Ho, *Hotel Pricing in a Social World: Driving Value in the Digital Economy* (Hoboken, NJ: Wiley, 2015).
- IDeaS Revenue Solutions blog, http://ideas.com/blog.
- OWL blog, www.forsmarthotels.com/hotel-analytics-optimization-blog.
- Cindy Estis Green and Mark Lomanno's book, http://demystifyingdistribution.com/about/.
- Kelly McGuire and Breffni Noone, "Price, UGC and Loyalty: How Road Warriors Choose a Hotel," Hotel Business Review, www.hotelexecutive.com/business_review/4808/price-ugc-and-loyalty.

NOTES

1. Some argue that regrets (representing price constraint, when the customer says no) and denials (representing a capacity constraint, when the hotel says no) are the right way to measure unconstrained demand. While this is entirely logical, the problem is that this data has to be collected "manually" using human judgment, which means it is notoriously dirty. When collected by an agent back in the 1990s it was always miscoded. Today, it is difficult to detect whether a shopper on the Internet has a true intent to purchase or is just "passing by," let alone ascertain in every case whether it was the price, product, availability, or any other factor that caused them to decide not to book. Mathematical processes extrapolate patterns in the data, so therefore are much more stable and less open to interpretation.

2. This section is referring to the BAR (best available rate) or base price by room type. That price is offered to the OTAs or used as the base for packages and promotional rates (i.e., breakfast included).

3. From the Center for Hospitality Research blog, https://sha.cornell.edu/blog/2016/05/11/chr-insights-distribution-costs-why-everyone-in-hospitality-needs-to-pay-attention-an-interview-with-mark-lomanno.

CHAPTER **9**

Analytics for Performance Analysis

Prediction is very difficult, especially if it's about the future.

—Nils Bohr, Nobel laureate in physics

I titled this chapter "Analytics for Performance Analysis" to encompass a few functions that leverage similar data for a similar purpose in the hotel and casino business. I am speaking of departments like finance and development that are responsible for analyzing the performance of units, brands, or regions, and identifying areas of opportunity. They can be responsible for developing new units or new locations, as well as reporting on the overall performance of the enterprise to stakeholders or shareholders. In some firms, this type of analysis and reporting function is referred to as analytics or business analytics; in others, it's called strategic planning and analysis, or financial planning and analysis. Some companies may have several of the departments that I named previously, but together they are responsible for the tasks and goals that fall under this area, including:

- Reporting on performance across the enterprise, including supporting quarterly earnings reports
- Supporting the process of convincing franchisees and owners to invest in the company's brands
- Determining locations or targets for new hotel development and identifying acquisition targets
- Understanding drivers of performance to build effective business strategies
- Anticipating changes in the operating environment and planning for future events
- Identifying areas of risk, where the organization might be in danger of missing a forecast or budget, and recommending strategies to mitigate that risk

One of the biggest challenges this function faces is fast and flexible access to clean and credible information. While every hotel and casino company has challenges with data storage and access, this challenge is exacerbated within the large global companies that were formed

258

through mergers and acquisitions. The various brands and properties from the original companies likely all used different source systems, or different versions of the same systems, which means that performance data is stored in a variety of locations with different formats, different data definitions, and different reporting processes. The people who work in these departments are constantly called on to answer questions from executives, owners, franchisees, or investors. Due to these data challenges, it is difficult to be responsive.

Our senior leadership team is very experienced and very charismatic. They are great as it is, but we always think about how powerful it would be if they had instant access to the right data, to answer any question that comes up in an earnings call or a negotiation on the spot with detailed backup from drilldown or data exploration.

—Executive from a global hotel brand, speaking to me about the importance of a flexible, integrated data and reporting infrastructure

In fact, the performance analysis function, whatever it may be called, is likely to be supporting all strategic decision making that happens at the enterprise level. It is crucially important that this function is able to access a single, clean, and credible source of the truth, defined by a common business language and available for any type of historical or forward-looking analysis.

There are two broad categories of questions that this group answers. The first is questions about current performance for executive-level reporting, strategic decision making, investor relations, or conversations with potential or current owners. The second category is forward-looking questions about upcoming opportunities and challenges, such as deriving the feasibility of projects that the organization is considering investing in, calculating revenue or pace into the future, or estimating performance in certain segments, markets, or regions.

DATA FOR PERFORMANCE ANALYSIS

The performance management functions live and die by core industry metrics like occupancy, average daily rate (ADR), and revenue per available room (RevPAR). One senior leader for a major hotel company told me that RevPAR is the very first metric his CEO looks at every day, so they will always pay particular attention (read: be more likely to invest in) to any initiative that can directly impact RevPAR (see my discussion about calculating RevPAR in Chapter 8. That is because RevPAR is the hotel- and casino-specific measure that Wall Street understands, and it is always reported on in hotel and casino earnings calls. Along with RevPAR, hospitality and gaming companies, of course, also care about profitability measures like EBITDA. Hotel companies develop expectations for future performance using the volume and velocity of advanced bookings, or *pace*. Benchmarking data from Smith Travel Research (STR), which provides information about a hotel or brand's performance against the market, is also used extensively. In particular, hotels care about RevPAR index and market share. When these metrics are above 100, the hotel is performing above the market in revenue and share.

▶ **NOTE**

STR benchmarking data has become ubiquitous in the industry as a measure of how individual hotels, brands, classes of hotels, regions, or countries are performing compared to their competitive set or the industry as a whole. These metrics are used in pricing strategies, written into management contracts, part of incentive plans, and even reported to Wall Street. There is always discussion about the real effectiveness of these metrics. Are they calculated properly? Are they measuring what we expect that they would measure? Is the RevPAR index incentivizing hotels to perform for long-term sustainability, or for short-term performance? As the industry evolves, it will be interesting to see how these metrics evolve as well. I addressed a potential alteration in this metric in the conclusion of the previous chapter on revenue management. It is also interesting to note that STR is not well penetrated in the casino market, which means there is very little benchmarking data available in Las Vegas.

STR metrics provide a lot of value to hotels and to the industry in general. The volume of data that STR collects can be used in all kinds of analyses where industry data is required. As with every metric, it is important to understand what these benchmarking metrics represent and how they are best used. As you apply industry benchmarks in your business, be sure to question whether they are incentivizing the kind of behavior you want to incentivize.

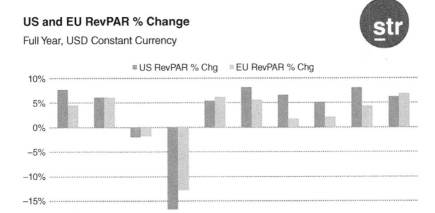

Figure 9.1 STR Reporting Example
This graph shows the kind of industry-level benchmarking that STR provides. Here you can see a comparison of RevPAR change between the United States and Europe.

Performance analysis is also concerned with cost information. In order to derive bottom-line metrics, they collect detailed information about cost structures of properties. This information is also used when evaluating the potential of future sites.

Beyond straight performance data, performance analysis also collects "demographic" information about existing and potential properties. This includes size, location, amenities, ownership structure, and any information that could potentially be related to performance. These characteristics are useful for determining what drives performance for the brand or location. Public hotel companies are frequently asked to report on performance according to these factors, so hotel companies must be able to slice and dice performance metrics according to all kinds of categorizations.

In fact, performance analysis requires many different sources of third-party data. The supply of hotel rooms in certain markets, especially the pipeline of future projects, is of great interest. Information about demand drivers like local industry and tourism, and forecasts for how those might change over time in target markets, is useful. Economic conditions in general are important indicators of potential future performance. Commodity prices, like oil, can impact travel patterns, especially for leisure or roadside destinations, where demand might increase when gas prices fall and travelers decide to take road trips, but fall as gas prices increase. As we saw in 2015 and 2016, it can impact travel patterns into oil producing destinations as well. As the price of oil dropped, hotel performance in the oil producing areas in the United States dropped significantly. Oil companies weren't making as much money, so they cut travel budgets. This cut was significant enough to impact RevPAR on a regional level.

Emerging Data Sources

Emerging data sources for the performance analysis function are similar to the emerging data sources that are of interest to other hotel departments. For example, reputation has been shown to have a relationship with performance, so many hotel companies are thinking about how to incorporate social data into their performance analysis. Forward-looking demand data by market has become available recently, and is of interest to hotels to help them understand whether they are capturing their fair share of market demand. Additionally, as I have spoken about previously, new information is emerging that makes it easier to collect and analyze distribution costs.

There are also pieces of information from other functions within the hotel that are of value, but not always easily accessible. For example, sales information, like future group and convention bookings, is useful to forecast performance, but the performance analysis function doesn't always have access to this information in real time and in flexible formats. Similarly, they may not be able to get to information about marketing's promotional plans or guest loyalty information. This could be about control, where departments want to be able to manage how their data is accessed and perceived, but it is more likely about the inability to easily share data across functional lines due to technology and data definition inconsistencies.

The development function for hotels and casinos builds financial models to evaluate the feasibility of future projects. These analyses look at all the factors that could contribute to performance and provide an expectation of future performance of a property, flagged with a specific brand, at a certain location. These estimates, based on the data I describe previously, are used to make the decision of whether the company wants to take on a project, or work with an owner. They can also be used in the negotiation of the sale of an asset. There is a whole art and science to these financial models, which I consider out of scope for this book. At the end of the chapter there are a couple of websites listed where you can go for more information. I will warn you, they are strongly biased toward the institution that I believe is best in class in this area.

ADVANCED ANALYTICS FOR PERFORMANCE ANALYSIS

The primary function of performance analysis is to answer questions about, well, performance (sorry, I tried to find another way to say that). This function spends a lot of time slicing and dicing the data to provide insight about past, current, or future performance. The way this area is typically run today, it is very much oriented to business intelligence. Historical performance reporting will always be an important, and likely primary, responsibility of performance analysis. However, there are definitely some very relevant and impactful uses of advanced, predictive analytics for performance management. Using the analytics continuum (see Figure 4.1), let's talk about some areas where advanced analytics can be used.

Statistical Analysis

Since statistical analysis is all about understanding the "why," it is particularly useful to performance management tasks. Correlation can be used to understand what factors are related to key outcomes, and regression modeling can identify the drivers of performance. You could test whether the size of a hotel, guest satisfaction, proximity to key demand drivers, brand, or ownership structure have an impact on performance. Hypothesis testing can determine whether differences in performance are statistically significant. For example, are hotels that just went through a renovation performing better than older properties? Do hotels from this brand in city center locations perform better than those in airport locations? Many analysts derive insights like this from viewing a report with the data sliced by certain key factors, but analytical hospitality executives know that a difference on a report might not be statistically significant, given normal variability in operations (as we learned in Chapter 4). Statistical modeling can provide the evidence that observed differences are statistically significant so the organization is focused on the factors that matter.

Forecasting

Forecasting is probably the most widespread analytical technique used in performance analysis, and this function is probably as obsessed with forecasting as revenue management, or maybe more so. Forecasting in performance analysis is typically performed at a higher level and over a longer range than revenue management forecasting, which is why a revenue management–developed forecast is not generally a substitute for a performance forecast. Uses for forecasting include budgeting (setting and tracking a goal for each hotel and the company as a whole), financial projections for individual properties or the enterprise, and financial reporting. In this area, expert opinion plays a large role in developing the forecast, so analytical forecasts are often overridden by a leader who has a different expectation of performance. Regardless of how it is ultimately developed, accuracy and efficiency in forecasting are very important for this function. It can be a cumbersome process to pull the numbers together, share them across key stakeholders, track any changes made by experts, and still manage the accuracy of projections.

It is probably time for a word about expert forecasting. You might think that an analytic hospitality executive would never succumb to the temptation to change a number just because "I say so." That sounds an awful lot like operating by gut feel, doesn't it? And isn't that exactly what your esteemed author has been telling you to quit doing? The exception is that when you have to build a projection for the performance of a brand new property, product, or service, analytics and data can only take you so far. After all the analysis using data from comparable properties, understanding the market, and evaluating the background and capabilities of the potential investors, owners, and stakeholders, a judgment call must be made. This judgment can only be speculation. Nothing will ever turn out according to the projection. Sometimes the "gut instincts" of an experienced executive who has a general feel for the market, and years of experience evaluating opportunities, is the only way to really come to the final decision. I have two examples of why relying only on analytics may cause a missed opportunity.

The first example is from the poster child for analytical decision making, Gary Loveman, former CEO of Caesars Entertainment. Loveman was a management science professor at Harvard before he joined Caesars, so when he took over the helm, he set the example in Las Vegas for the benefits of fact-based decision making. Yet, he is the first to admit that his biggest mistake as CEO was not relying on the gut feel of the market when it came to investment in Macau. In 2006, Caesars had the opportunity to invest in one of six gaming licenses in Macau, but passed because Loveman's analysts could not make the numbers work. They simply could not analytically derive enough potential in the market. As I will describe in the next chapter, the Macau market has exploded. Now, Las Vegas Sands, a competitor of Caesars in Las Vegas, is making exponentially more money in Macau than in Las Vegas, as are the other six companies that purchased the gaming licenses.[1]

Hilton Worldwide set a record for the largest single property hospitality real estate deal in history when they sold the Waldorf Astoria building in New York City to Anbang, a Chinese insurance company, for nearly $2 billion. Any model you run on that sale might never have predicted that the building would sell for that price, but Hilton found a buyer who valued the ownership of the asset, and presumably had plans for the building that would justify the price tag.[2] If the Hilton executives didn't have the instinct and experience to suspect that there could be a buyer like this in the market, they might have taken a lower offer sooner.

The point is that when you are speculating on an opportunity with no precedent, the gut feel and good instincts of an *experienced* executive can trump the analytics—the problem is, it doesn't always work that way. But that's what business is all about, isn't it? Taking and mitigating risk.

NOTE

David Schmidt, Vice President Marketing Analytics Strategy at Beckon, Inc., said in one of his blogs on AllAnalytics.com, "It's a false choice to place the gut-based decider and the data-based analyst in a tug-of-war. This is because decision makers are supposed to use their guts. Nearly every decision of consequence operates in a gray area. The great decision makers figure out how to reduce the gray to make a more informed decision, but in the end they have to use their guts to navigate whatever gray is left."

I would say that Hilton carefully evaluated what the asset was worth, and fully understood the profile of a potential buyer, and then let their guts guide them to the right buyer and the highest price. Caesars, after running the numbers, could have let a trusted advisor's expertise help them understand why the numbers were not telling the full story. Either way, it is important to remember that there's a time for analytics and there's a time where despite what the numbers might tell you, you still need to take that risk based on expert opinion.

▶ **NOTE**

Malcom Gladwell's book *Outliers: The Story of Success* addresses this phenomenon of how talent, effort, and experience combine to form expertise, achievable after at least 10,000 hours of practice. It's a great read, as are all of his books.

Predictive Modeling

Predictive modeling is an emerging area of opportunity for performance analysis. One very relevant use for predictive modeling is to review performance data against the characteristics of existing properties to predict performance of a new location. As hotels consider new investments, predictive modeling can help to identify which brand might be most successful in a certain location, or which ownership structure will be most advantageous for a property. Predictive modeling is very useful in site selection, where the model will predict the performance of a specific brand or type of hotel in that site based on relevant characteristics, or determine the ideal size and type of hotel that would best exploit the potential of the site. While there are regulations that govern negotiations with potential franchisees, predictive modeling can also help to guide discussions as franchisees decide whether they want to invest in a brand.

It is easy for managers to make excuses about the unique operating characteristics of their environments when put to the test about the performance of their properties. You can point to the size of a property, the demand drivers, the brand, and the age all as excuses for why this property did not achieve the same level of performance as others in the system. Predictive modeling is the great equalizer. The model can control for all of the factors that make a property unique, and determine the expectation of performance, which will clearly show whether that unit achieved its potential, or not.

Optimization

I have not really seen optimization used in this area, but there are some potentially very useful applications of this technique. There are many constraints in the performance analysis problem, like budgets, agreements with existing franchisees and ownership groups about cannibalization, potential of area-demand generators, and competitive factors. Hospitality companies desire to maximize their return for a given project or across their portfolio, or minimize their risk, cost, or exposure. An optimization algorithm could help hotels decide where they want to invest with what brands or locations, given the operating constraints. Optimization will probably never take off in this environment, especially with the uncertainty and need for expert opinion, and in my opinion, despite how much I love it, it probably doesn't have to. However, there is always the chance that a bored data scientist (if there is such a thing), and a creative analytic hospitality executive, will find a great use for optimization and provide a huge competitive advantage for their organization.

BENCHMARKING PERFORMANCE ANALYTICS CAPABILITIES

Since performance analysis is so heavily connected with data and reporting, I'm going to focus more on data infrastructure and visualization here than in previous chapters. The ideal for performance management is to be able to rapidly produce answers to business questions that impact company strategy or investor relations. Many hospitality and gaming companies are hampered by legacy, disparate selling systems, a highly manual environment, and an overburdened IT department that is focused more on keeping operational systems working than longer-term business strategy.

Beginners. At the lower end of sophistication, hospitality and gaming companies are operating in a highly manual performance analysis environment. They use Excel extensively as a data aggregation and reporting tool. It takes a long time to create operating reports. Forecasting for budgeting is a very laborious process, prone to mistakes as it is managed again through an Excel spreadsheet. There is no data governance, no visualization technology beyond Excel.

Average. The average hotel or casino company has or is in the process of creating a data warehouse and a data management strategy that includes some type of data governance. They are making efforts to consolidate data from disparate systems, or to build a strategy for identifying the source of record. They have invested in a data visualization tool (sometimes multiple tools), and are using them to automate and speed up the process of creating key operating reports. Overloaded information technology (IT) departments are still a roadblock in many cases, so any analyses outside of routine reporting tasks can still be manual, and still take time. These companies are planning investments in deeper analytical tools, or may have a few analytical resources on staff that can perform statistical analysis or forecasting.

Most sophisticated. The most sophisticated hospitality and gaming companies already have a data warehouse in place, and in some cases are going through a modernization effort to make the environment more flexible and responsive. They could be investigating data virtualization and big data strategies like Hadoop. They extensively use data visualization tools, and have a process in place for responsive ad hoc analyses. Performance analysis functions are using advanced analytic techniques like statistical modeling, forecasting, and predictive analytics. They are building robust models to drive their development strategies.

I haven't spoken much about IT in this book so far (this is not an accident, the book is targeted at the business). IT clearly plays a crucial role in the implementation of data analytics programs, and most especially, I believe, in this area. Given the pace of technology development, effective performance analysis requires a strong partnership with a strategic IT department. The data challenges faced by the performance analysis function are tremendous, and so they require infrastructure support, and also the ability to be relatively self-sufficient in terms of accessing data and creating reports, especially when they are under pressure to provide insight quickly. Hospitality and gaming IT departments are slowly evolving to meet these needs, but there is a gap that needs to be filled before this function can meet its true potential.

TECHNOLOGY AND PEOPLE INVESTMENTS

In this section, I will provide some recommendations for the technology and people required to support this function. Most organizations have well-established departments in this area due to financial reporting requirements. However, most of the analytical resources are focused on reporting and historical analysis as opposed to more advanced analytical opportunities.

There is a tremendous opportunity today for organizations to leverage their data to build a strong analytic program that can create a competitive advantage in cost savings, risk mitigation, and, most important, value enhancement. To accomplish this, organizations need strong analytical leadership who understands the metrics cross-functionally, so that they can act as air traffic control while challenging results. It's become too easy to be siloed, ignoring cross-functional perspectives from subject matter experts across the business. Organizations that have strong analytical leadership who enable and enforce constant communication will be able to incorporate this cross-functional thinking to best leverage analytical outcomes across the business.

—Jess Petitt, Vice President, Global Business
Analytics, Hilton Worldwide

Technology

I think it's pretty clear from the discussion in this chapter that performance management functions need strong data and visualization support. Technology needs include:

- **Flexible and adaptive database structure with a strong data governance program.** Since performance reports are consumed by senior leadership, it is important that the data be clearly defined and stored in such a way that facilitates any level of reporting or analysis.

- **Data visualization.** The performance analysis function needs a robust data visualization platform that facilitates the automation of routine reporting tasks, but also allows the flexibility for ad hoc analysis and exploration. Some light analytics like trending, correlation, and basic data mining could also be very useful here for business analysts to be enabled to respond to queries at the speed of business. Performance analysis needs to be able to slice and dice the data according to the questions being asked, which will require that the tool has the flexibility to quickly adapt to different hierarchies and data views. Hospitality companies can no longer afford to wait for IT to create a new OLAP (online analytical processing) cube to answer a question that might be asked in the next earnings call or owners' meeting.

- **Forecasting or data mining technology.** Excel has its limits as an analysis tool. Most performance analysis functions, particularly in larger companies, would benefit from more advanced forecasting or data-mining technology for deeper insights than data visualization alone can provide. Investment in these tools will also require investment in a resource that has expertise in these techniques.

People

Performance analysis is one of those departments where domain specific training is a huge benefit. You will want to recruit a resource that understands finance and real estate. Even better if they know the hospitality problem. Look for strong reporting and model-building skill sets—someone who is very comfortable building financial models in Excel (which, by the way, it was actually created to do).

Someone, perhaps many, in the department should become a power user in whatever data visualization platform the company has invested in. The department will be called upon to build all kinds of reports. Accessing the data, providing a different view of the data, or configuring the business intelligence tool used to be strictly the domain of IT. This means that even the simplest of reports end up stuck in a long queue. Visualization tools, because the data storage has become more flexible, permit more self-service from the user base. Once the data infrastructure is put in place (no small task by the way), the users are free to configure any view of that data they need to run their business. This drastically reduces time to insight, and frees up valuable IT resources.

As the analytical capabilities of the department advance, a forecasting or data-mining expert might be beneficial. You could share this resource with other departments, particularly at first. The case study in this chapter shows the benefit of a resource that understands data mining. The more powerful, and therefore, more accurate, forecasting and data-mining tools require a user who understands how to define, build, and interpret the right algorithms, and a strong partner on the business side that can help to formulate the problem and interpret the results.

CASE STUDY: PERFORMANCE MANAGEMENT, DAVID SCHMIDT, IHG

For a multibrand hotel company operating in a complex global marketplace, understanding what drives hotel performance is both crucial and complex. Data is in a myriad of disparate systems across the enterprise, and there are many factors that can contribute to the success or failure of a property. David Schmidt's group at IHG was responsible for providing these types of insights to brand managers, development teams, and potential owners. David, who was Director of Performance Strategy and Planning at the time, applied data-mining techniques to uncover insights about hotel performance under a wide variety of conditions in a global market. He cites

(continued)

(*continued*)

as an example an analysis that he and the team did on the factors that drive top-line performance for a specific brand. Using data-mining tools from SAS, he was able to unearth an insight into how the nearby presence of certain competitors affected the performance of the brand's hotels. Before using SAS, doing this analysis was too labor-intensive. "The amount of effort that it would take to evaluate every one of those competitors' brands and to see which ones even mattered just wouldn't have been possible," David said.

In addition, his group was able to gain more confidence in the information they produce. In the past, the tedious process of trying to get the data together left concerns that something was missed. "The way we're assembling our data is more reliable and robust, so we spend less time questioning how we put that data together. We have the tools that really help us provide robust models and extract insights that we have much more confidence in than we had before."

I adapted this case study from the information David provided in a SAS success story. What he didn't tell SAS, but what I observed from spending time with David over the years he was at IHG, was that he was able to leverage the success of his projects into higher visibility within the organization for the team, but also for himself. He would never say this, but as the word got out about the value of the analyses he was producing, his reputation for analytics execution excellence, both internally at IHG and externally in the market, grew as well. More high-visibility projects were brought to his team internally, and David had more opportunities to spread the message about the value of analytics externally as well. I consider his journey similar to Jeremy TerBush's experience, which I describe in Chapter 11, in which small impactful projects with good publicity raised the profile of analytics, and the analytical champion, within the organization. David has great insight into how the analytics function within an organization should work with the business. I encourage you to look for his blogs on AllAnalytics.com and seek him out if he's ever speaking at a conference. David has moved on from IHG, so when I refer to his insights in this book, you'll see me list his new title.

Source: "Dramatically Boost Brand Performance: SAS Helps Intercontinental Hotel Groups Compete More Strategically," SAS, www.sas.com/en_sg/customers/ihg.html.

CONCLUSION

The performance analysis function clearly has many data challenges, exacerbated by disparate systems that are often cobbled together from various acquisitions through the years, all collecting and storing data in different formats with different definitions. Making sense of this data, let alone the business rules that surround it, is more challenging than it appears on the surface. Think back to Dexter Wood's story about Hilton's efforts to build a common business language from Chapter 2. Understanding the definitions of data sources, data definitions, and key performance indicator formulas is no small task, yet it is easily underappreciated and underestimated by someone who has not been through it. The amount of time I personally have spent in my career trying to figure out why my number doesn't match the business unit's number, when presumably we all started with the same data, seems crazy in the modern business environment. Yet it happens all the time. It's because this analysis is hard.

The technology exists today to support a single source of the truth, and a common business language. The effort to get the data prepared will be significant, but well worth it. I always tell revenue managers to be the catalyst in synchronized, cross-departmental decision making. I will start calling on performance analysis functions in hotels and casinos to lead the charge in pulling the organization together to establish a common business language and bringing discipline to the data. After all, they are the group that the executive leadership generally looks to for providing business insights that support earnings calls, owner negotiations, internal budget reviews—all of the critical decision-making points for hotels and casinos. I think every analytic hospitality executive would much rather spend their time in meetings working on solutions as opposed to arguing about data points. You have your charter now. I will get down from my soapbox and move on to discussing analytics for gaming in the next chapter.

ADDITIONAL RESOURCES

- Center for Real Estate Finance, Cornell School of Hotel Administration, https://sha.cornell.edu/centers-institutes/cref.

■ e-Cornell Coursework on Real Estate Finance, http://www.ecornell.com/ certificates/hospitality-and-foodservice-management/hotel-real-estate-investments-and-asset-management.

■ Michael C. Sturman, Jack B. Corgel, and Rohit Verma (eds.), *The Cornell School of Hotel Administration on Hospitality: Cutting Edge Thinking and Practice* (Hoboken, NJ: Wiley, 2011), pp. 247–352.

NOTES

1. Karl Taro Greenfeld, "Loveman Plays New Game at Harrah's after Tapping F-16s of Debt," Bloomberg, August 6, 2010, www.bloomberg.com/news/articles/2010-08-06/loveman-plays-new-purely-empirical-game-as-harrah-s-ceo.

2. Charles V. Bagli, "Waldorf-Astoria to Be Sold in a $1.95 Billion Deal," *New York Times*, October 7, 2014, www.nytimes.com/2014/10/07/nyregion/waldorf-astoria-hotel-to-be-sold-for-195-billion.html.

CHAPTER 10

Analytics for Gaming

*The laws of probability, so true in general,
so fallacious in particular.*

—Edward Gibbon, English historian

I n previous chapters, I have discussed analytic applications that are useful for both casinos and hotels. The analytics that can be used for operations, marketing, sales, revenue management, and performance analysis in casinos are very similar to those for hotels, with the nuances that I mentioned in those chapters. There is, obviously, one area in casinos that is drastically different from hotels, and that is the operations of the casino floor. The casino floor is the primary and most profitable source of revenue for gaming companies—moving the needle even a little bit there can have a big payout.

In this chapter I will talk about specific analytic applications for managing and optimizing the performance of the casino floor. Hotel executives may still be interested in the problems I describe here, and find some inspiration in the analytical solutions. Plus, some find a certain glamor to this industry, and always enjoy hearing about the inner workings of casinos. I know I do.

The gaming industry has been expanding and evolving since the late nineties. Traditionally, casinos were located in destination markets like Las Vegas, but recently the number of local markets has been increasing dramatically, as states within the United States, and increasing numbers of countries outside of it, begin to issue gaming licenses. This has intensified competition around the globe. As competition increases, casinos are beginning to diversify their offerings. With increasing focus on developing offerings outside of the casino floor, nongaming revenue is outpacing gaming revenue in some markets, reaching a broader mix of potential patrons.

There are several different models for casino operations. The most complex are integrated resort-style casinos, which, in addition to the casino floor, include hotel rooms, restaurants, retail, golf, shows, and even theme park attractions. Some casinos strictly offer a gaming floor, or sports betting parlor, with very few nongaming amenities. Online gaming, although not broadly available yet in the United States, due to some complex interactions of federal and state regulations, is big business in Europe, where there are fewer brick and mortar establishments. At their core, all of these companies rely on gaming revenue from games of chance as the primary driver of revenue and profits.

The casino industry, particularly gaming operations, is highly profitable, but also highly regulated. Each jurisdiction that has approved gaming has its own regulatory body and its own rules. This includes everything from taxes to the number of licenses that will be issued, to the amount and types of games, and even who is allowed on the casino floor. For example, Canada issues licenses by province. Therefore, the casinos in Ontario do not compete with those in British Columbia. There are no countrywide casinos, or foreign investment. Singapore issued two gaming licenses for two large integrated resorts (whose combined gaming revenue exceeds that of the Las Vegas strip). However, Singapore, in an effort to protect its citizens from problem gaming, requires that Singaporean nationals pay a cover charge of around $100 to access the casino floor.

Policies from countries that do not allow gaming within their borders also impact casino operations in neighboring regions. China, a huge feeder market for casinos in Asia, does not allow gaming within its borders, and is very restrictive in permitting citizens' visas to travel to gaming destinations. In 2015, China started to crack down on corruption, placing an increasing focus on cash transactions from corporate officers in particular. Some of the Macau high rollers have pulled back their gaming spend to avoid attracting attention from the government, whether their gaming spend was from illegal sources or not. This caused a huge dip in gaming revenue in Macau and around the region.

Given the amount of cash that changes hands in casinos, most of the rules that govern casino operations are designed to prevent money laundering by criminal elements ranging from members of organized crime to drug dealers to terrorists. These regulations govern the levers that casino floor operators can pull to generate revenue, and can be highly restrictive, varying greatly by location. For example, the hold percentage on slot machines, the house advantage, is highly regulated in the United States and needs to be reported on regularly. Regulatory controls put pressure on reporting functions, as casinos are required to demonstrate compliance with regulations like responsible gaming, terrorist watch lists, and anti–money laundering regulations. For example, Canadian casinos are required to demonstrate that they are enforcing responsible gaming regulations by restricting access to patrons who have put themselves on the problem gaming list. If these patrons are able to access the casino and gamble, the liability is on the casino rather than that patron.

All of these forces combine to create a very interesting dynamic and highly profitable business. The scale of the revenue-generating potential for these kinds of businesses makes the effort to comply with local regulations more than worth it. However, between consumer behavior, the probability associated with the games, and regulatory pressures, casinos can be quite complex to operate. They are simply crying out for data analytics!

In this chapter, I talk about three highly related areas where analytics are applied slightly differently from hotels: calculating patron value for marketing purposes, gaming floor optimization, and fraud and anti–money laundering. As in previous chapters, first I will talk about data gathered by gaming operations, then analytics that can be leveraged by casinos specifically to drive casino floor revenue, and then I finish with the systems and resources that can be used to apply data analytics to casino floor operations.

GAMING DATA

Casino companies were among the first to implement rewards programs to track and reward player behavior. These programs provided incentives for gaming patrons to consolidate their play where they could earn more of their preferred benefits, while giving the casino company access to player behavior and value. Total Rewards, from Harrah's Entertainment, now Caesars Entertainment, is a good example of a successful early implementation of a casino rewards program. (I know I've mentioned this several times before, but in case you are skipping around, here's another description.) This program was designed around a tiered structure, rewarding patrons with special access and shorter lines as their status (and spend) increased. Since patrons earned points for every gaming dollar, they were incentivized to track all of their gaming play. More important, when Harrah's analyzed this data, they realized that their most valuable gamers were not the high rollers who came to Vegas a couple of times a year, spending tens of thousands of dollars, but rather, the consistent, frequent gamer in their locals markets who drove to the casino a couple of times a week and gambled a couple of hundred dollars per visit. The Total Rewards program was, therefore, designed to attract and retain these high-frequency players (Davenport and Harris 2007).

Most casinos use the information from the loyalty programs to calculate the value of their patrons, and incentivize them to continue to stay and play at their properties. Along with play behavior, casinos collect demographic information about these patrons, which allows for more effective targeted marketing. This data can also be used to understand revenue-generating patterns on the gaming floor, and to tie together behavioral indicators for fraud and anti–money laundering programs.

As the gaming industry has evolved, these programs have had to adjust as well. In addition to tracking gaming behavior, casino rewards programs are beginning to expand to consider nongaming as well, building a true 360-degree view of the patron. This has been challenging for casinos for the same reasons we've been talking about in previous chapters, such as disparate selling systems that might not have originally been designed to capture card data. Further, many gaming companies have started partnering with third parties to operate the retail or food and beverage space, which means they have to convince their partners to collect and share the information. Technically, this also means the casinos will be rewarding the patrons for spend that doesn't go into the casino's coffers. Still, it is proven that gamers play where they stay, so encouraging them to use the entire enterprise has benefits to the casino, even if the casino doesn't directly see revenue from the retail and restaurant outlets.

Casinos also track the performance of their casino games. Hold percent (the house advantage) is regulated by game, but there is some flexibility to manipulate this figure in slot games in some areas. The hold represents profitability for the casino, so it is carefully monitored.

Table 10.1 Casino Game House Edge*

Game	House Edge
Blackjack	0.80%
American ("double-zero") Roulette	5.26%
European ("single-zero") Roulette	27%
Craps	0.60%
Three Card Poker	3.4%
Pai Gow Poker	2.5%
Caribbean Stud Poker	5.26%
Baccarat (for banker)	1.17%
Baccarat (for player)	1.63%

*"House edge" represents the advantage that the house has based on the underlying probability structure of the game. The higher the edge, the worse for the player

Casinos track the speed of play at both slots and table games, which also has an impact on the amount of revenue a game can generate. The popularity of certain games is tracked as well, to ensure that popular games are available for the right patrons, and less popular (or profitable) games are cycled off the floor.

Emerging Data Sources

In terms of emerging data sources for casinos, casino floor operators can use social media activity to understand what is driving players to the casino floor, whether it's specific games they prefer or other activities around the gaming floor. Social media data, along with reviews and ratings collected both for the casino and their competition, will assist in uncovering valuable information about market-wide preferences and how the casino is stacking up to the competition. Location information can be used to track traffic patterns around the casino, as well as to influence patrons either through advertising along popular paths or by creating diversions that purposely route patrons past attractions that the casino operators want to feature.

ADVANCED ANALYTICS FOR GAMING

Casino games are, in general, quite profitable for the casino. Impacting the revenue on the casino floor, even a small amount, can result in tremendous gains for casinos. While Las Vegas and Atlantic City (in its glory days), have been established markets for a while, I have heard incredible stories from casino floor managers about the early days in markets that had just opened to casino gaming, like the Native American casinos in Connecticut or Oklahoma, where the wait for a blackjack table was three deep. In Macau, the first few casinos that opened on the Cotai strip (a new development in that market) were so packed that the crowds in the back row around the baccarat table started betting with each other based on what was happening on the table. (Without getting into the details of the game, the rules of baccarat actually make it easy for these kinds of side bets. Obviously, that practice was strongly discouraged by the casinos, as they saw no revenue from that practice.) There was a real "if you build it they will come" mentality in many markets, meaning that casino operators were more worried about crowd control than revenue generation. Unfortunately, I rarely hear these kinds of stories anymore. Increased competition in all markets, combined with some of the regulatory activities I mentioned previously, have resulted in casino operators being under more pressure to improve performance on the casino floor. Just look at what happened to Atlantic City as more markets opened in the region. Casinos are starting to turn to advanced analytics as the best way to continue to drive revenue and profits.

Statistical Analysis

Casino floor operators can use statistical analysis to determine the drivers of patron value. Statistics can be used to calculate expected revenue from the casino floor or for any individual player. Remember that all casino games are based on probability theory, which is a branch of statistical analysis that analyzes the occurrence of random events. I won't get into probability theory here (it's some pretty hard math), but there is a reference at the end of the chapter if you are interested in learning more about calculating "odds." It's a really good way to understand exactly why the house always wins. Based on probability theory, the expectation of player theoretical value can be calculated. There are several ways to calculate this player win or loss rate:

- **Theoretical win.** Thought of from the house perspective, theoretical win represents what the house will gain from a particular player or a particular game. Remember, all of these calculations are based on probability, so this figure is an estimation, hence "theoretical." This metric is calculated as average bet × hours played × decisions per hour × house advantage (Kilby and Fox 1998).

  Theoretical win can be thought of differently by game type. I describe why you might want to think of this differently in the next section, where I talk about table and slot optimization. For these next metrics, I use the term *loss*, which is, from the player perspective, what you expect a patron to lose over time as they play these games. Some casinos use one and some use the other, but most understand the term *player theo*, used to represent the theoretical value of that patron in gaming revenue.

- **Patron theoretical loss table.** This metric is calculated as average bet × time played × speed of game × house advantage (hold percentage). The speed of the game is similar to the term "decisions per hour" in the previous metric. It matters here how fast the game is played—whether it's hands per hour, rolls per hour, spins per hour—the faster the dealer or machine operates, the faster the patrons lose, and the more money the casino makes.

- **Patron theoretical loss slots.** This metric is calculated as coin in × hold percentage. It might also consider player behavior on the specific slot machine type. For example, if the player always plays the max bet they have a chance at winning the jackpot, or some of the smaller prizes that are available only at max bets. If they don't play max, they won't win, so there's less risk for the casino.[1]

As you can tell, these player theoretical value metrics can get quite complex. These seem like straight equations, but statistical analysis can identify patterns of behavior that change the expectation of player theo. For example, casinos might adjust this value based on the duration of a trip, or based on current behavior combined with previous behavior.

CASE STUDY

CASE STUDY: PLAYER VALUE, FANIE SWANEPOEL, MARINA BAY SANDS

Fanie Swanepoel is Vice President, Revenue Optimization, at Marina Bay Sands, which is a 2,500-room integrated resort in Singapore. The property includes a 1.3-million-square-foot convention center, an 800,000-square-foot shopping mall, a museum, two large theaters, a skating rink, and the world's largest atrium casino. Fanie's team includes hotel room revenue optimization, casino floor revenue optimization, and marketing analytics. Having these three groups in the same division paints a complete picture of demand and revenue potential. Working together, they can identify opportunity periods, and know how to incentivize the right demand, across the resort, profitably. They can set up operations on the casino floor using the levers they can manipulate, like minimum bets, to take advantage of predicted demand and guest mix. One of the key inputs to decision making is the potential value of a guest. I asked Fanie how his team thinks about guest value as they are making decisions like promotion planning, setting room rates, or casino floor layout.

"We think of guest value in two ways. There's the lifetime value of the guest and then the expected spend per trip. We can expect a certain percentage of spend across the integrated resort from our retail guests, but the casino guests' spend is more volatile," he told me. "Therefore, the shorter-term expected spend per trip has better predictability. We use lifetime value to determine the reinvestment in the guest, in other words, the benefits and perks they get to encourage them to keep visiting our integrated resort. The expected spend per trip is used more to determine who to invite during certain periods."

As for how they calculate guest value, well, obviously that's intellectual property, but he did describe their high-level process. "We have a dozen or so variables for each homogenous segment of guests that are a pretty accurate determinate of future behavior," he said. "We also think about the 'share of wallet' we may be achieving from an individual, by comparing their performance with the rest of the group. If they are performing on par, that's fine. If not, we need to think about why that might be and take the appropriate action."

Forecasting

Much like other functions within the hotel or casino, for budgeting purposes, casino floor operators forecast casino floor revenue over a longer term time horizon. Demand forecasts can help to schedule labor like cocktail servers, dealers, security, and maintenance. Demand forecasts can also help in forming a plan for raising and lowering the minimum bets on the table games. A forecast of slot performance can identify which machines should be replaced with options that are either more attractive to patrons or more profitable for the casino.

Predictive Modeling

Predictive modeling is the basis for calculating patron lifetime value. The theoretical value of players (player theo) is an input into patron lifetime value, but these algorithms extend that player theo over the lifetime of the relationship with that player, generally estimated to be 10 years. Segmentation analysis, also described in the marketing chapter, can help to split the patrons into groups with similar behavior or characteristics beyond player value for better targeting. Predictive modeling can also be used to understand the performance of certain games in certain locations on the casino floor. For example, certain games may be more profitable if they are located by high-traffic areas. Others might be better off located in the middle of banks of machines, so that players have to search them out to find them.

Simulation analysis, as I described in Chapter 5, is also useful for this casino floor design problem, as it can help to assess the impact of changes in this very complex system. Note that many jurisdictions have rules about how often you can change the configuration of the casino floor. In some places you have to apply to the gaming board for approval, and in others games need to be staged in a back area for a period of time before they are able to be moved onto the casino floor. This makes predictive modeling even more important, as it can help to reduce the risk of time- and resource-consuming changes.

Optimization

There are several applications of optimization in casino floor operations. Just as I described in Chapter 5, optimization can be used to calculate the optimal deployment and schedule configuration for casino floor staff. It can also be used to figure out an optimal schedule for opening and closing table games and raising and lowering minimum bets.

 NOTE

At SAS we worked with a Canadian casino company on a solution to help them optimize the replacement of slot machines on their casino floor. Due to jurisdictional regulations, the slots were staged for two weeks in the back of house of the casino before being deployed on the floor. There was limited capacity in the back of the house, and also on the casino floor. This optimization algorithm produced a schedule for type and number of games to order as replacements to maximize casino revenue, considering the popularity and profitability of games, the capacity of the front and back of house, and the time lag before the games could be deployed on the floor.[2] As you can see from this example, an optimization can consider any of the unique operating constraints in a specific environment, along with standard inputs and outputs.

CASINO FLOOR REVENUE OPTIMIZATION

As I mentioned in the introduction, casino floor revenue optimization is a particularly important application of analytics that encompasses predictive modeling, forecasting, and optimization. From the definition of revenue management in Chapter 8, the casino floor fits the necessary conditions for a revenue management problem.

- **Limited capacity.** Only so many square feet for games, so many slot machines available, so many seats at table games.
- **Perishable product.** If the seat at that table at that time is empty, it won't generate revenue. If no one is playing the slot machine between 6 p.m. and 7 p.m., it won't generate revenue.

Figure 10.1 Increasing Casino Floor Revenue
There are two ways to increase casino floor revenue:
manage the capacity (games) or manage the demand
(patrons). Operations has responsibility for the games,
marketing has responsibility for the patrons. Obviously,
it's important for these activities to be synchronized.

- **Time variable, segmentable demand.** There are peak and
  off-peak periods at the casino and patrons can be grouped by
  price sensitivity, theoretical value, and game preference.

- **Low cost of sale, high fixed costs.** The cost of adding one
  more patron to a seat or on a machine is minimal as compared
  to the overhead for running the property.

Certain areas of the casino floor represent more of an opportunity than others, and certain areas fit the classic revenue management
problem better. For example, table games, with the constrained number of seats and ability to raise and lower minimums probably follow
the classic problem a bit more closely than the slot floor, where the
option to change price on the machines on the fly is more limited. Still,
thinking about this as a revenue management problem of generating
the most possible revenue from the limited amount of space is a useful
way of evaluating the potential of this area (Figure 10.1).

Table Game Revenue Management

Compared to a slot machine, a table game in general is capable of generating more revenue in the same period of time because of the size

of the bets, the capacity of players per space, and the ability to raise and lower rates. In the United States, in general, table games represent about 20% in general of casino floor revenue, and slot machines roughly the other 80%. In Asia, this statistic is reversed. Therefore, you tend to see casino operators in the United States more concerned about managing the slot floor, whereas in Asia, the table games are of primary focus.

For table games there are a couple of levers that can be pulled to generate revenue.

- **Number of available tables for each game type.** This problem starts with the right mix of games, although this is regulated in some areas. Calculating the right mix of game types involves understanding demand for each game type, the value of that demand, and the number of tables that can fit in the allocated space. This decision will only be made periodically, as the configuration can be difficult to change out once it is implemented.

- **Number of open tables.** The casino can control when they open and close tables. The cost associated with opening the table is primarily staffing, which, compared to revenue potential, could be minimal. It's not nothing, though, so casinos do not really want to open tables when there are no interested players.

- **Minimum bet.** The minimum bet represents the amount that a player must wager per round in order to play. The casino has the option to raise or lower these bets at any time. Most casinos have moved to digital signage, so the change is a matter of flipping a switch. Many casinos will allow players to continue playing the original minimum if the minimum is raised while the player is still playing.

- **Number of seats at the table and number of patrons in the seats.** Many table games come with a preconfigured number of players, which is indicated on the game top. However, the play experience can be impacted, positively or negatively, when all the seats are full. Casinos need to decide at what point they want to open more tables in order to spread out the number of players, or if it's better to concentrate the players at a few tables. A social game like craps might generate more money when there are more players egging one another on and winning together, whereas a crowded table at a dealer-intensive game like blackjack could get slowed down to the point where it impacts revenue generation.

■ **Velocity of the game.** Since the table games are dealer driven, the casino has some control over the speed of the game. The faster the dealer manages a round, the more rounds per hour and the more revenue that can be generated.

Maximizing revenue from table games becomes a balancing act (read: optimization) considering all of these factors. The problem starts with a forecast of demand by game type and value. Then there are a few strategies to consider, and predictive modeling can help the company arrive at the answer. You might fill all the seats at all the tables if you keep the minimum bets low, but you could be diluting revenue from players who prefer to play at lower bet tables, but who would play at higher-minimum-bet tables if lower options are not available. The same situation occurs for those players who prefer blackjack but will play roulette, which is more profitable for the casino, if blackjack is not available. You might want to restrict the number of certain game types to push players to more profitable games.

It may seem like good practice to plan to fill every seat at the table, but there is a point where a full table slows the dealer down too much, so that it's actually more profitable for the table to be at 80% or less capacity. Finding that inflection point is a key determinant of how many tables should be open. The impact of all of these factors depends also on your mix of business and patron preferences. An optimization algorithm can help to balance all of these factors, provided the casino has the data for the inputs, of course.

The problem gets complicated because there isn't really a good way to track the revenue from the table games in real time, which could be a key input to the problem. Players do not always bet consistently, so the amount of revenue generated per specific player is hard to determine. In slot machines, the amount of *coin in*, or the amount the patron adds to the machine, as well as their winnings, and what they return to the machine, is tracked perfectly. Not so at a table game, where the casino really can't tell how much players sit down with, particularly if they arrive with chips already, tracking their buy-in at the table is manual, and there isn't a good way to track how much they bet per hand. All of these key metrics are tracked through observation and manual data entry. The manual nature of the data collection makes accuracy in this problem challenging.

While the analytics department can provide some insight and expertise, today effective table game revenue generation depends on the speed and acumen of the dealer and the experience of the pit boss (table game manager), who is responsible for decisions to raise and lower bets on the fly. I am very interested to see whether advances in technology, radio frequency identification (RFID) chips, for example, will change data collection and improve our ability to solve this problem. If you are able to tie chips to a player, and a player to a table, then create gateways where the chips are bet and pass back and forth from player to dealer, you could theoretically exactly track the value of each bet, and how much the player is winning or losing. This will require investment in technology at the table that can track the RFID, and a process that ties chips to a player and a table. It is potentially a very cool opportunity, though.

Slot Floor Optimization

In North America, slots generate by far the most revenue on the casino floor. Over the years, slot machines have evolved from the famous "one-armed bandit" with the mechanical arm and spinning wheels, to computerized, animated experiences that are themed, with multilevel jackpots. Slot machines are designed based on probabilities, and just like table games, there is a hold percentage that represents the house advantage. While this figure is regulated by jurisdiction, there is some variation allowed. The "tighter" the slots, the more profitable for the house, and the "looser," the better for the patron. Some games have a progressive jackpot that grows over time. These are attractive to players who are hoping for a big hit, even when the jackpot payoffs are very rare. However, when that jackpot hits while players are in the casino, and it creates a big stir, they may gravitate toward the machine in hopes of achieving a similar result. To create the excitement that keeps patrons playing in hopes of achieving that eventual big payoff, casinos put a mix of machines on the floor, so patrons can see payouts from time to time, even if they don't actually get one themselves.

The levers that casino managers have on the slot floor are the denominations of the machines (the amount per spin can range from pennies up to $10 or much more), the hold percentage, the mix of machines, and the location of the machines on the casino floor. Speed of play also matters for slot machines.

There are two ways to optimize the revenue from the casino floor: optimize the mix of machines and optimize the placement of machines in the space on the casino floor. Casinos need to constantly evaluate the performance of their machines, understanding which are profitable and which are popular. Forecasting performance trends for these machines can identify which machines are declining in popularity (which will likely lead to a profitability decline as well). As I described previously, there could be a long lead time before casinos can replace machines on the floor or adjust the floor configuration, so forecasting performance for planning purposes is crucial. Optimization algorithms can help to optimize revenue potential, taking into account constraints like space, timing, profitability, guest preferences, and regulations.

Optimizing the configuration of slots on the casino floor is a very interesting problem. Casino managers know that different locations on the floor have different patterns in terms of patron play behavior. For example, machines near restrooms have short duration and low coin in play because they tend to be played while someone is waiting for a companion. Casinos may want to locate profitable machines (tighter machines), next to the restrooms, to take advantage of this play behavior. Machines on aisles may get more play than centrally located machines, because they are more visible. It could be that less profitable machines in these locations will draw patrons to play the more profitable slots in the center of rows, because patrons see the others winning on the aisle. Popular games can draw traffic through less popular areas, encouraging patrons to discover new games, if they are placed in less accessible locations, but this strategy could backfire if they are too hard to find. Areas outside of attractions might get more play during certain periods; for example, those located outside the entrance to the in-house show might get more play during immediate pre- and post-show time periods. Therefore, particular machine types may do better depending on location.

Heat maps of the casino floor (see the description of heat maps in Chapter 3), calculated by time period, can provide insight into the performance of machines, and the drivers of performance. Statistical modeling can validate whether these patterns are statistically significant. These performance metrics are then used to determine where machines should be placed on the floor. Simulation analysis can help with understanding the impact of changes before they are implemented on the floor. The profitability and popularity of the game would be treated as inputs, along with traffic patterns throughout different sections. This is a complex system to model, but changes on the casino floor are expensive, and can have huge profitability implications. Understanding the impacts in a lower risk arena clearly has benefits. It is also important to track performance over time after changes, as behaviors might not evolve as expected, or may change as the games age.

CASE STUDY: SLOT PERFORMANCE, DAVID KOCH

CASE STUDY

David Koch, a data scientist who developed analytical capabilities in a casino in Canada, emphasizes the importance of a more dynamic view of casino floor performance. David told a pretty compelling story at a gaming summit, and I asked him to reprise that discussion for this book. You'll find the entire story in Appendix 3.

One of my favorite examples from his talk was the impact of changing a game location. He presented the graphs shown in Figures 10.2 and 10.3 and explained what they found.

(continued)

(continued)

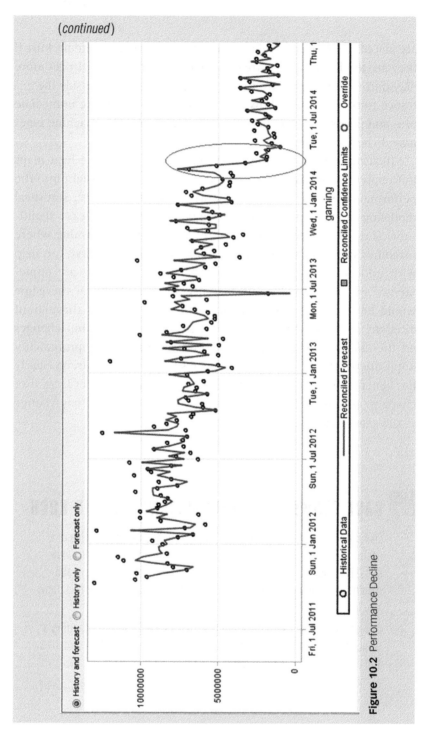

Figure 10.2 Performance Decline

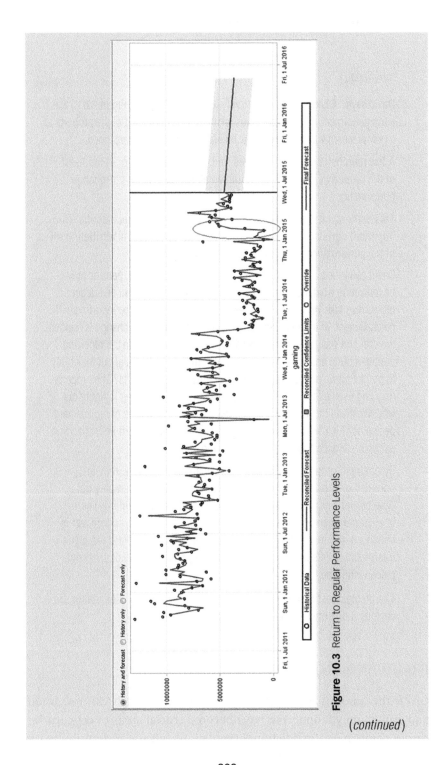

Figure 10.3 Return to Regular Performance Levels

(*continued*)

(*continued*)

David says, "Change is an opportunity to learn. This game (Figure 10.2) was a top performer until one day it was taken from a central part of the property to a new place only a few steps away. Its player appeal quickly declined.

A few months later it was returned to its previous location, in the heart of the property (Figure 10.3). It immediately resumed its pre-change performance.

This demonstrates how decisions by the property can affect results. One important corollary that follows from this: Be careful about attributing all of the performance of an asset *to* the asset."

David continued: "There is meaning in change. In particular, patrons may be indicating what they like and don't like. Some changes will be sudden; others may take years to be manifested. Static, period-in-time reporting will be challenged in trying to surface long-term change. When change is sudden, the pre- and post-change results will be amalgamated within the reporting period, muting and thereby obscuring any impact. And what about the ability to predict future performance from these amalgamated results? The property may find itself either under- or overpredicting and later trying to figure out why. What will this mean when determining the effectiveness of replacement decisions? Finally, what kind of progress will be made toward understanding patron preference and developing (growing) the business?

By contrast, graphical depictions are dynamic. Ultimately, they are bounded only by the limits of available history. Cycles can play out. Whether long-term or sudden, change is more clearly evident. There is a natural opening for statistical application. The ability to forecast is enhanced and made more reliable. Context is given. Direction is given. Interpretation is strengthened. The evolving short term takes its proper place within the long-term picture.

The greatest test is the test of time. In numbers, relationships matter. Be curious. Look underneath. Ask why and how."

FRAUD AND ANTI–MONEY LAUNDERING

Given the amount of cash that is exchanged through casinos, fraud and anti–money laundering have become crucial areas of concern for casino companies. Jurisdictional regulations put the responsibility on casinos to make sure that illegal activities like money laundering or terrorist funding is not facilitated by the casino. Casinos also have to keep a close eye on fraudulent activities perpetrated by employees or patrons, as they can also have significant profitability implications.

Recently in the United States, casinos have faced an increasing amount of attention from FinCEN, the U.S. Department of Treasury's Financial Crimes Enforcement Network, the Internal Revenue Service, and various other state entities with regards to their Anti–Money Laundering (AML) compliance programs. This activity is motivated by the U.S. Patriot Act, which was established in October 2001, mandating that banks and other financial institutions have robust AML compliance programs. Prior to this legislation, banks were similar to casinos today, in that they had individuals within the organization who were very skilled at detecting and mitigating potential money-laundering activities. However, very few banks had a systematic, analytically driven approach to detecting money-laundering activities. Under increasing regulatory scrutiny, it did not take the banks long to realize that they could not keep up with the demands of these programs manually. They needed to leverage data analytics to minimize their potential risks; risks that not only included losses from bad actors, but also included the risk of significant fines for noncompliance.

Today, under the increased scrutiny of FinCEN, risk management professionals in most casinos are struggling to keep up with the wave of inquiries, and are burning valuable resources in the explanation and proof of prior actions and decisions. Every moment spent on inquiries can hinder the discovery of new risks. Analytics can automate the process of detecting patterns that indicate potential violations. Data and analytics programs can also provide workflows that automate the process of reporting that casinos are required to fulfill to demonstrate regulatory compliance. One of the major hurdles preventing the introduction of analytics regarding AML risks is the age-old issue facing all analytical programs: the amount of disparate data throughout the organization.

Money laundering, for those who have not yet watched the AMC series *Breaking Bad*, refers to the process of making large amounts of cash that were obtained illegally (like through drug deals, black market transactions, bribery, etc.) appear to come from a legitimate source to avoid government detection. It could also be used by business owners attempting to disguise business earnings as casino winnings to avoid taxes. In the TV show *Breaking Bad* (spoiler alert), the lead characters purchased a car wash and rang up fake car wash transactions paid in cash. These transactions could be reported on the company P&L, and, for a small tax hit, the owners could avoid governmental scrutiny. Similarly, given the large volumes of cash that move through a casino, there is an opportunity for the bad guys to use the system to their advantage. Whatever the cash source, the idea here is to make the cash look like winnings associated with gaming or simply a cash-out of chips used in gaming activity. A patron could deposit cash in exchange for chips, and then exchange the chips for clean cash. The patron could also insert cash into a slot machine and immediately cash out a voucher, perhaps repeating this activity across the casino. There are some tracking and regulations that casinos follow that need to be manipulated by the bad guys, which makes the process slightly less straightforward than simply buying and selling chips, or cashing in vouchers, but the opportunity is there if the bad guys understand the system.

Detecting money-laundering activities requires tracking patron behavior over time. For example, *structuring* is a method of arranging with the casino a series of transactions that are less than the ten thousand dollars that require filling out a Currency Transaction Report, which would result in the transaction being registered with the IRS. To avoid detection, the bad guys recruit actors to launder on their behalf. Therefore, a patron who routinely gambles small amounts at a time, but suddenly shows up with thousands of dollars, might be suspicious. Patrons who cash out large amounts of chips without a log of associated play could also be a trigger to investigate. Casinos issue credit, and frequently receive and transfer funds on behalf of their high-value patrons. Funds wired into a casino and transferred to another organization without being cashed out are also suspicious. Criminals have become very creative in the ways that they organize these activities, and there are some fascinating, if scary, stories on this topic.

Fraud is another fascinating area in the casino space. Fraud refers to the act of illegally taking money from the casino, or taking money under false pretenses, which makes it a slightly different problem than money laundering. Fraud activities can be as simple as trying to pass a bad check or cash in fake chips. They can also get infinitely more complicated, like organizing rings to "cheat" at casino games. Many are familiar with the movie *21* and the book *Bringing Down the House*, which is the story of a group of MIT students and their math professor who organized a plan that resulted in their winning millions at blackjack. If you haven't read the book or seen the movie, it's a fascinating look at probability theory and the casino industry. These mathematicians were simply working the probabilities, which isn't technically illegal. However, casinos consider this type of activity cheating, and it goes under the heading of fraud. Casinos have the right to refuse service to anyone, which is what happened. The MIT gang was banned from playing in Las Vegas casinos for life. In other cases, it could be employees colluding with patrons to steal money at the tables, in restaurants, or in other outlets.

▶ **NOTE**

I had a friend who managed what was the hottest nightclub in Las Vegas at the time. They did a significant amount of cash business, so there were many checks and balances in place to ensure that the bartenders were not stealing cash. There were cameras installed to ensure that any cash that the bartenders handled went into the register, the drawers needed to be balanced every night, and even bartender tips were carefully managed to ensure that the bartenders weren't dumping stolen cash into the tip jars. Still, my friend suspected that the bar just wasn't bringing in the cash that he would have expected. He carefully monitored the staff to figure out if there was some behavior he could detect that indicated they were stealing. Finally, he noticed that the bartenders were bringing candy into work and moving it from bags to glasses with regular patterns during the shift. He realized that the bartenders were putting extra cash into the register from giving patrons duplicate checks during routine transactions, so the cameras detected no anomalies, but then the bartenders had to remove the cash they placed in the register before they balanced their drawers at the end of the night. Drawers that were off by even five dollars were heavily scrutinized, so they had to know exactly how much cash they were storing in the register during the shift. They were dropping pieces of candy into a glass by the register so they knew how many 20-dollar bills to pull out at the end of the shift. When my friend figured this out, he stopped by his bartender's drawer to check in, and during the course of the conversation, he grabbed a handful of candy from

(continued)

(*continued*)

the glass, and watched the bartender's face go white, knowing he had been caught (mean, but awesome, right!?!). There were several bartenders involved in this scam, and they were all prosecuted by the casino, since it was determined that they had probably stolen over a hundred thousand dollars from the nightclub.

Analytics supports the detection of these anti–money laundering and fraudulent activities by automating the process of detecting patterns in the data. Analytics can detect a betting pattern, or a buying-and-selling-chips pattern that is significantly different than what would be expected from that patron. They can look for rings of operators, patrons, and employees who happen to be in the same place when the table goes on a winning streak. They can match patron activity to watch lists or problem gaming lists, so that patrons who aren't supposed to be in the casino are not given access. Analytics could even identify when revenue drops below an expected level, or costs rise without revenue to balance them (which would have helped my bar manager friend). All of these activities require a consolidated view of patron activities across the casino property, or even the casino company if there are multiple locations, combined with operational information. The industry is simply too large and too complex for individuals to manually detect and surface these patterns.

I have seen interest in these areas grow over the last few years as governments start to crack down on corruption. In most industries, investment in these areas only happens when the risk of getting caught and fined outweighs the cost of investment. In other words, these solutions only become important when it is an emergency. Still, there are well-documented cases recently of casino companies facing significant fines over this. Most famous, probably, is the $47 million fine levied against Las Vegas Sands to settle a claim that they failed to report suspicious activity by a Chinese drug lord who lost $84 million in their casino; specifically, they failed to report money that was wired through suspicious connections.[3] I know that you are doing the math here, calculating that LVS might still have come out ahead in the deal. Keep in mind, this negative publicity might scare away other high rollers who don't want this kind of attention on them, whether they are legitimate or not.

BENCHMARKING GAMING ANALYTICS CAPABILITIES

Much like hotels, casinos demonstrate varying levels of analytical capabilities, both from company to company and also from department to department. Marketing in casinos tends to be more mature in their use of analytics, since so much of the revenue that is generated on the casino floor depends on patron relationships. While casinos are perceived as having vast resources, they tend to invest in programs and facilities that will drive business to the casino floor, rather than investing in technology infrastructure to support data and analytics, but this is changing as competition becomes fiercer.

Beginners. The less sophisticated gaming organizations are highly manual for data access and very Excel driven for analysis. They may be able to pull together a patron profile, but the data is not well organized and has missing values. Marketing is not targeted, and while they may be able to keep track of high rollers, they have very limited visibility into what might be driving profitability in other patron segments. Rooms, restaurants, and other revenue-generating outlets are definitely considered amenities for players, and there is no strategy for gaining a 360-degree view of the patron. Operating reports take days to pull together, and decision making tends to be highly reactive. Managers on the casino floor operate through gut instinct, and possibly by reacting to historical data that is at minimum several days old.

Average. For casinos that are about average in their analytical capability, the marketing department is probably building segmentation models, predicting patron value, and incorporating likelihood to respond in targeted marketing campaigns. They have a fair amount of data on their patrons, and may be working toward a more holistic view of patrons, planning to incorporate nongaming revenue. Some of these casinos are using data visualization or business intelligence to automate the process of distributing operating reports, so managers have better access to information that drives their businesses. There could be a revenue management department managing the retail room rates and group business after the casino department gets their room block. There is likely a group called revenue optimization whose responsibility is to manage revenue generation on the casino floor. They track and report on floor performance, might do some forecasting and trend analysis, and probably provide some intelligence to floor mangers regarding the best schedule for the table games. This schedule is static, but it does provide directional guidance for the pit bosses.

Advanced. The most advanced casinos have very sophisticated marketing operations. They have started considering nongaming revenue in their patron value calculation, either by mining the guest folio or facilitating patron identification at the outlets around the casino. They are using advanced analytics for predictive modeling of patron behavior. They can predict lifetime value, do deep analytical segmentation, and predict churn, acquisition strategies, and next best offer. These organizations are starting to move toward real-time decisioning, interacting with patrons when they card-in to a machine, use a kiosk, log on to the website, or are speaking with an agent. They have an active social media monitoring program, and are moving toward sentiment analysis and text mining (mostly using third-party vendors rather than internally). There is a robust patron database, which also contains some operational insight. They are planning for location-based marketing through Wi-Fi access or beacons. Hotel revenue management generally uses a system that takes player value into account, as I described in Chapter 8, and are balancing casino rates with retail and group business. On the casino floor, the revenue optimization team is leveraging advanced forecasting and optimization techniques to plan the schedule for table games, and to track and plan deployment of slot machines. As yet, I have not seen a casino be at the point of executing this revenue optimization in real or near real time. They still rely on the pit bosses to make on-the-fly decisions based on flow of business due to the data challenges I described previously.

TECHNOLOGY AND PEOPLE INVESTMENTS

Casinos will definitely see benefit in investing in the marketing technology and resources that I suggest in Chapter 6. Given how important it is to understand the impact of patron value, and to nurture the relationship with your best patrons, investment in this area will definitely generate a return. In addition, considering the amount of revenue that is generated by the casino floor, any efficiencies gained can have a massive payback as well. The following are my suggestions specifically for casino floor operations.

Technology

Casino floor revenue, as I described previously, can be increased by attracting more patrons to the floor, encouraging each patron to gamble more, or increasing the turnover, or utilization, of the assets on the gaming floor. This is why many casinos invest so heavily in their marketing programs. At a minimum, to compliment the efforts of casino marketing (see the technology section in Chapter 6), casino floor operations, regardless of the size of the casino, should invest in the following analytical technologies:

- **Data visualization.** Detecting a common theme, right? The ability to quickly visualize trends on the casino floor, by machine, table, or location of a group of machines. These insights are key to driving performance on the floor, even if there are no predictive analytics associated with them. However, as David Koch's example illustrates, being able to identify a trend in slot machine performance and predict it into the future is extremely valuable when it comes to understanding and managing casino floor performance. Many of the slot machine manufactures provide some level of business intelligence or data visualization capabilities, which provides easier access for smaller casinos that are already working with these vendors. Just keep in mind that there's an added level of flexibility associated with a data visualization package that sits on top of all of your transactional data as opposed to precanned views provided by a vendor. Still, something is always better than nothing.

- **Forecasting.** The ability to forecast revenue at a detailed level is essential to understanding trends and anticipating opportunities. Forecasting frequently must come with a resource that can conduct this kind of analysis properly, but that should be well worth the investment.

Visualization and forecasting will provide a significant advantage to casino floor operators, both for understanding current performance and anticipating future opportunities. However, to truly get the most out of the casino floor, I would strongly suggest investing in predictive modeling and optimization technology and resources. As I described earlier, moving the needle even a little bit on casino floor revenue can make a big difference, and optimization technology can provide the capability to do that.

People

At a minimum, casinos need an analyst or two dedicated to casino floor performance. These analysts should at least be able to manipulate data to produce both routine and ad hoc reports, as well as identify and understand the drivers of performance. They should be relatively comfortable with numbers, probably with a strong business background, and some foundational statistics classes. For this role, you could train someone who has an aptitude for numbers in the casino business, rather than look for someone with a casino background. This could be an entry-level position, if you have an analytically minded manager on the floor. Otherwise, you might want someone with maturity and seniority who can guide strategy.

As the casino floor operations get more sophisticated, casinos should think about investing in some forecasting and optimization resources. Typically, it can be difficult to find someone who is good at both of these areas since optimization is such a highly specialized skill set, but those resources do exist. Prioritize the optimization resource, as your casino floor performance analyst can probably help out with forecasting. You could always outsource this kind of modeling, but you would want someone internally who can understand the business, as well as the appropriate techniques and their implications, to guide development of any outsourced models. As you can tell from my discussions earlier in the chapter, optimization is valuable because it actually provides a decision that managers can take action on, which will help them achieve their goals. Generally, it is always worth the investment to bring on a full-time resource internally.

CONCLUSION

Casinos have always been considered very glamourous, and some-times thought of as a mysterious insider game or a license to print money. I must say that in my career in analytics, my favorite stories have always come from my casino colleagues, and some of my favorite personal experiences have happened either directly or through obser-vation in some of the breathtaking (and maybe not so breathtaking) casino properties globally. For someone who is interested in the inter-section between consumer behavior and revenue generation, there is no better testing ground than casinos.

Despite the mystique, casinos are struggling with some very real issues in today's market. Competition is stronger than ever before, and governmental scrutiny is causing high rollers to pull back, whether it's individuals slowing down their trip frequency or the conferences and events that got such a bad reputation dur-ing the economic downturn. Many casino companies are also see-ing what they consider an alarming shift in patron behavior. The upcoming generations, while they enjoy the nongaming aspects of the casino floor, appear to not be as interested in the traditional slot machines (or even new iterations) as previous generations. For North American casinos in particular, this is a dangerous trend, as they rely on the revenue from the slot floor for sustainable performance.

Casinos are struggling to figure out what kinds of activities will attract the next generation of gamers. They are starting to investigate skill-based games, where the players think they have some control over the outcome. These can be as simple as basketball free-throw tournaments, but also include what could be thought of as typical vid-eo games as well. Monetizing this area will be a challenge, of course. Even more of a barrier, however, are regulations. Currently in the U.S. market, regulations implicitly prohibit casinos from profiting from any games that are not inherently governed by chance. For example, while poker players can gain skill at playing the game, and following probability rules at blackjack provides some advantage, the cards that are dealt are governed by chance. This is not the case in a video game or a free throw. It will be interesting to track this trend in the next few years. If you want to hear more, *Planet Money* did a great podcast on this issue in Episode 619, "The Free Throw Experiment." (Actually, *Planet Money* is a great podcast for analytic hospitality executives. They produce fascinating stories about how the economy works.)

Analytics presents a huge opportunity for casinos to maximize the performance of their casino floors, and drive profitability through challenging times. As with every other area of the industry, it will require a mindset change from top executives, but I am already seeing encouraging signs in this direction.

Speaking of changing mindsets and growing analytical capability, in the final chapter of the book, I describe how to get started with an analytics program, how to organize analytics within the company, and how to integrate data and analytics for cross-departmental decision making. I also provide a few examples from some inspirational analytical leaders.

ADDITIONAL RESOURCES

- Scott Sutton, "Patron Analytics in the Casino and Gaming Industry: How the House Always Wins," white paper 379-2011, SAS Global Forum, 2011.
- Clayton Peister, "Table-Games Revenue Management: Applying Survival Analysis," *Cornell Hotel and Restaurant Administration Quarterly* 28(1)(2007): 70–87.
- Clive J. Pearson, *Double Down on Your Data*, 3rd ed. (Mustang, OK: Tate Publishing, 2012).
- Ben Mezrich, *Bringing Down the House: The Inside Story of Six MIT Students Who Took Vegas for Millions* (New York: Atria Books, 2003).
- Catalin Barboianu, *Probability Guide to Gambling: The Mathematics of Dice, Slots, Roulette, Baccarat, Blackjack, Poker, Lottery, and Sport Bets* (Craiova, Romania: Infarom, 2006).

NOTES

1. This calculation can get complex. For example, the progressive machines can be categorized on four levels, each with different profitability and appealing to potentially different groups of patrons. Progressives can be categorized by:

   1. Number of levels
   2. Whether standalone (one machine) or linked to the bank of machines, or across casinos
   3. Whether mystery and/or symbol driven (as in, how do you know you have won?)

4. The relationship of the wager to the jackpot
   - The likelihood of winning increases with the wager (proportional)
   - Betting the maximum is a condition of winning (binary)
   - The jackpot varies with the wager (variable)
   - The jackpot is the same no matter the wager (invariable)

2. "Analytics and the Modern Casino: A Game Changer," Canadian Gaming Business, www.canadiangamingbusiness.com/AnalyticsandtheModernCasinoAGameChanger .aspx.
3. James O'Toole, "Las Vegas Sands, Resolves Laundering with $47 Million Deal," CNN Money, August 27, 2013, http://money.cnn.com/2013/08/27/news/companies/ las-vegas-sands/index.html.

CHAPTER 11

Pulling It All Together: Building an Analytical Organization

All models are wrong . . . but some are useful!

—George E. P. Box

The final piece of the puzzle is execution. Now that I have convinced you of the many, many opportunities to apply analytics in your organization, the natural next question is "How do I get started?" (Or, if you've read all of my chapters closely, you might say: "Okay, fine, I get it, I bought a data visualization package, now what?") There are a few decisions that need to be made as you grow your analytic capability. None of the initial decisions you make need to be permanent, but they do need to be thought through carefully. You will want to pick an organizational structure that makes sense for your company and current resources. You need to decide in what functional area you want to get started and with what project, and also build a roadmap for the next several years. The roadmap should include the problems you want to tackle, but also your technology and capability strategy, whether you want to partner with vendors or consultants, or whether you want to build everything yourself—or maybe it's a mix.

Much of this chapter will be dedicated to providing you with the pros and cons of various options for these decisions. There are a few best practices, but in most cases, there's no exact right answer. Most organizations I've worked with have adjusted their philosophies, structures, and strategies as the business and their capabilities evolved. I have also seen some organizations make a sudden and dramatic decision to create an analytics group from the ground up and make a massive investment in people and technology to support it. That can work too. How this will evolve in your organization will depend on the goals and business strategies of your company (or the ones you begin establishing after you've read this book).

This chapter includes some perspectives from industry leaders I admire. They have pioneered analytics in modern hospitality and gaming, and continue to lead the charge in this area. They won't talk about the specific models they built or strategies they are developing. This is (obviously) because innovations in analytics have resulted in so many benefits for these organizations that they are considered among their most important competitive advantages. In fact, this is not what you

308

want to hear from them anyway. Any one of these leaders will tell you that copying someone else's strategy or letting a vendor or consultant dictate your strategy for you won't work. You need to define the analytical opportunity and roadmap for yourself, making it part of your unique business strategy to address your unique business problems. What you do want to learn from them is how to get executive attention for your vision, how to organize for success, and how to attract and retain the best talent. That's what you'll hear here.

GETTING STARTED: WELL-DEFINED, SMALL PROJECTS FOR MAXIMUM IMPACT

Unless you are in one of the very lucky few organizations where the executive team wakes up one morning and says "Right, we're starting an advanced analytics program today, and you can do whatever you need to make that happen, cost is no object," or you have the benefit of being hired into an organization that already has this mandate (like me), you are probably going to have to figure out how to do this practically from scratch with a small team, a limited budget, and very little support or recognition. Don't worry, the most successful programs and departments started this way. It is harder work, but it will be much more sustainable than if you get a mandate and fail to produce a silver bullet at the speed the executive team expects (and they will always expect it way faster than is actually reasonable). Keep in mind that when I talk about building up analytics capabilities, I am talking about statistical analysis, forecasting, predictive analytics, and optimization, in other words, deploying advanced analytic along with building reports and ad hoc historical analysis. You want to go beyond what your organization is probably already considering and add some forward-looking intelligence.

It will sound obvious after I say it, but you need to start with a small, well-defined project, where the data is not too messy and a key executive would care a lot about the outcome. This is harder than it sounds. The project has to be small and well defined, because scope creep happens with every project. If you start too large, or aren't clear on what you are trying to do, timelines increase, and you can lose focus and momentum. Data is a huge time suck, so the more confidence you have in the quality of the data initially, the more likely you'll be to get results while people are still paying attention, and, of course, executive-level support is what will propel the project, and future investment, forward.

> *But for my team, as we strive to bring a new level of analytics to our stakeholders, tools and data are literally the last things on which we'll be working. That's because in my own experience and in observing others, I've seen too many analytics initiatives fail because they started with the data.*
>
> *I'll repeat it until I'm blue in the face: analytics is about questions. I don't care how well you think you know your business, if you don't first start with your decision makers and really get inside their heads, you're going to come up with solutions that miss the mark. Everything pivots on having clarity on the questions that need to be answered.*
>
> —David Schmitt, Vice President, Marketing Analytics Strategy, Beckon, Inc.

Let's take a minute to talk about what I mean by project, well defined, and small. The best projects are ones where you use the data to discover an opportunity, you find a way to take advantage of that opportunity in the operation, and then you measure the success of the implementation. It's much better if a change or a new decision is made based on your initial analysis, and that decision has demonstrated success in the field. Yes, I just made this harder.

A well-defined project starts with a burning question, as David's quote above suggests, and has a measurable outcome. It is not "Hey, let's see what's in this data set." It's not "I wonder if . . ." It's more like "How can I increase response rates to our campaigns? Why is revenue down in the Northeast? How can I increase revenue on Tuesdays? Who are my best customers? Which email subject line results in more openings? What image best drives conversions?" You want to pose questions or hypotheses that are discrete and deterministic, not open-ended or exploratory (save those for after you have demonstrated some success).

Small is equally as important as well defined. Small keeps the project in scope. Pick one property, one region, one segment. Limit the number of factors you will include in the analysis. Do whatever can be done to make the scope extremely targeted. You may be concerned that this is limiting. It isn't. It's focused. You will be much more successful in recruiting a partner that is happy to test out any changes you suggest, and will work with you on the data collection, if you keep things small. The interpretation of the data will be easier if it is smaller. Controlling the factors that could bias results will be easier if it's small.

As I described in Chapter 2, it is typical that analysts spend 80% of project time preparing data and only 20% on the analysis. This is why you should start with a data set that you feel comfortable with. Make sure you chose a data set where you understand how the information is collected and what all of the fields mean. This will make it much easier to interpret the results, and it will save some time. You should still plan for more time than you think you need for the data preparation, but choosing a familiar data set should help you to move things along.

An executive-level sponsor who has a stake in the results will help to raise the visibility of your project, and can help you convince their peers to continue investment or at least help to identify your next project. Make sure you, along with your executive, evangelize the results loudly and often. The higher the visibility of your success, the more likely the right people in the organization will notice and be curious to see what else can be done.

You will probably have to repeat this exercise many times over a few years before there's any kind of enterprise-wide mandate. If you are located within an individual department, you can certainly prove value by leveraging your business knowledge on high-impact projects. Just be sure that you are taking opportunities to build awareness outside of your department as well. I am hopeful that moving an organization toward a strategic analytic culture won't take as long today as it did for those who started even 5 or 10 years ago. The word is out about the value of advanced analytics, and the pioneers are demonstrating so much value for their organizations that others are now eager to keep up. Regardless of whether you have to fight your way to awareness or you are asked to jump in with both feet, keep my advice in mind. It pays to find a well-defined, high-impact, small-footprint project right out of the gate so you can quickly demonstrate value. If you've read the rest of the book, you surely can see that there is plenty of low-hanging fruit in our business.

CASE STUDY: GETTING STARTED WITH ANALYTICS, JEREMY TERBUSH, WYNDHAM DESTINATION NETWORK

About three-quarters of the way through writing this book, I had an opportunity to join Wyndham Destination Network as Vice President of Advanced Analytics. I made that decision in no small part because of the level of commitment the leadership at WDN has to analytics. I had already planned to include WDN's story in this book, and, particularly, my new boss's part in that story. It's very exciting to be able to experience the results of the team's hard work from the inside.

Wyndham Destination Network, formerly Wyndham Exchange and Rentals, is the world's largest provider of professionally managed, unique vacation accommodations—from houseboats and cottages to rental homes and timeshare resorts. Its network comprises more than 110,000 properties in over 100 countries and consists of a collection of renowned brands including RCI®, The Registry Collection®, Wyndham Vacation Rentals, Hoseasons, Landal GreenParks, Novasol, cottages.com, and James Villa Holidays. Last year, Wyndham Destination Network sent more than 10 million people on the vacations of their dreams. Together, these companies represent about 30% of Wyndham Worldwide's revenue, which makes us slightly larger in terms of revenue than the hotel division (at about 21% of Wyndham Worldwide's revenue).

Jeremy TerBush is Senior Vice President of Global Analytics for Wyndham Destination Network. Jeremy leads a team of around 35 data scientists, analysts, and developers who provide analytical solutions for risk analysis, valuations, business intelligence, digital marketing, and advanced analytics. This group is centralized at corporate, and acts as a shared service for the various lines of business that make up WDN. Advanced Analytics (my team) has built custom pricing and revenue management solutions for all of our vacation rental companies, as well as the analytics behind the valuations in RCI's exchange market. We also work on projects in owner recruiting, Net Promoter Score modeling, inventory distribution, and digital marketing. Analytics are named in the strategic vision for the company, with the value recognized and supported all the way up through the C-level. Jeremy reports to the chief financial officer.

Of course, it wasn't always this way. Jeremy and his team's success at WDN is the product of a lot of hard work and evangelizing. Jeremy started with RCI as an inventory analyst, and progressed to manager and then director in revenue management. These were relatively small groups within RCI, dedicated to driving incremental revenue in RCI's exchange network. The group was doing good work, but it was mostly manual. Still, the group was gaining a reputation for delivering value, and this reputation was elevating their visibility within the organization.

In the RCI exchange market, members can deposit their timeshare vacation weeks and exchange that inventory for a different vacation experience. In order to maintain member satisfaction, and encourage more trading, the valuation of the deposits and the exchanges needs to be accurate and fair. Executing this dynamic valuation accurately requires forecasting supply of deposits (6 million region/week forecasts), usage (15 million region/week/product forecasts), and demand (15 million region/week/product forecasts), and determining the optimal value of each deposit and exchange.

"At a certain point we realized that we needed a more automated approach to the exchange valuation process. Based on what we had seen of the success of pricing and revenue management in hospitality, travel and retail, we knew there was an opportunity, but this problem was a bit different to the more traditional applications," says Jeremy. "We were going to have to make a pretty major investment in time, resources, and technology to build this dynamic, automated system internally because there wasn't anything commercially available to solve this problem. If we hadn't already had a demonstrated track record of success, and a reputation for execution in the department already, we could not have gotten the necessary executive buy-in to make this investment for RCI."

The new system generated $11 million in revenue in the first year due to an increase in volume of trades, with deposits, occupancy, and average weekly rates all increasing as compared to recent trends. Starting with pricing and revenue management was a good strategy for Jeremy and the team, because of the direct impact on revenue, as well as other key metrics that executive leadership understands and values. The team made sure to focus on those metrics and measure success against them.[1]

(*continued*)

(*continued*)

It didn't stop there though. By loudly evangelizing the success of the revenue management system internally at RCI (winning the INFORMS Pricing and Revenue Management award in 2011 didn't hurt either), Jeremy and his team were able to convince the organization to apply these techniques to other lines of business. Jeremy's group was separated from RCI's revenue management group, which remained to focus on the business of managing the exchange market based on the output of the analytical system. Jeremy's team became a shared services organization at the corporate level of Wyndham Exchange and Rentals (as it was called then). Revenue management at RCI became a client, and Jeremy's team started working with the other rental companies. Pricing solutions developed internally were rapidly rolled out across several of the larger rental companies with great success, so investment in people and resources to grow the group continued. It should be noted that Jeremy himself, based on his leadership during the success of these analytics initiatives, rapidly rose through the ranks at WDN, becoming senior vice president in 2015, in a department and a role that was created for him and his team because of their demonstrated success.

I have found that even with executive commitment, our internal clients still need to be able to justify the resources and time they invest during development and implementation of the pricing solutions we develop for them. These lines of business have their own goals and priorities. Therefore, we still need to be able to sell the benefits of analytics to business stakeholders to obtain the right level of buy in to move forward. Jeremy works hard to maintain our internal reputation and our status as trusted advisors to our stakeholders. He pushes the team for excellence in every deliverable and also in responsiveness to our clients. We are constantly educating, demonstrating benefits, and collaborating with our clients.

Before I started working with him, every time I sat in on a conference session where Jeremy was presenting, I'd be the first to raise my hand and ask him to talk about how he was able to grow the visibility and impact of the team internally.[2] This is the advice he always gives:

- **Prioritize impact.** Work on high-impact projects first, looking for quick wins within the projects. "Perfect is the enemy of good," he always tells us. When you work with high-powered analytical talent, there is a natural tendency to want to develop the perfect algorithm or the most robust solution (because it's fun for them). Jeremy pushes us to find a good balance between accuracy and time to value. Getting something in the hands of decision makers that drives some value in the short term is better than waiting around for the most robust solution. There's always a roadmap after the first deliverable to continue to refine the model.

- **Cultivate an executive sponsor.** Some of Jeremy's early managers grew with the company and took him, and the analytics, with them, so to speak. They understood the value, and were willing to advocate for investment, but, of course, he had to deliver.

- **Demonstrate excellence.** The team had to deliver high-quality, impactful work to gain a reputation of having the answers. This helps to build our reputation as trusted advisors.

- **Understand the business.** We have a group of engagement managers that act as integration points with our clients. They are experts in a client's business, and they can translate those business requirements back to the analytical teams. They also act as consultants and trusted advisors through the implementation and afterward. Not that the data scientists, analysts, and developers wouldn't also have to know the business, but it is very helpful to both credibility and execution to have designated business experts in our team.

- **Network and communicate.** Jeremy spends much of his time these days speaking with the senior leadership team across the lines of business, and he encourages his entire team to keep lines of communication open. He is always talking about the projects we've delivered on and hunting for new opportunities to add value.

"I have been very fortunate to work for and with some brilliant analytical people, and I've learned from every one of them. We have been successful because we have created a culture of curiosity and creativity combined with humility. In order to deliver successful solutions, you need your clients to invest their most important resource, their time, in you. They'll do this because they want to work with you, not because you're the smartest person in the room," says Jeremy.

ORGANIZING YOUR ANALYTICS DEPARTMENT

You should start having conversations early on about how you plan to organize your analytical resources. As important, probably more so actually, as the data foundation and the tools they will use to do their jobs are the resources you bring on board. Their ability to be effective in executing on the strategy is somewhat dependent on the organizational structure you choose for the analytics group.

There are six different organizational model options for analytics teams.[3] Each option has strengths and weaknesses and may be better suited for particular kinds of organizations or stages of maturity. The structure you decide on is going to be up to your organization's goals and strategy, and it will probably evolve over time.

Decentralized Analytics

In this model, analyst groups are associated with business units and corporate functions. There is no corporate reporting or consolidated structure for analytics. For hotels and casinos, this might mean analytic capabilities at each property, within the brands, and within the functional areas at corporate (marketing, finance, revenue management). The hotel analysts have no corporate support, and the analytics functions within the lines of business at corporate are independent of each other as well.

- **Advantages.** Analysts are close to the business, so they can be very responsive. They are also likely to learn the nuances of the business very quickly.

- **Disadvantages.** It is difficult to set analytics priorities across the organization. It is also difficult to develop staff, and take advantage of specialized skills sets across the organization. There is almost always a lack of communication between analytics groups in this model.

- **Best fit.** This type of organization is best fit for a diversified corporation where the multiple businesses have very little in common. Reading between the lines, it's probably not the best option for a hotel or casino company, although many are set up this way currently due to organic or grassroots growth.

The decentralized model is highly siloed, and is frequently the product of a grassroots effort to get analytics off the ground. Analysts can feel isolated, and it is difficult to share innovative solutions or even best practices across the organization. Many hotel and casino companies may start here, but probably should evolve from this.

Centralized Analytics

In this model, analysts are all part of one corporate organization. They may be assigned to business units or functional areas, but they report to the corporate unit, and the corporate unit sets strategy and priorities.

- **Advantages.** It is easy to invest in specialized resources because they can be deployed for key projects across the organization. Supporting high priority projects is also facilitated in this model, as it is easy to reprioritize and deploy analysts wherever they are needed. Analysts can build a community and gain new skills. It is generally easier to recruit talent, because there is a demonstrated corporate commitment and an established community to join.

- **Disadvantages.** Distance can be created between analysts and the business problems if the analysts are all located at corporate.

- **Best fit.** It is easiest to deploy this model if there is already an organizational precedent for shared services at corporate. If there isn't an existing awareness of the value of analytics, and the benefits of working with this group, the group may not have enough "work" from the field to sustain operations. Further, it may be difficult to work with lines of business who feel as though analytics are being "done to them" instead of controlled by them.

This structure is best deployed when there is executive support and an existing pipeline of analytics projects. If you plan to reorganize into a centralized model by pulling together the pockets of established advanced analytics capabilities from across the organization, you can expect some disruption as the analysts settle into these new roles. Extra effort will need to be made to keep lines of communication open between the centralized analysts and the business. In addition, since they are not embedded in the business, analysts will need to put extra focus on learning the business and staying close to major issues as they arise.

Functional Analytics

In this model, there is one major analytics group in the organization that reports into a business function that is the primary consumer of analytics. This unit may also act as consultants for the rest of the organization. In hotels, the revenue management function may behave this way today. For casinos, it could be the casino marketing group.

- **Advantages.** Analytics are deployed against key business initiatives, and the analysts stay really close to the business, so they can be highly responsive and build local knowledge. However, they are also available to support projects in other areas as they arise.

- **Disadvantages.** Opportunities to apply analytics in other functional areas may be missed with this laser focus on one functional area.

- **Best fit.** For organizations that are just starting on their analytics journey, this model could be good. It provides focused attention on high-valued business initiatives, but there's some flexibility to solve other problems. Additional focused groups could be added as new projects are identified, or the group could be redeployed.

In this model the functional home for the analyst groups could migrate over time, as projects are completed or organizational priorities change. Still, the singular focus is liable to cause the organization to miss out on broader opportunities to gain advantage from analytics.

Consulting Analytics

Analysts work for a central organization, and business units "hire" analysts to work on their projects. This is a bit different than the centralized version because here the analytical priorities are set by the lines of business as opposed to centrally.

- **Advantages.** Key analytic resources are positioned to solve problems across the organization. The right fit skill sets can be deployed against key projects. Analysts who are deployed to lines of business can build close relationships with decision makers.
- **Disadvantages.** If enterprise focus and prioritization activities are weak, analysts may not be deployed on the projects that deliver the most value, but instead become focused on the projects for whatever line of business executives yell the loudest.
- **Best fit.** The analytics organization must understand the value of the work provided, and be able to set priorities. It will be crucial to market and sell to internal clients to keep building the project pipeline.

Analysts in this model need to be able to effectively educate and advise their business partners about how to utilize analytics, and need to build sustainable solutions. As the projects demonstrate value, the organization needs to be prepared to prioritize future work, which will be difficult without a corporate entity to serve as an arbitrator.

Federated Analytics

This model is a collection of decentralized analytics groups that report to business units, but have formal ways to collaborate. This could be a steering committee or a chartered enterprise governance committee, but there is an organization that ties the groups together.

- **Advantages.** This model has an immediate enterprise view, with coordination on priorities, initiatives, resource deployment, and analyst development.
- **Disadvantages.** Committees may lack clout in the organization. It could be difficult to establish standards, set priorities, and share resources for corporate analytics initiatives.
- **Best fit.** This model works well in large and complex organizations where business units share some, but not all, things in common.

This model could work well in hotels, particularly at corporate, where there are some common elements across functions (guests, channels, properties). If there are already decentralized analytics groups, a federated model could be a good method for bringing these groups together for some measure of coordination and collaboration.

Analytics Center of Excellence

Decentralized analyst groups are embedded in lines of business, but are also members of a central coordinating structure that builds a community of analysts at the enterprise level.

- **Advantages.** This structure builds a community of analysts that can share experiences and best practices, and creates opportunities for learning and development.
- **Disadvantages.** This is a less formal arrangement than the federated model, so this group, while good for best practice sharing, rarely has the power to assess corporate analytics needs, prioritize projects, and manage analyst career paths.
- **Best fit.** Organizations can adopt this model as a first step on the path toward a centralized, consulting, or federated model. It is useful for organizations that want to promote community learning and development, but don't yet have a mandate for any corporate level initiatives.

There needs to be clear value to the participants in this model, since the reporting lines are not formalized. Businesses need to decide how much control or responsibility the center of excellence has over development paths or project priorities.

The main differences among these six options are who controls the priorities, the lines of business or corporate, and how formal the arrangement at the corporate level is. As I alluded to, some of these organizational styles are on an evolutionary path as organizations grow in their analytic capabilities, investment, and maturity. It is reasonable to expect that an organization would try out several options before deciding on the one that fits.

CASE STUDY

CASE STUDY: ORGANIZING ANALYTICS, DAVE ROBERTS, MARRIOTT INTERNATIONAL

I had a chance to catch up with Dave Roberts, Senior Vice President of Revenue Management and Revenue Analysis for Marriott International. Marriott is well known for being a leader in analytics in the hospitality industry. They were the first to publically adopt revenue management, following the model that Bob Crandall started at American Airlines, and they have become quite advanced in applying analytics to other functional areas, like marketing, as well. As with most organizations, analytics grew up at Marriott in the various functional areas across the organization. Though most disciplines involve some analytics (for example, finance, operations, and many more), Marriott has consolidated top-line analytics into two departments—one focused on the customer experience, and the other focused on revenue performance of the hotels.

I was curious to understand the drivers of this decision and what advantages and disadvantages Marriott has found as they consolidated analytics. Dave's view is that there are significant advantages to consolidating analytics, including:

- **Opportunities for learning and development.** As Dave pointed out, a centralized analytics team allows analysts to both challenge and help each other. Though their projects may be different, they can share data sources/nuances, techniques, software, and problem-solving approaches. With proximity and day-to-day contact, it is easy to collaborate and learn from one another.

- **Diversity of skills.** A centralized analytics team can bring in a wider variety of skill sets and backgrounds than any individual department could on its own. This specialized expertise can be easily shared across functional areas.

- **Staffing efficiencies.** As Dave told me, "If a particular department has only two analysts, and one leaves, this creates a staffing challenge. If the analytics organization is centralized, we can more easily cover for these gaps while we are attempting to hire a replacement."

- **Project efficiencies.** A centralized group is better able to leverage project efficiencies as well. As Dave explained,

(*continued*)

(continued)

an analyst might be trying to evaluate the effectiveness of a promotion from marketing, and it could take five days to source the data, formulate the problem, do the analysis, get feedback, and make adjustments before delivering the final product. If we then want to analyze the effectiveness of a banner ad, the project timeline for this shrinks significantly because the analyst is already comfortable with the data sources and analysis approach. This also leads to comparable assessments across multiple functional areas.

I figured there must have been a downside. In fact, Dave said that the functional areas can be, rightly, concerned about losing control over the prioritization of projects. Once analytics become centralized, different disciplines may need to compete for analytics resources. Marriott addresses this by ensuring that analysts are primarily dedicated to certain functional areas, like sales, marketing, revenue management, or digital. The analysts could be leveraged for any project, but as soon as a request comes in from their area, they prioritize that request. This also helps to ensure that analysts build up business knowledge over time, which makes them more effective at delivering results that can be immediately consumed by their stakeholders.

If set up and executed properly, a centralized analytics team is a clear benefit to individual stakeholders. As analytics advance within an organization, it becomes important that the leaders of those analysts are experts at managing analytics and analytical resources. Not that a sales leader or a marketing leader couldn't necessarily manage the analysts in their organizations, but there is a point where guidance and development from someone who specializes in analytics is much more effective in moving the organization forward and achieving meaningful results. In fact, Dave believes (as do I) that a centralized organization with a strong leader is essential to attracting and retaining analytics talent today.

"With the high demand in the market today, data scientists, analysts, statisticians, and anyone who is passionate about analytics will go where they have support, development opportunities, and a strong organizational commitment to analytics. It is absolutely essential to attract the right talent," he told me.

This, of course, brought up the issue of what talent an organization should look for as they build their analytics department. Dave had an interesting perspective. He told me that while obviously quantitative/mathematical skills are important, what he feels is even more essential is someone who is just plain passionate about analytics. He said that anyone can learn software and data manipulation, as long as they love analytics. "Generally I can tell within about 60 seconds of an interview if that passion is there. If I ask them about the business analysis they did for their last project and I can see them getting excited about it, I know they have the kind of passion they need to be successful. This is even more important than any specific educational background, in my opinion."

The other key skill to look for, in Dave's opinion, is the ability to formulate a problem, to translate the business need into an analytical model. The math can sometimes be hard, he readily acknowledges, but the constraint most of the time is not in doing the math, it's in properly defining and constructing the problem such that it provides a useful result. It takes a special skill to ensure that the business need is well understood, the data is in the right format and level of detail, the model construction suits the question being asked, and the outcome measures are clearly defined. And, as the revenue manager in Dave pointed out, you have to figure out how to eventually make some money from this analysis.

Dave said, "There are several great statistical software packages out there that can crunch through the math. You can even hire consultants or vendors to write the code and execute the models, if you want. But you need your analysts to be able to frame and formulate the problem—otherwise even the best modeling in the world won't help you."

Finally, I asked Dave about building an analytics culture in an organization. Of course, Marriott has been at this for a while, so the value of analytics is well established through many departments in the organization. Dave emphasized the importance of close collaboration with stakeholders. "If a stakeholder doesn't understand the analytics on a particular project of theirs, that's on me, and on the whole team. Similarly, if an analyst doesn't understand the business context of a problem, they need to spend more time with the stakeholder. Communication is key, and is, unfortunately, often the Achilles' heel in analytics. One of

(continued)

(continued)

Dave's favorite quotes is from George Bernard Shaw: "The single biggest problem in communication is the illusion that it has taken place."

Dave's admittedly biased view is that you can't do much in the business world without sound analytics. He believes organizations should think in terms of a series of controlled experiments. He is a firm believer in the importance of test and learn, the A/B testing that we talked about in previous chapters. He believes that no one in the organization should be launching anything significant, from an email campaign to a lobby redesign, without thinking about test and control experiments. He also said that it's the analytics function's role to make sure the entire organization is "fluent in A/B testing."

It can be very helpful at times to work with outside partners that can help you with analytics, data management, advanced modeling, or controlled experiments. But note Dave's advice to hoteliers: "Don't outsource your thinking! The business problem definition, and the decision making that should result from analytics, must be owned internally." I couldn't agree more!

THE BUILD VERSUS BUY DECISION

As you are thinking through the decision about how to organize your analytics function, it's also important to think about your technology strategy. In Chapter 2, I defined various types of technology deployment options, including the option to create technology solutions in house. This decision about whether to build technology systems or buy them is a struggle for most companies, particularly when it comes to analytical solutions. It's one I struggle with myself. Until now, I have always worked for technology vendors, and I became biased toward thinking that hospitality and gaming companies should outsource as much of their technology footprint as possible, to allow them to laser focus on doing what they are best at, delivering excellent service (profitably).

This attitude, let's say, *evolved* during my time at SAS and certainly since I took my current position at Wyndham Destination Network. There are some clear competitive advantages to building an analytics solution internally that is purpose fit to your specific problem and your organizational goals and strategies. When it comes to data and analytics, it is really difficult for one size to fit all. Revenue management system vendors struggled with this for years, and still do. Revenue management systems, when they were first introduced, were really good at the full-service hotel problem. Extending these solutions "as is" to limited service (which tends to have much more need for price optimization), extended stay (a different forecasting problem), or all inclusive (a different way to think about room rate) was a difficult fit, let alone trying to retrofit the hotel solution to a related problem, like cruise lines or show tickets. The question becomes: Are organizations that have a different flavor of the problem better off starting from scratch with internal resources and technology, trying to fit their problem to the available vendor-built solutions, or working with consultants to build and deploy custom solutions?

A build decision requires organizational commitment to invest in the right resources and the right technology platforms. This takes time and a budget. Many of the larger hospitality and gaming companies took this on by necessity in the early days, particularly in the area of pricing and revenue management, when there was nothing suitable in the marketplace. Some have since decided to work with vendors. Others, like my team at Wyndham Destination Network, continue with internal development for all analytics projects. For us, it was out of necessity. The vacation rental and time share exchange businesses are very different from any of the traditional pricing problems, so there were no commercially available pricing solutions. After building up analytical capabilities internally to deliver pricing solutions, it seemed natural to use the team to tackle other problems, even those where there might be an existing commercial solution. We now have the resources and mandate to continue our own development, so we can take advantage of the ability to customize every analysis and system to our own unique operating environment. In most cases, the ability to design the solution specifically for our unique problem provides us with better results than we may have gotten from a commercially available solution. Where it might not, we at least have a cost savings, because we use technology and resources we already own.

The team, and the technology investment to support us, did not happen overnight. Over time, the organization, as my boss describes in the story in this chapter, saw the value of continuing the investment, and now considers our analytical capabilities a core competitive advantage and a key part of our strategic platform. (A bit jealous of me, aren't you? Well, you should be!)

If the organization doesn't have the resources or commitment to build, buying has its advantages too. The development and implementation cycles should be shorter, so you can start seeing benefits sooner. The vendor is responsible for upgrades, support, enhancements, and, particularly if you are deploying a cloud-based solution, service level agreements. Vendors can help with training and change management. There are best practices associated with these solutions, and some won't require you to invest in expensive specialized analytical resources (right away). Since most analytical solutions are designed for decision support, even if you are using a commercially available solution, the business processes around how you configure the solution, and most important, interpret and use the analytical results, can differentiate you from the competition.

There is a hybrid option, of course, and that is to acquire the building blocks and work with a consultancy to build out the solution. This has the advantage of being able to acquire a custom-built solution without a payroll commitment. Presumably, you can hire a consultancy with experience where it might be difficult to find and afford the right skill set for internal development. Projects with consultants can have scope creep, and can be expensive. You do not control the resources, so the staffing on the project may evolve, and you may lose some experience and expertise. A third party may never know your business as well as you do, and over time, the momentum of the project and quality of the solutions could decline.

System selection and strategic technology investments are among the most crucial decisions in an analytics roadmap. It can be challenging to evaluate whether the tool or solution will fit in your business process, or even whether it functions as advertised. The investment in time and money in systems is generally considerable, and it is easy for projects to grow in scope, miss milestones, and lose momentum. The technology might work great on its own, but not really fit within your existing technology environment, causing integration problems. Be sure you have a stringent process for evaluating technology investments. For some major technology acquisition projects, it is probably worth it to work with an external consultant that has experience with system selection and systems integration. Of course, you have to take as much care in selecting that partner as you would in selecting the technology, but this decision is perhaps less complicated. I could write an entire book on the nuances associated with requirements gathering, system selection, and system integration. I'm nearly done with this book. Perhaps I will do that next.

INTEGRATED DECISION MAKING

Regardless of how you have decided to organize the analytics resources, and what technology projects you take on, there is significant benefit in breaking down silos and synchronizing decision making, from the property level up through the brands and corporate.

Half of this book is about how individual functional areas within the hotel or casino can best apply analytics to their business problems. Every hospitality or gaming company needs to start somewhere, but it is easy to lose site of the bigger picture as you are bringing individual functional areas up to analytical competency and analytical decision making. There are significant advantages to departments sharing data and results, and collaborating for more holistic decision making. In fact, in today's complex digital environment, lines between disciplines are blurring, so working together is becoming a necessity rather than a luxury. Think about the personalization initiatives that many companies are planning for as of the publication of this book. It is a good example of how digital is blurring lines and corporate initiatives are beginning to span functional responsibilities.

Personalization Blurs the Lines between Functions

Figure 11.1 shows a typical guest journey from search to book, through the experience, and then into the post-stay. Every interaction with

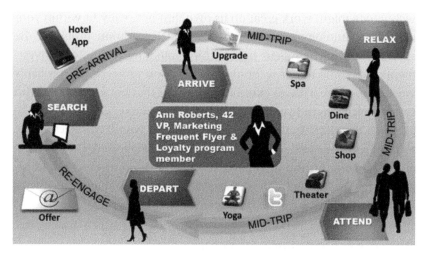

Figure 11.1 Typical Guest Journey

the hotel, either through technology or a live person, is an opportunity to collect data about this guest and potentially provide some intervention that will cause them to take an action that benefits the hotel. This is a complex technology, data, and analytics picture, but it's also more than that.

If you think about it, marketing owns the pre- and post-interaction with the guest. They control the messaging and branding on the website, the brand promise, and the communication style and cadence. They plan interactions through social channels, emails, and the app. However, once the guest arrives on site, operations takes over in delivering on the service promise. The entire operation needs to be lined up not only to execute on the service promise, profitably, but also to collect the data that can be used to continue to foster a longer term relationship with that guest. If revenue management hasn't properly priced the rooms and other ancillary services, as well as fostered a revenue culture throughout the hotel, then profitability will also suffer (Figure 11.2). Each area has a crucial part to play if this initiative is to be successful.

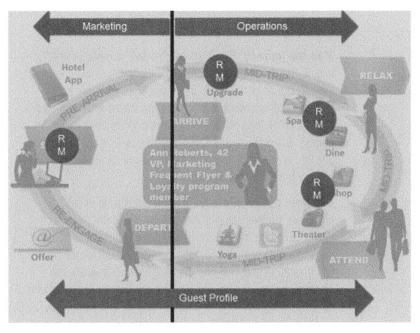

Figure 11.2 Everyone Has a Role in Personalization

CASE STUDY: ANALYTICS AND THE CUSTOMER JOURNEY, ANALISE POLSKY, SAS BEST PRACTICES

Do you want to send out more timely, relevant offers to guests while they are browsing online or at your property? What if you could reduce the average purchase time from four minutes to two by using your mobile app?

If you want answers to these questions or others, then it's time to consider the guest journey.

The journey—in its simplest form—is the set of interactions a guest has with you as they embark on a business transaction with your company. A journey can take place across multiple channels and lines of business. When you understand the journey, you strengthen guest satisfaction and improve the guest experience. Here are seven best practices to get you started:

(continued)

(continued)

1. **Map the journey.** Pick just one objective or initiative and map it. Be sure to account for the duration of the interaction, the expectation of the guest, the touchpoints—in person or online—and systems and processes associated with each step of the journey. Also note where guests might get stuck (friction points). The exercise of journey mapping may involve more than one line of business. It can be a great way to stimulate conversations and identify duplicated efforts.

2. **Cultivate guest intimacy.** Invest in knowledge of guest behaviors, preferences, and intent. Armed with this behavioral data, you can create smaller, more refined segments and have more relevant conversations with guests. Account for the depth and breadth of guest actions. Clicking an advertisement is a discrete, measurable activity. Reading email and interacting with advertisements between the hours of 12 p.m. and 1 p.m. (say, lunchtime) adds insight that will further shape understanding of the guest.

3. **Contextualize the data.** Circumstance shapes individual behaviors and actions. Have you considered what factors truly influence your guests the most? What moments or activities act as pivot points in the journey? This is what I call the "widen to reveal" part of the guest journey. Is that person running because they love fitness or because they are outrunning a bull in Pamplona? If we look at running in isolation, we miss the bigger picture.

4. **Mind your metrics.** Journey mapping may reveal natural congruencies between departments that were once disparate. Which individual metrics need to be in place? Which can be shared? For instance, who should get credit for new guest bookings or a group that came in through an online channel? Sales? Marketing? The call center? Or all of the above?

5. **Think analytically.** New tools allow you to optimize the journey and further evolve the guest experience. The key is anticipation and responsiveness. Knowing there is an opportunity to interact

with the guest is different from having the means and speed to do it. Some call centers have used analytics to decrease response time to complaints from weeks to 24 hours.

6. **Implement standards of behavior.** The guest experience is incomplete without a set of standards and principles that serve as a social contract between you and the guest. What do you do to protect guest data? Just how transparent are your data policies? The same protections and standards apply to the business as well. Employees must embody the value of the business and know how to tactically ensure they can protect guest data.

7. **Tell a story.** Ultimately you decide how information should be expressed back to your internal constituents and guests. Weave the threads of data together in a meaningful way that reflects the guest beyond his or her purchase experience.

So much of the stay experience is based on how guests feel they are being treated. You don't need to know everything, but the more information you have, the better your guest interaction and outreach will be.

Aside from massive, cross-departmental initiatives like personalization, there are advantages to working more closely together on day-to-day activities as well. The first step toward figuring out which decisions will be improved by collaboration is to simply start talking to each other. Sit down and talk about your responsibilities and goals, and share and explain your data and the kinds of analyses you tend to create. This is highly manual, but it can easily come before any organizational changes or incentive realignment (although those issues will likely need to be addressed at some point). In the next section, I will provide some examples of how departments can benefit from data and analytics that are under the provenance of other departments. I also describe the benefits of a phased approach.

Marketing and Revenue Management

The industry has been talking for years about the benefits of integrating the data and analytics from revenue management and marketing.

Revenue management holds key information about demand patterns, and knows when demand is needed or when inventory needs to be protected for the highest-paying demand. Marketing can use this information to improve the placement, segmentation, and timing of promotional activity. Marketing can also provide information about these promotions, including discount levels and expected lift, so that revenue management can incorporate that demand into their forecasts and ensure that they are not restricting rates and availability for this incentivized demand.

As is already happening in casinos, hotel revenue management could benefit from understanding customer lifetime value, and potentially favoring the most valuable guests in the revenue management decision. This is tricky, of course, because guests could react badly to any perceived inequity in the distribution of prices. Hotels will have to think carefully about how to deploy customer lifetime value-based pricing.

I have written extensively on this particular topic, as I think it is really important in today's digital environment. I dedicated an entire chapter to it in *Hotel Pricing in a Social World* (that's my first book, if I haven't mentioned that before), and I provide some references at the end of this chapter where you can get some additional information.

Operations and Revenue Management

Operations needs to understand revenue management's demand and revenue generations plans so they can set up their systems to properly handle the opportunities. As a simple example, if revenue management is planning a program to sell upgrades at the front desk, obviously the agents need to be well trained. Housekeeping also needs to know. Housekeeping prioritizes cleaning rooms that are going to be occupied that night. If they don't know that some of the upgraded eligible rooms might be occupied, they will save them until last. This means that front desk would not be able to sell the room upgrades, because there are no clean rooms to check the guests into.

Revenue management should lead the charge in building a revenue culture throughout the hotel. To make that cultural shift successful, operations needs to share their experience and the data from other revenue-generating assets across the property, to help revenue management work with them to identify further opportunities to generate incremental revenue and profits from the asset. With the whole organization working together to identify and exploit revenue opportunities, the enterprise moves closer to the vision of total hotel revenue management.

Operations could benefit from revenue management forecasts, particularly if revenue management is doing arrivals or occupancy forecasting. Operations could use that information for everything from scheduling housekeeping and the front desk to supply ordering. Operations can also assist in building attractive packages by providing demand and profitability information about restaurants, spa, retail, and golf. Revenue management can ensure that they are creating incremental demand for these outlets instead of blocking full-paying demand during peak periods (for example, understanding that discounted spa packages should be offered only on weekdays because the spa is busy serving local demand on weekends).

Marketing, Operations, and Gaming Floor

Most casino floor operations are supported by a casino marketing department, so the integration is, relatively speaking, already in place. However, there isn't always a tight integration between casino marketing and the rest of the operations teams. Casino marketing leverages all of the assets in the casino to drive business, but if they do that without involving the operational managers, they could overload the outlets, displace higher-paying business, or send out offers that there isn't capacity to redeem. Good lines of communications between casino marketing and operations will help ensure that the operations are prepared for any promotional activity, or that casino marketing doesn't overincentivize patrons who end up not being able to be accommodated.

Gaming floor managers can also work with casino marketing to help them understand the popularity and profitability of games, and flow of business through the casino floor and to particular types of games. For example, if the table games are generally busy in the evenings, a daytime table game promotion would be a better way to generate incremental revenue. Casino marketing should keep gaming floor managers up to date on the preferences of high rollers, so sufficient capacity is available for the best players. Much of this sounds obvious, but since so much of the data collection and aggregation in hospitality and gaming is manual, and operations can move so quickly, it can be difficult to find a platform or cadence for sharing information.

Performance Analysis: A Centralized View

Since performance analysis tends to pull together results from across the organization, good relationships and good understanding of business processes are required to effectively interpret results. As the case study from Dexter Wood in Chapter 2 illustrates, pulling together a cross-functional team that is responsible for defining key metrics and important data fields is a crucial first step toward ensuring that cross-functional performance discussions at the executive level focus on strategy and not arguments over where the numbers came from.

Building strategy also involves understanding what levers need to be pulled to drive desired results. Early access to sales information, such as pace of group bookings or status of corporate contracts, will help the hospitality or gaming company foresee any upcoming soft spots where a different strategy might be required. Visibility into marketing initiatives, including guest loyalty programs or campaign strategies, will provide insight into incentivized demand patterns that could improve performance across certain markets or sectors, or could explain past performance. The point is that senior leadership doesn't just need to know the "what" to make the right decision, they need to know the "why." Access to data and, more important, expertise from all the functional areas across the enterprise provides this crucial insight, which can help to justify past performance and set strategy to move forward.

Phased Approach

Our industry is at a crucial inflection point where analytical talent must keep pace with technology (and vice versa) to be successful.

—Jess Petitt, Vice President, Global Business Analytics,
Hilton Worldwide

The journey toward integrated, cross-departmental decision making won't happen in a single step. You are likely just beginning to instill an analytical mindset in many departments, and are uncovering opportunities within those departments for the first time. It is a lot to ask to suddenly require collaboration with other groups. I strongly suggest the phased approach to integrating departmental data and analytics that I introduced in Chapter 1 and explain in more detail next and in Figure 11.3.

- **Establish.** In the establish phase, the enabling technologies for analytical automation are introduced department by department. Users become accustomed to incorporating system results into their decision making. As the analytical culture grows in these departments, the enterprise begins to prepare for the organizational and cultural changes required for more holistic and synchronized decision making. This could mean changing incentive plans or reporting structures. It could also mean questioning business processes or improving data collection mechanisms. Or, it could simply mean introducing analysts and managers from different departments to each other and starting a regular series of meetings.

- **Integrate.** The integration phase is about manual information sharing. This is probably the phase where the cross-departmental team responsible for data governance is taking a strong role in ensuring a clean, credible, and unified version of the truth in the database. Departments begin to manually incorporate one another's data into decision making. For example, revenue management might share a report detailing demand patterns with marketing, so that marketing can schedule promotions when they are needed. The integration phase is crucial because this is where the understanding and trust in the data is built.

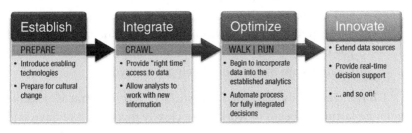

Figure 11.3 Phased Approach

Users become comfortable with how their decision making will change with access to new data. They understand how the level of detail and formatting of the data might need to change for it to be usable by other groups. New fields or expanded definitions might be added to existing data sources to make them more generally useful. A good deal of institutional knowledge is gained at this stage, which cannot be replicated elsewhere. Any investment in time here will pay off later.

- **Optimize.** The optimize phase is where cross-departmental data sources are included in the automated systems, changing analytical results. For example, promotional lift could be automatically incorporated into the revenue management system, so that forecasts are adjusted based on incentivized demand. Because the organization spent time in the integration phase understanding how promotional lift is calculated, and potentially manually adjusting the forecast accordingly, users are comfortable with the impacts of the new information. It is possible that some data will not be valuable or some departments will not need to incorporate these external data sources into their automated processes. There are certain types of data better shared outside of an analytical system. However, where it makes sense, decisions should be automated to save users time and effort in manual adjustments.

- **Innovate.** After routine decisions are automated and users are operating on a single source of the truth for synchronized decision making, it is time to think about innovation. Organizations can think about new data sources to incorporate, or new initiatives like real-time decisioning or location-based marketing, which requires different access to data and analytics. The innovation phase might bring the organization right back to the establish phase if new technologies or new departments need to get involved, but with an established process like this, the innovations are much more likely to succeed.

I have really only scratched the surface here of what is possible when departments begin to work more closely together. As I have said repeatedly, the digital economy is blurring lines between functions.

Hospitality and gaming organizations must now look at their businesses more holistically, or they will miss out on huge revenue opportunities. Data and technology can be the glue that binds departments together, but there will also be organizational and cultural changes required to achieve the vision of integrated decision making. However, as I always tell analytic hospitality executives, there's no time to wait around for the technology or the organizational changes. Now is the time to start opening lines of communication and understanding where there are opportunities to drive profits through collaboration.

CONCLUSION

Tom Davenport and Jeanne Harris suggest in their book *Competing on Analytics,* that organizations should strive to develop "analytic capabilities that are hard to duplicate, unique, adaptable to many situations, better than the competition, and renewable."[4] This is a tall order, particularly in industries as traditionally oriented to operating on the best instincts of experienced (or maybe not so experienced) managers, such as hospitality and gaming. However, the operating environments for hotels and casinos have become so complex and so competitive that it is nearly impossible to operate without analytics. Uncertain economic conditions, increased competition from nontraditional lodging and alternative entertainment options, merger and acquisition activity, mobile and social technology changes, rising costs of distribution, changing consumer behavior, digital innovation, and increasing volumes of complex data—all of these elements contribute to an environment that is more dynamic, more volatile, and harder to interpret than ever before.

I hope that this book has given you some inspiration about how to get started or where to look next. Data analytics can be an intimidating concept, and the field is evolving quickly. My intention for this book is to increase your comfort level with key points and important decisions, so that you can begin to have conversations with analysts, vendors, and consultants about the right solutions for your organization that fit with your strategy. I will leave you with a few pieces of advice to think about as you plan your analytics journey. These are a set of things that I believe the industry needs to stop doing, start doing, and do more of in order to survive and thrive in this complex environment. I believe that if you follow this advice, not just in your analytic efforts but across your management responsibilities, the way forward will become clearer!

Stop:

- **Acting in silos.** As I allude to in this chapter, it's time to break down the silos in hotels and casinos. Departmental barriers and conflicting incentives are holding us back. Hotels and casinos must start synchronizing decision making across marketing, revenue management, finance, development, and operations, and need to be supported by a collaborative and business-focused IT organization. Some companies have moved in this direction by consolidating some or all commercial functions under one leader, for example. Organizational changes will go a long way to facilitating more coordination. Beyond consolidating related functions under strong leaders, however, we must foster cross-departmental decision making and reward decisions that holistically benefit the organization.

- **Relying on gut instinct.** I guess you could say that the entire book is about this point. I hope I have convinced you. Data and analytic systems have become more accessible. There is no longer any excuse to rely strictly on guesswork or gut instinct. Hospitality executives need to foster a culture of fact-based decision making, or risk falling behind. I am not suggesting that a revenue management system or a data-mining platform can replace an experienced revenue manager or marketer. In fact, it's quite the opposite. The systems are there to provide decision support, but the manager needs to make the decisions through the lens of their experience and business acumen, based on what the data tells them. I've been encouraged to see more hospitality organizations investing in data and analytics systems and people over the last few years. This must continue.

Start:

- **Preparing for the future.** This business isn't getting any easier. Consumer behavior is changing rapidly, as alternatives for research and booking flood the market. Technology continues to evolve, creating more data sources and more operational complexity. Recent hotel company acquisitions will change the competitive landscape. It is up to each of you to prepare yourselves and your organizations for this change. You need to stay updated in the latest trends in technology and consumer behavior. You need to learn how to evaluate a technology investment from a business perspective, and communicate those needs clearly with the IT organizations that support you. You are taking a great first step by reading this book. Attend conferences (some outside of the industry), read articles, look at software demos, ask for proof from vendors and consultants, and interface with your peers. Most important, however, is to keep asking questions. Don't take anything at face value. With all the noise out there, it is up to you to cut through the hype and determine what will be most effective in moving you and your organization forward.

■ **Becoming more prescriptive.** As I described in the first chapter, with more and different data available and as the influences on our business grow and change, it's not enough to be able to predict what will happen, you must be able to prescribe solutions to achieve desired outcomes. It's great that your revenue management system can tell you that you will get to 90% occupancy next month, but what if business goals require you to be at 95%? In the current climate it can no longer be about knowing what will happen, it's about knowing what to do about it. A prescriptive manager can synthesize a wide variety of inputs, read the market, and work with other departments. Start asking the questions "So what?" and "What do you plan to do about it?" of your managers and analysts now. This is useful during any economic climate, but think about how powerful it will be if you were already practiced at this kind of business decision making as we move into the (seemingly) inevitable next downturn.

Do more:

■ **Automating.** Another major theme of this book is that we can't afford to waste our talented resources and time wading through reams of data to produce a routine analysis or report. There is simply no reason anymore for analysts to spend large portions of their time on data gathering and cleansing, or for managers to have to wait days to access operating reports. These routine analyses should be automated through business intelligence and analytic applications. You should have an automated revenue management system, a reputation management system, a business intelligence application, and an automated marketing execution system, so that the organization can focus on interpretation and prescriptive decision making. When analysts and IT are not stuck on routine tasks, they have more time for more strategic or ad hoc analyses.

- **Strategic thinking.** It is easy to get caught up in the day to day and not leave enough time to look forward. You should know where you want your organization to be 3, 5, or 10 years in the future, and make a plan to get there. Follow trends and understand impacts. While you are at it, think about your own career. Where do you want to be five years from now, and what will it take to get there?

One of my favorite analytic hospitality executives always reminds me about "unintended consequences," the ones that are hard to see coming, so they take us by surprise.[5] In a complex environment like hospitality and gaming, it's easy for an action to cause an unanticipated impact on the business. With a strong culture of fact-based decision making, you will be able to anticipate opportunities and hedge against risks–and hopefully avoid being taken by surprise. There will be challenges ahead. There always are. Arm yourself with the tools and the people who will give you the best chance to survive and thrive. I wish you the best in your journey to a strategic analytic culture!

ADDITIONAL RESOURCES

- The International Institute for Analytics (http://iianalytics.com) was founded in 2010 by Jack Philips and Thomas H. Davenport, as an independent research and advisory firm to work with organizations to build strong and competitive analytics programs. They provide unbiased advice with no influence from hardware or software vendors, consultants, or system integrators. If you are looking for help in getting started or sustaining a program, I suggest you look into this group.

▓ Tom Davenport, Jeanne Harris, and Robert Morrison, *Analytics at Work: Smarter Decisions, Better Results* (Boston: Harvard Business Review Press, 2002).

▓ Kelly McGuire, "Revenue Management—Optimal Decisions: Using Integrated Marketing and Revenue Management Analytics," *Hospitality Upgrade*, October 1, 2011, www.hospitalityupgrade.com/_magazine/magazine_Detail.asp?ID=682.

▓ Success story about the RCI Exchange Analytics, www.sas.com/en_us/customers/wyndham-exchange-and-rentals.html.

▓ Srinidhi Melkote, Dasong Cao, Preeti Modgil, Sneha Thakkar, and Ryan Connelly, "Optimizing Vacation Exchange" *Journal of Pricing and Revenue Management* 11(2012): 625–631, www.palgrave-journals.com/rpm/journal/v11/n6/full/rpm201236a.html.

▓ Kelly McGuire, "The Role of the Guest in Total Hotel Revenue Management, Hotel Executive," www.hotelexecutive.com/business_review/4466/the-role-of-the-guest-in-total-hotel-revenue-management.

NOTES

1. "Accurate Valuations, Forecasts Increase Revenue: Wyndham Exchange & Rentals Generates $11 Million in Incremental Revenue in First Year, SAS, www.sas.com/en_us/customers/wyndham-exchange-and-rentals.html.

2. Jeremy also believes in sharing success externally as much as possible, without giving away a competitive advantage, obviously. He believes that the more others hear our story, the more likely WDN is to attract not just new owners, but also top analytical talent. I can attest to the fact that these are challenging and interesting business problems. The tenure on my team is high because we keep finding new business problems for our data scientists and developers to solve, and we give them the resources they need to do it successfully.

3. "Six Models for Organizing Analytics Teams," International Institute of Analytics, 2016, http://iianalytics.com/analytics-resources/six-organizing-models-for-analytics-teams.

4. Tom Davenport and Jeanne Harris, *Competing on Analytics: The New Science of Winning* (Boston: Harvard Business School Publishing, 2007), pp. 48–49.

5. The concept of unintended consequences dates back to John Locke and Adam Smith, but it was popularized in the twentieth century by sociologist Robert K. Merton in his 1936 paper, "The Unanticipated Consequences of Purposive Social Action."

Case Study from Infor: Analytics Opportunities in Operations

Infor builds beautiful business applications with last-mile functionality and scientific insights for select industries, delivered as a cloud service. With 14,000 employees and customers in more than 200 countries and territories, Infor automates critical processes for industries including healthcare, manufacturing, fashion, wholesale distribution, hospitality, retail, and the public sector. Infor software helps eliminate the need for costly customization through embedded, deep-industry domain expertise.

▓ ▓ ▓

Bernard Ellis, Vice President of Industry Strategy for Infor, provided the following perspective on analytical opportunities in operations.

▓ ▓ ▓

Hotels have been practicing revenue optimization relatively effectively for the past decade or so, to the point where revenue-managing rooms has become a game of small incremental adjustments. Particularly recently, with rates at historic highs, there just isn't that much further to go in driving room revenue. Yet all of the revenue optimization expertise at hotels, and casinos, tends to be narrowly focused on managing room rate. It's time to switch to a broader enterprise-wide effort to move the needle on revenue and profits, what I call hospitality enterprise optimization.

This may sound very similar to total hotel revenue management or total hotel profit optimization, where revenue management techniques are also applied to all ancillary revenue sources, like spas, restaurants, and retail. This is important, of course, but hotels need to also be focused on the costs associated with bringing in that revenue. Hospitality enterprise optimization (EO) doesn't limit itself to the demand management side of the picture, though, but also examines the costs associated with delivering the experience that actually earns the revenue, which can sometimes be much greater. As its name would suggest, it has as its universe the entire hospitality enterprise. Any input, output, or business practice that can be made to yield a more optimal result by applying observation, science, and technology is fair game for EO.

In such a complex business, so many parts of a hospitality enterprise feature business practices and customs in which individual goals are not aligned with those of the broader organization and have a high probability of dragging down profit margins. If these goals and incentives are aligned, profit margins increase. Let's look at some examples of how EO can find more profit in unexpected places.

A valet parking manager is responsible for scheduling hundreds of hours of labor. When peak demand is not met, the valets are at the receiving end of the ire of angry guests who are getting to their functions late, missing their flights, or otherwise being severely inconvenienced. Because of this, despite full awareness of the impact on payroll costs, the valet manager will be conditioned to schedule to potential peak demand levels in order to avoid putting his staff, or himself, in this position.

An unbelievably high number of labor schedules are created based on very rudimentary business driver assumptions, whether the schedule is based on early forecasts of occupancy and expected arrivals and departures, or just because that's how you staff a Wednesday. The schedule in this example may have been made as much as a month in advance, and in the meantime, perhaps demand from a large group did not materialize as expected. If the business unit does not have the latest information about property-wide demand, they can only schedule to their intuition or self-protection.

Instead, through the prism of EO, updated rolling forecasts from revenue management would be distributed to all department heads, and, more importantly, the department heads would be told how to interpret them. Systems can be built with sophisticated business drivers to calculate how staffing levels should change based on changes to the revenue management forecast, but human insight still has a crucial role. For example, a human might know that the group picked up only 50% of its block because an emergency government legislative conference siphoned away drive-in attendees from the local region. The remaining attendees were almost exclusively fly-in, arriving by third-party shuttle, Uber, or taxi. The right answer was to reduce valet parking staff not by only the 50% that the group fell short, but actually by 75%, which would still run little risk of not meeting peak demand.

A bar manager who also works shifts could take the opposite view of our valet parking manager. By scheduling fewer bartenders than truly required, she will make more in tips by sharing the pool of customers with fewer colleagues. Service may be a little slow, but should be adequate enough for the food and beverage director not to notice. So, the bar manager and the rest of the staff have a great night for tips but service is mediocre, and beverage sales decrease because people were not offered refills quickly enough.

This is also a common way for profit to evaporate before it makes it to the bottom line. In this case, instead of having the bar manager create the schedule based on gut or self-interest, an EO perspective would have uncovered that the expected mix of business in-house that night typically correlates with very high sales of signature cocktails, with an average of 2.2 per person being sold. These are high-margin items, but they are laborious and time-consuming to prepare. With this business mix in-house, the bartender couldn't work at a fast enough pace. Guests may not have gotten to the point of being frustrated with service, but many would have purchased a second or third cocktail had they been offered. But they usually weren't, cutting the beverage sales for the night by *fully half*. Ironically, the bar manager is pleased with the tip jar contents as a percentage of sales, but glad she didn't have too many people with whom to share them. This disastrous result could have been avoided by just giving the bar manager a clearer picture of what kind of guests were expected, and, more importantly, what to expect from them and how she stood to benefit.

A hotel chef's signature dish is a Burgundy-braised short rib of beef, which is especially popular with older male business travelers visiting local firms. The food cost of the short rib varies greatly from week to week, and sometimes supplies are limited at practically any price. At times, the chef is forced to pull the dish altogether, much to the disappointment of regular guests. The hotel's main meat supplier offered the chef an opportunity to make an advance purchase of a large shipment of short rib, which he naturally took advantage of. Unfortunately, the usual crowd who loves the dish was participating in an emergency government legislative conference that week, and instead the hotel was forced to accept a price-sensitive children's sports group.

The chef was creative enough not to waste the short rib, but instead used it in lower-priced short rib sliders and quesadillas that were offered as specials for the sports group. There are many easy ways that food costs can turn out to be much higher than forecasted, even when there is no wasted product. In fact, there may be many cases where higher food cost is highly correlated to certain market segments, even when everything else is seemingly constant. Careful analysis will show that purchasing food in smaller lots on more of a just-in-time basis, even at higher prices, could drive significant gains in profitability. If an ingredient's availability and price are unpredictable, then relegate it to being an occasional special of the day only when conditions warrant. Otherwise, buy filet for the businessmen and ground chuck for the sports group.

The biggest barrier to hotels achieving this vision of EO is the simple fact that today it's rarely someone's job to pursue it. Service operations analysts may be doing their best to drive efficiencies, and revenue management and marketing may have carefully targeted the market mix that's expected, but each department's analysis tends to be limited to its own silo, driven by its own key performance indicators and incentives. As revenue managers continue to gain more trust in the automation of their routine forecasting and optimization tasks, they should have new time available to find new questions to answer and optimal results to find. This will be especially true if the distribution landscape in the post-parity world won't be so much about the endless goose chase of matching prices and mastering the shell game of constantly changing commission models, but rather about broader marketing reach and savvy, for which most hoteliers are more than willing to sacrifice margin.

Revenue managers shouldn't expect their revenue management system to provide all of the answers, but it should help to shed light on the questions. The forecasts it generates and regenerates on an ongoing basis should be dynamically shared with other departments via an enterprise performance management system that not only assesses past performance and defines future expectations, but helps the enterprise to constantly stay in alignment with changing demand levels. And the revenue management system is already gaining more and more assistance from the Internet of Things to supply the enterprise performance management system with dynamic data inputs for everything from water and power usage on a dishwasher to employee uniform laundering and replacement costs to the fuel consumption of each airport shuttle van in the fleet to precise time and attendance of service delivery personnel. There will be countless discoveries of opportunities to reduce costs, with little or no effect on guest service or employee morale, and they will often be property-specific. A flexible enterprise performance management system will allow future monitoring of those opportunities to be automated, allowing time for the next one to be discovered.

Case Study from IDeaS: Meetings and Events Revenue Management

Kate Keisling, Product Manager, New Business Development for IDeaS—A SAS Company, provided the following perspective on analytical opportunities in meetings and events.

▩ ▩ ▩

INTRODUCTION

Industry experts have been talking for years about optimizing function space. In rooms, we settled on a core set of metrics we all agree are the best tools for measuring success, and these are widely reported. Basic metrics like occupancy, revenue per available room (RevPAR), and average daily rate (ADR) are widely accepted across the hotel industry. Somehow, we haven't done the same with function space. These room metrics provide the base for so much of our decision making. Other sources of income, specifically food and beverage, can make up nearly equal portions of a hotel's revenue budget and are not represented in these metrics.

The other complicating factor is the sheer volume of data in areas like food and beverage. Without tools to manage the size and complexity of the data in food and beverage, many hoteliers make meeting and event decisions based primarily on rooms and topline revenue factors. While this can provide limited success, it doesn't provide the whole picture. Food and beverage can also represent one of the most significant cost areas in the budget. To get the most out of meetings and events business, sellers and managers need to understand profitability.

As you take steps to improve your results from meetings and events, you will likely find lots of areas that can be improved upon. The most important step is to create a vision for the end state you would like to see. That vision will equip you to assess your current state and determine what will contribute to that vision and what is getting in the way of achieving it. As you complete that assessment, the steps you should take toward achieving that vision will become clear. This plan may involve taking some simple steps to update processes and staff skills or it may involve creating some basic spreadsheet tools or even selecting a decision-support tool. Included here are some focus areas for your assessment where many hoteliers face challenges.

Function space is a bit like a jigsaw puzzle, both in reality and metaphorically. You have pieces for the various team members involved. Meetings and events business touches almost every department in the hotel and they all have a potential impact—some more than others.

Then there are the pieces that represent the systems that meetings and events business touches. These systems include the sales and catering system in which the business gets booked, all the way through the point of sale (POS) system where the banquet check for each event is created. Each system has unique data elements necessary to understand demand, revenue, and profit conditions.

And of course there's the fact that you don't have a single price for function space; there are lots of interdependent revenue streams involved. What impacts one revenue stream will likely impact another, sometimes in ways that might not be obvious without a little bit of data. You need to understand how they fit together to predict whether those impacts will combine together in a positive or negative result.

If you take a simple but strategic approach to the analysis and work your way through each element, you can fit them all together and find ways to generate more positive results. Before you jump into collecting data and compiling spreadsheets, take a step back and look at current processes. Take into consideration all of the pieces involved in delivering meetings and events. Talk to each of the departments or team members involved from initial contact through reporting on actuals. Do a basic inventory of your current reports and methods for forecasting, evaluating business, and measuring results. Look at each of the systems involved in those processes. You might be surprised at what you find. As you do, the adjustments needed will reveal themselves.

EVALUATING GROUPS

Group business evaluation in the absence of a revenue management system often consists of a first-come, first-served approach. It is tempting to take the first group that wants the rooms or space if you don't have empirical data to show you that a better and more profitable group may be on the way. It is possible to do some basic evaluation without a system, but evaluating groups effectively requires comparison to established baselines and/or thresholds. Establishing those baselines and thresholds will depend on clean meetings and events data.

There are several baselines that can be established to help give a quick guideline on which to base a decision. They include identifying demand patterns by season, day of week and segment, and historical averages of revenue and profit. However, they all depend on clean data.

Data Quality

There is an abundance of rich and critical data in a sales and catering system. That rich data is often obscured by unclean data that may prevent the critical points from rising to the surface. The data can be organized at various levels to find the trouble spots and make a plan to clean them up.

Accounts

In sales, response time is critical. In an effort to be fast, there are often details that are skipped and never get revisited or are entered in ways that make patterns difficult to identify. One of the worst habits is having a large onetime account under which all sorts of different bookings are attached. These bookings can be from any number of different market segments, each with a different purpose for the event such as celebrations, trainings, reunions, and so forth. Often, a booking can be considered SMERF business, but it's impossible to determine whether something really should have been considered a onetime event once it gets lumped into a giant catch-all account. Alternatively, creating an individual account for each and every booking may not be necessary either. Instead, break down these likely onetime events into accounts that provide indicators of their behavior, such as by purpose of booking or time of year.

For all other accounts, make a point of doing regular data audits to catch simple things like:

- Address errors
- Market segment classification
- Industry classification

The list goes on and on for all sorts of different reasons, but these three will help you to correctly identify patterns of demand within their associated business. Address information will help you identify sources of business data. This data can help you penetrate new markets. If your hotel is impacted by any sort of geopolitical activity, this data will become invaluable. Understanding where prior business originated and where to look for leads from previous clients can aid in identifying untapped demand.

Market segment and industry are powerful on their own, but when combined they can help you see new patterns. For example, you may know that corporate business generally books within a particular lead window. But you may also find that corporations within the pharma industry fall earlier in that lead window and have a particular size and date pattern in their profile that fits a gap you need to fill.

Bookings

Information collected at the booking level, also referred to as the group header or booking header, can also fall victim to speed over quality when it gets entered. A particular example that is incredibly important is booking types. Most sales and catering systems have a classification on the booking level that often gets mistaken for a duplicate of the market segment field, but this allows you to do so much more. Using the earlier example, a corporate account in the pharma industry may have any number of reasons to block guest rooms and/or space at a hotel. Assigning it as only corporate doesn't tell you anything. Instead, make sure the list reflects the various purposes of bookings. With clean data you could, for example, identify patterns for corporate pharma holiday parties versus corporate pharma executive board meetings versus corporate pharma product launches. The profile of each of these three types of bookings is very different, but the information is often buried in a sales and catering system because the right classification hasn't been assigned.

Status transitions present another problem area that can keep you from seeing data patterns. Some examples might include:

- Bookings sitting with a prospect status well past the decision due date
  - Each of these should be set to the appropriate lost status with a reason, if it's known.

- Inconsistent criteria for updating booking statuses, especially from tentative to definite
    - Consistency in standards for upgrading or downgrading the status of business are critical to correctly identifying demand patterns and ultimately to forecasting.
- Timeliness of status changes
    - Updates to status should be made on the appropriate date to accurately reflect times from initial contact to conversion of business or to loss.
- Inconsistent tracking of lost business reasons
    - While lost business is often considered "dirty" data when it comes to forecasting tools, it is still a valuable source of leads if the information is maintained properly.
- Request for proposal (RFP) channels that create prospect bookings for each incoming RFP
    - This can create a sudden influx of what looks like new demand from that channel when it is initially activated. This is because much of it represents business that human sellers may never have entered when they were receiving the RFPs via email.
    - Make sure these incoming RFPs are properly sourced to their respective channels and can be separated for independent analysis, especially in the early days with the new channel.

Guest Rooms

If you have a sales and catering system that is a module of or is integrated with a property management system, chances are your data on guest rooms will be fairly clean. If not, an integration will save a lot of data entry in the following areas.

- Accurate pickup
    - Pickup for each room type for each occupancy level (e.g., single or double).
    - This information should be updated daily while the block is open for reservations and upon departure.

- Accurate rates
  - A daily rate value for each room type in the group block.
  - A daily rate value for each room type the group ends up consuming.

Events

Event detail is the area where the volume of data is highest and the likelihood of dirty data is also the highest. For revenue management purposes, we are primarily concerned with two areas:

1. Space allocation
   - The block start and end times and the specific space blocked should be verified throughout the life of a booking. Variability in tracking of things like setup and teardown times or of how foyers used for setting up breaks or registration tables are booked can make it difficult to get a true picture of how much space was actually used. The team should follow consistent standards to allow the data to represent a clear picture of the demand.
   - Events created as a second option in addition to behind the primary space holder should be cleaned up once it is determined that a group is not able to procure the space. Otherwise, depending on how the information is analyzed, it can be difficult to avoid double-counting space needs.

2. Revenues
   - Prior to arrival, in order to get accurate revenue forecasts, take advantage of default average check features offered by most sales and catering systems. This allows you to set average per-person spend amounts that are applied to the event by default once an event type is selected. This also makes it easier for you to understand how a new group being evaluated adds to or takes away from the overall revenue picture for a day or set of dates with less data entry by the seller.
   - Actuals should be updated in the sales and catering system after an event, either manually or via integration with a

POS system. Depending on how well the revenues were maintained prior to arrival, the actuals can end up varying greatly from what was initially booked, especially if default average checks have not been used. This makes it impossible to benchmark average spending as a reference point.

Regular Audits

Clean data doesn't happen overnight unless you are starting from scratch. Changing habits and developing a culture of strong data tracking will take time. Most important, it won't happen unless and until the team understands the impact of having good clean data and why it helps them to succeed. To get the process rolling, approach it as a team effort rather than making one person the enforcer. A little contest and some prizes can go a long way.

Demand Patterns

Once you've gotten your data cleaned up, you can have more confidence in what it is telling you. The cleanup is the tough part. The payoff is in finding the patterns that will help you to fill gaps in low-demand periods and drive profits in high-demand times. In many sales organizations, knowledge of demand patterns is the biggest opportunity for improvement. With it, you can price dynamically and release function space to event-only business when group demand wanes, preventing unsold or undersold space. You can also better target profitable business that is still within their lead times that matches the openings in your inventory. Without knowledge of demand patterns, you are basically playing the odds.

Lead Time

One of the most important things to understand when evaluating a current piece of business is how it compares to patterns in the past and the profile of similar previous business. It's not enough to know the average lead time by market segment; you also need to know which segments book during which season over which days of the week.

This will help you to determine whether a piece of business represents new demand or whether the current pace from a particular segment is ahead of or behind the pace from previous years. Knowledge of pace can help you to manipulate the mix of business in your hotel on higher demand days in your favor by taking advantage of more profitable segments. It can also prepare you for releasing space to catering to give them more time to sell and shift your room efforts toward transient when it's clear that groups will not materialize.

The restrictions around release of function space to event-only business, generally referred to as free-sell restrictions, are often based on limited data. A typical set of restrictions in a hotel with a lot of corporate business would allow the catering team to sell space on Friday evenings through Sunday evenings, and often on weeknights as well. Catering sellers are not allowed to sell daytime midweek events without approval from the director of sales outside of 45 days or sometimes even 30 days. In many hotels, these rules are followed religiously and catering opportunities are not even considered midweek outside of that window just in case a group does materialize. This is based on the desire to fill the hotel with groups that use both rooms and meeting space, which are generally more profitable. If, however, demand for groups using both rooms and meeting space does not exist, it will cause more damage to hold on to the space rather than letting catering have a longer selling window to drive better revenue.

With lead-time data in hand, however, you could have a better understanding of whether demand seen for the same date in prior years is still within their booking window. If you are outside of that booking window, you are better able to confidently decide whether it makes more sense to take the event or wait for the potential group.

Seasonality and Day of Week

In addition to understanding the lead windows of particular types of groups, it is also important to understand who books in which seasons and on which days of the week. When necessary, this allows you to do some more targeted hunting for business that fits a particular profile. Let's say you have a cancellation for a Monday-to-Wednesday pattern during the third week of October and you are 60 days out. With the clean data and the right reporting, you can search your historical data for groups with a Monday-to-Wednesday pattern, inside their booking window who have booked October or even late fall in the past.

Let's take it a step further and say that cancellation was for just the ballroom but no breakout space. That is a pretty specific profile. If you can also count on clean data with respect to which space was used in the past, you can quickly identify groups that needed only the ballroom over similar dates in the past to find a match.

Demand Calendars

Once you have the basic data available, it becomes easy to create a simple chart that can help your sales team get a concrete picture of the demand. The team may all intuitively know that September is always busy, but do they know that it is specifically busy on weekends and short Tuesday/Wednesday patterns but there is still some potential to drive business on shoulder dates? A simple color-coded chart can show high/medium/low average space usage by date. It takes some effort to initially create this type of chart, but is very easy to maintain it on an ongoing basis. You might even break it out by ballroom and breakout space and eventually add details for things like daytime versus night-time usage, actual attendance, event types, or special events. Noting whether the space was used by groups or function-only business can also help you to get more dynamic with the release of space to catering where a mix of transient rooms and catering events might be a better fit for the demand that exists. A little effort can lead to a robust tool that helps your selling team make better decisions about which dates need more business and when they can push rates and event minimum spends harder based on demand.

Spend Pattern

Once you've got a clear understanding of the demand patterns, you can take advantage of changes in demand to price more dynamically. Historical spending patterns will provide a strong indicator of willingness to spend in the future. Breaking down the revenue data by revenue stream (e.g., rooms, food, beverage, etc.) using the same techniques you did for identifying demand patterns will help you match the spending habits with the corresponding demand.

Just as we've established with demand, not all business in a single segment will act the same way, and they won't have the same budget either. A company planning an executive board meeting may have a very different price point than they will if they are planning a sales kickoff or a training seminar. Looking at the historical spending by revenue stream, by segment, by industry, by season, and even by day of the week, you will start to see where meeting and event planners are willing to spend a little more and where you might need to flex your rates and pricing to make the dates more attractive.

METRICS

No matter what your vision is, it will require a set of performance metrics. This is where your work to clean up the data is really important. These metrics can be used not only to evaluate past performance, but also to manage the business on an ongoing basis. Making them a regular part of your weekly revenue meetings will give them the emphasis they deserve and get the team thinking more about the overall impact of their meetings and events.

Utilization

Even the smallest hotel operators would have a hard time managing their business without understanding both historical and forecasted occupancy. However, we ask directors of sales and catering to do this every day when it comes to function space. They are forced to rely primarily on the function diary for knowledge of what happened in the past and to predict what will happen in the future. Few hotels have a strong reporting capability when it comes to function space usage; even fewer have tools that allow them to forecast function space usage.

Room occupancy is generally pretty easy to calculate. Most hotels, with the general exception of airport locations, would rarely rent a room multiple times in the same day. Meeting rooms, on the other hand, can be combined in different configurations and sold multiple times per day. There may also be seasonal space that is only available during the warmer months that impacts the capacity used in that occupancy calculation.

Hotels may have many spaces represented in their function diaries that are only there in order to prevent conflicts but that do not generate revenue. These might be things like a chef's office that is used for menu tastings, or storage areas that can be reserved by a group, but no event will ever be held there. Also included in the function diary will be public spaces and/or restaurant outlets that are not exclusively used for banquets and catering events.

The first step in getting to an occupancy metric is deciding the fixed amount of space that should represent capacity. Typically, this includes the spaces that are advertised on a hotel's website as part of their meeting space and for which there are fixed dimensions that can be measured. Seasonal spaces make this challenging, but beware of double-counting. If a space requires a backup indoor space to be held as well, it should not be included in the capacity amount as its use would always inflate actual usage figures.

Calculating the actual function space utilization requires accurate event actuals from your sales and catering system. Last-minute cancelations for which the event never got deleted from the function diary or other last-minute changes may cause these numbers to be inaccurate. Make sure you have cleaned up this type of data before relying on the metric for decisions.

To calculate utilization:

1. Calculate available space by multiplying the available area (in square feet or meters) by the number of hours being evaluated.

2. Calculate the occupied space by determining the area used in each hour and summarizing that for the hours being evaluated.

   a. If a space is used for any portion of the period being evaluated (e.g., a day), it should be considered blocked for that entire period. If a room is sold more than once during that time, it will help with the next two metrics that look at profit, but in terms of utilization, it is not a factor.

   b. Utilization should include the total amount of time during which the event was not available for use by other groups. This includes both the actual event times and any nonstandard setup/teardown time required for the event during which it is out of inventory.

3. Divide the used space by the available space to determine the utilization percentage.

$$\frac{\text{Total area of occupied space for the time period}}{\text{Total area of capacity for the time period}} = \text{Function space utilization for the time period}$$

Depending on the amount of function space at your hotel or the size of your team, this type of calculation may not be feasible in a manual environment. The simple color-coded chart mentioned earlier, showing each day of the year and whether an indivisible meeting room was used or not, would go a long way toward helping the team understand the demand patterns in the space. Day-of-week patterns can be easily visualized, as can seasonality, with such a visual chart. Answering questions like "How often did that meeting room go empty on a Tuesday night in December?" can also be invaluable when making dynamic decisions about whether to release space to event-only business.

Profit per Occupied Space/Time

For guest rooms, we have ADR to indicate the average selling price for guest rooms. In measuring function space, it's a little trickier. A meeting room can be used multiple times per day, in combination with other meeting rooms or not, and can also be used for different types of events that combine different revenue streams.

Price is really a misnomer in the case of function space. Two groups could pay the exact same amount for the same amount of time in identical meeting rooms, but they could have had very different events. This is why it is important to understand the spending in individual revenue streams, because groups will have very different contributions. A group using a meeting room for three hours with a projector and screen paying room rental might generate the same revenue as a group using the room for three hours holding a luncheon, but the meeting might be significantly more profitable due to room rental. A comparison of a group to a historical average of what has been achieved in the past, using this metric, can help you to make sure space is being used more effectively.

Profit per occupied space/time, or ProPOST, allows you to understand the contribution of an event based on the space they are consuming, just as ADR does with rooms.

To calculate ProPOST, follow these steps:

1. Isolate the events that took place during the time period you're evaluating.

2. For each revenue stream, total the revenue associated with those events. The revenue streams would include food, beverage, audiovisual, and meeting room rental revenue.

3. Apply the profit percentage to each revenue stream total to determine the amount of profit from each category. This is where many hoteliers try to get too detailed. Using the profit percentages for these top-line revenue groups from the P&L gives you enough detail to start. If you decide to get more detailed later, by all means go right ahead.

4. Once you're down to profit amounts, add them all together to determine the total profit for that time period.

5. Next, determine the total square units (feet or meters) that were occupied during that period of time from the area of each space that was used.

6. Divide the total profit by that number to arrive at the ProPOST.

$$\frac{\text{Total event profit for the time period}}{\text{Total area occupied for the time period}} = \text{ProPOST}$$

Understanding ProPOST in different time slices or even for particular segments gives you a comparison against which you can evaluate future business to see if it will improve, maintain, or erode your performance.

Profit per Available Space/Time

The well-known guestroom metric of RevPAR helps us to understand how well we've used the inventory available to us in both busy and nonbusy times in order to generate revenue. In function space, as we saw with ProPOST, we need to look at profit because each of the revenue streams involved could have a widely variable contribution to the bottom line.

Visibility into this metric of profit per available space/time (Pro-PAST), especially when used in conjunction with function space usage, will help you understand the efficiency with which you are allocating space. If a group has been granted use of function space for move-in or move-out days without being charged rental, this metric will suffer. Alternatively, if your team is able to push room rental fees for such activities, the metric will show a marked increase, as will your bottom line.

To calculate ProPAST, follow these steps:

1. Isolate the events that took place during the time period you're evaluating.

2. For each revenue stream, total the revenue associated with those events.

3. Apply the profit percentage to each revenue stream to determine the amount of profit from each category. As with Pro-POST, start with the profit percentages from the P&L.

4. Once you're down to profit amounts, add them all together to determine the total profit for that time period.

5. Next, determine the total square units (feet or meters) of function space capacity during that period of time using the area of each space.

6. Divide the total profit by that number to arrive at the ProPAST.

$$\frac{\text{Total event profit for the time period}}{\text{Total area available for the time period}} = \text{ProPAST}$$

ProPAST allows you to understand the profit generated by the meeting space inventory being managed, just as RevPAR does with revenue generated from rooms inventory. ProPAST is a terrific metric for measuring your team's success with respect to function space because it's a great equalizer. While a particular group may have a terrific ProPOST figure, if the day pattern makes it difficult to sell around, you could end up sacrificing the ProPAST of the entire week for one juicy booking in the middle that ends up bringing your overall numbers down. If you're able to look at the same week in prior years and see the day patterns associated with that demand, you might be able to shift that business to a more appropriate week or shift it to the pattern within that week to make it a better fit, ultimately improving your ProPAST metric.

OTHER FACTORS INFLUENCING SUCCESS

You have many team members involved in selling, planning, and executing events. At each step in the cycle, your team members have the ability to impact the profitability of a group or even a single event. This is also an area of the business where there are habits and processes that have been in place for ages. Intuition plays a heavy role in meetings and events decision making because there have been so few tools to analyze the data and prove that intuition right or wrong. This is changing, but there is still a strong pull toward those old habits. Next are some areas to include in your assessment.

Incentive Alignment

Most sales team members are primarily incented to deliver room nights and sometimes have an overall revenue goal. Revenue-driven actions by sales and catering team members that are primarily focused on rooms can lead to less profitable or less optimal business mix decisions. A rooms-only incentive structure for sales can also contribute to a less collaborative culture between sales and catering. Catering is generally incented on food and beverage (F&B) revenue, but may not get the space to sell that F&B revenue until free sell restrictions have passed. If F&B revenue, or even profit margin at time of contract, is not part of the incentive plan for all sellers, they will not make holistic decisions and areas outside of rooms will suffer.

Knowledge and Structure

Your staff can only be held accountable for doing what they have been taught. First and foremost, you need to be sure they've been given the knowledge to make the right decisions on behalf of your hotel. If your team is fantastic at creating exceptional experiences that will delight the meeting planner but do not understand the cost of what they are delivering, you will have happy clients but may end up losing money in the process. They need to have a healthy appreciation for the cost behind the various elements of service so they can still make decisions that keep those guests delighted while keeping your hotel's bottom line intact.

SUMMARY

Knowledge really is power. Your systems and standard processes need to support the efficient collection of the data you require to understand the demand patterns and spending habits of your business. The entire selling and servicing team has to be invested, both financially and emotionally, in success. Revenue management principles and concepts should be applied to all the revenue streams and should be a part of each person's job. Building a strong revenue management culture doesn't happen overnight, but the more knowledge your team gains and the more success they see from its application, the faster it will build toward revenue breakthroughs in your meetings and events business.

APPENDIX **3**

Why Dynamic?

I presented at a gaming summit with David Koch, who was then data scientist at a casino in Canada. Our session was about evolving analytical capabilities in casinos. I set up the discussion, much like I have done in this book, by describing the characteristics of an analytically driven organization and providing a roadmap to achieve that vision. David followed, with findings from a database for slot performance management he developed.

Much can be learned by examining a game's history. The database exhausted all years of available production data but pared it to existing assets (machines) only. Asset attributes captured in production were cleaned and new ones introduced for better product differentiation. Capable of regeneration from production in moments, a rich, up-to-date historical database was always available. Not only the basis for forecasting, these game histories would prove insightful when viewed graphically against time.

Under the theme of the importance of asking how and why, following are findings David presented at the summit. For the purposes of this book, he has re-created here relevant portions of the presentation, with further discussion.

■ ■ ■

Context comes from a long-term perspective. Play is not constant. There are cycles.

For this first game (Figure A.1), season of the year was a determining factor in its betting activity. Note the recurring January (and sometimes July) lows.

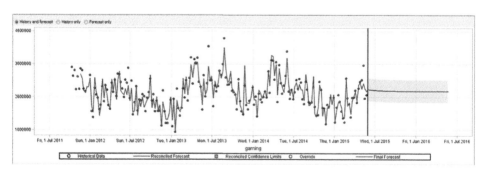

Figure A.1 Seasonal Demand

At the same time, broader changes may be taking place. The long-term view of this game (Figure A.2) again reveals seasonality, but this is a game in secular decline. Note the successively lower Januaries. Its appeal with players is waning.

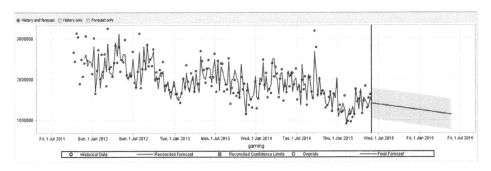

Figure A.2 Low-Demand Periods

Imagine the disappointment if, after considering a recent (say, quarterly or year-to-date) report on the profitability of this game, the property had decided to purchase more of the game. Being in secular decline, the future performance of this and any newly purchased versions would never achieve that of this game's past.

So, too, this game (Figure A.3) has recurring January and July lows, but in this case the downturns are deceptive. They are short-lived and belie the broader rise taking place. In fact, this is a game with rising appeal.

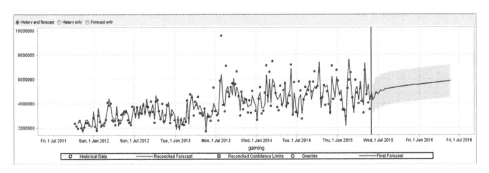

Figure A.3 Forecasting an Increase in Demand

Here (Figure A.4) is a game rediscovered. In decline for a time, followed by a period of plateauing, it turns around. Changes in the environment (property) can affect a game's performance. After all, games are in competition with other offerings in the property, especially like-games. A change in the long-term performance of a game, such as what is displayed in Figure A.4, may be reflecting new arrivals of like-games or their disappearance. This, then, illustrates a new dimension of game performance; that is, the arrival of new games can have implications for preexisting (unchanged) games.

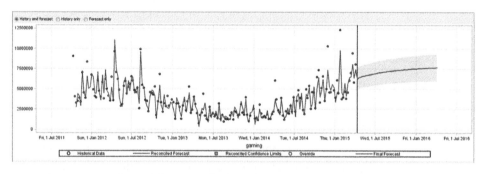

Figure A.4 Coming Back from a Decline in Performance

Therefore, "Embrace the change!" because decision making based on static measures, especially when they're short-term, is risky. In particular, there is a risk of discarding the game in Figure A.5 because it

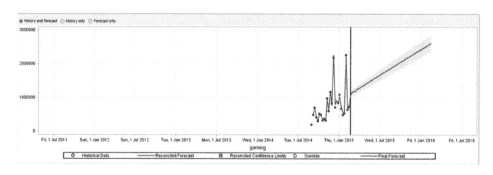

Figure A.5 Should We Get Rid of This Game?

does not fare well against some static target, and retaining or buying more of the game in Figure A.6 . . . because it does!

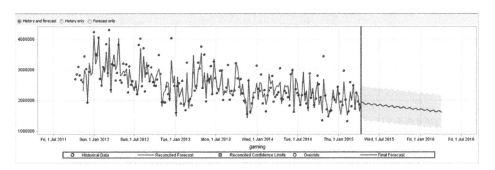

Figure A.6 And Keep This One?

Change is an opportunity to learn. This game (Figure A.7) was a top performer until one day it was taken from a central part of the property to a new place only a few steps away. Its player appeal quickly declined.

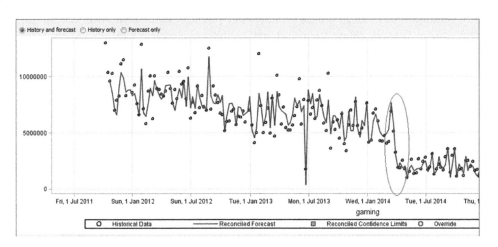

Figure A.7 The Impact of Moving a Top Performer

A few months later, it was returned to its previous location, in the heart of the property (Figure A.8). It immediately resumed its pre-change performance.

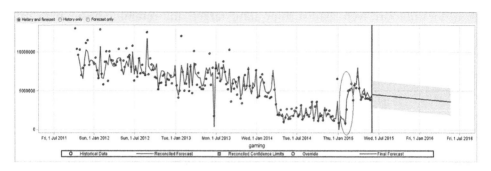

Figure A.8 And Then Moving the Top Performer Back

This demonstrates how decisions by the property can affect results. One important corollary that follows from this: Be careful about attributing all of the performance of an asset *to* the asset.

This game (Figure A.9) was performing poorly in relation to others in its game family. At some point in the past, the button deck had been changed such that there was no longer the ability to vary the credit multiplier; it was always 1 times the chosen line count. Suspecting the betting options were too limited, the row of multiplier buttons was changed to 1, 2, 3, 5, and 10 times per payline, consistent with peers. There was an immediate and striking change in the fortunes of the game, placing it on par with its counterparts.

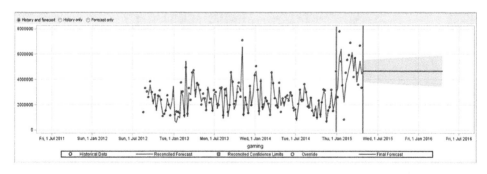

Figure A.9 Impact of Change in Multipliers

In this case then, configuration *was* a limiting factor in the asset's performance. An incomplete understanding leads to missed opportunities and wasted resources.

This game (Figure A.10) was changed only in that a standalone two-level mystery progressive was added, at the point indicated by the red line. Note the increase in the mean and the variance of betting activity. As a result of the increase in variance, results will be less consistent from week to week; meanwhile, higher (mean) betting activity will accompany it.

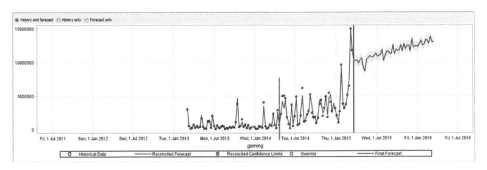

Figure A.10 Adding a Mystery Progressive

A series (bank) of games underwent a change of progressive. Some were given a new, standalone two-level mystery version, while the others retained a linked four-level. Here (Figure A.11) is one of the changed games after the change. According to the forecast (grayed area), the change is met with little enthusiasm.

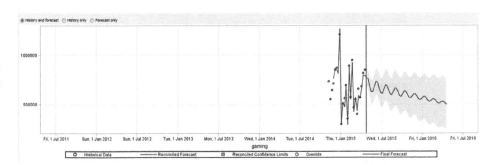

Figure A.11 Change Didn't Help This Game

Meanwhile, here (Figure A.12) is the very same game apart from the progressive (unchanged). After the change to its counterpart, indicated by the red line, this version attracted new play.

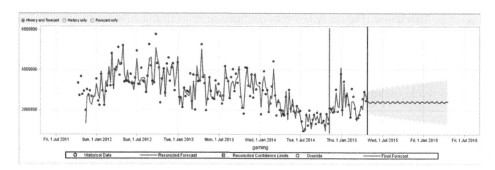

Figure A.12 Change Didn't Help This Game

Is it more levels, the linked configuration, or some other feature that patrons prefer? This would be a question for further study, and the answers could shape future purchase decisions (Figure A.13).

Figure A.13 A Sign Post for Analytics

Context, then, is the beginning. It helps facilitate understanding and delineate change. It is the basis by which change is measured. It requires history.

Organizations may possess more history than they use. It may be common practice to discount all but recent history, believing it's all that matters. Decision making may be based on predefined "where-when-who-what" tabular reports. The "when" may correspond to calendar or budget cycles, which may be part of the allure.

But consider this. Is customer behavior in sync with the business's budget cycles? Is the information telling of the future? Where seasonality exists, is a year-to-date measure indicative even of full-year results? Comparisons will be made to the last reporting period. Where results vary, is it seasonality, random variation, or true change? How much information can two numbers alone convey? Where is the context? Does such reporting lend itself to understanding what is causing the results to be what they are?

There is meaning in change. In particular, patrons may be indicating what they like and don't like. Some changes will be sudden; others may take years to be manifested. Static, period-in-time reporting will be challenged in trying to surface long-term change. When change is sudden, the pre- and post-change results will be amalgamated within the reporting period, muting and thereby obscuring any impact. And what about the ability to predict future performance from these amalgamated results? The property may find itself either under- or over-predicting and later trying to figure out why. What will this mean when determining the effectiveness of replacement decisions? Finally, what kind of progress will be made toward understanding patron preference and developing (growing) the business?

By contrast, graphical depictions are dynamic. Ultimately, they are bounded only by the limits of available history. Cycles can play out. Whether long-term or sudden, change is more clearly evident. There is a natural opening for statistical application. The ability to forecast is enhanced and made more reliable. Context is given. Direction is given. Interpretation is strengthened. The evolving short term takes its proper place within the long-term picture.

The greatest test is the test of time.

In numbers, relationships matter. Be curious. Look underneath. Ask why and how.

Chapter
Questions

CHAPTER 2

1. Describe why unstructured data is particularly difficult to manage within a traditional data architecture.
2. If you were charged with starting a data governance program, what functional areas would you invite to participate and where would you get started?
3. Why is data virtualization potentially useful to hospitality organizations?
4. For each of the following data sources, apply the list of questions from this chapter, come up with the list of information you would need from the data provider to be certain of the value of that data, and determine how it might be useful within the organization.
   a. Forward-looking demand data (benchmarked reservations on hand for a defined market for the next six months)
   b. Text from all the reviews on TripAdvisor with the associated demographic and ratings data
   c. Performance benchmarking data (like STR), including your ADR, occupancy and RevPAR, as compared to the competitive set
   d. Web shopping data from your website
   e. Guest lifetime value
   f. Competitor pricing
5. Which of the data cleansing techniques described in this chapter would you apply to your guest data warehouse?

CHAPTER 3

1. Describe the advantages of visualizations over spreadsheets.
2. What are some best practices for building an effective visualization?
3. Review the following visualizations. What issues do you identify, and how would you change each visualization to make it more effective?

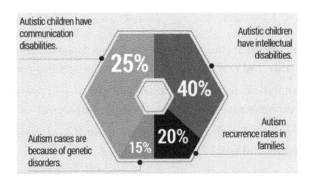

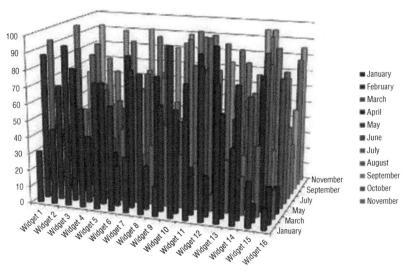

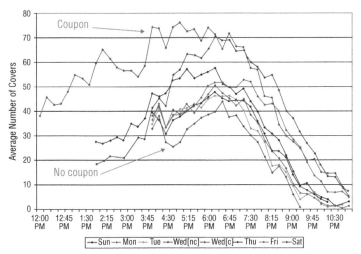

CHAPTER 4

1. What analytical technique would you use if you wanted to know which banner ad was most effective in driving traffic to your website?

2. What analytical technique would you use if you wanted to improve response rates to your marketing campaigns?

3. What analytical technique would you use if you wanted to improve your food cost?

4. What is the difference between data mining and predictive modeling? What is the difference between data mining and machine learning?

5. Describe the advantages and disadvantages of SaaS versus on-premise delivery.

CHAPTER 5

1. What are the two ways to think about time in the context of operations? Why are each important?

2. Describe the inputs for a staffing forecast for the valet stand. How would you collect this information?

3. What queuing method would you employ for the front desk of a convention hotel? Describe the advantages of that method. Which of Maister's propositions would potentially apply to this format, and how would you mitigate against those impacts?

4. You have just been hired to be the vice president of analytics for food and beverage for a large casino company with at least a dozen food and beverage outlets. This is a brand-new position, and you want to make an immediate impact. Where would you get started with data analytics?

5. How can operations best use location data? What advanced analytics techniques do you anticipate using to support your use cases?

CHAPTER 6

1. What is the difference between web analytics and digital intelligence?

2. You are the manager of a ski resort brand with six locations. You have been asked to design a loyalty program to increase engagement and repeat visits. What type of data would you want to gather from your guests, and how would you go about convincing them to give it to you?

3. You are managing the corporate loyalty program for a mid-size hotel chain, and you get to hire your very first analyst. What skill set would you target, and why?

4. Describe how marketing can use review data. What business problems can be addressed with this information? What techniques would you use to analyze that review data, and what technology might you have to invest in?

5. Describe how to set up an A/B test for a marketing campaign. Why is this important?

CHAPTER 7

1. Name three reasons the sales function is slightly different from other functions when it comes to their analytical needs.

2. What analytical results might a salesperson need to support a negotiation with the meeting planner for a large convention?

3. What metrics are important to sales, and how are those collected?

4. If you were hired to run a sales team for a small hotel chain, what technology would you invest in first, and what resource would you look for to manage it?

5. How should sales work with the other functional areas in the hotel like marketing, operations, and revenue management? What data would sales share, and what information would be useful for them to know from other departments?

CHAPTER 8

1. When is price optimization appropriate, and when is traditional inventory optimization the right approach?

2. What is the goal of the optimization algorithm for revenue management? What constraints might be included in that optimization?

3. Describe the revenue management analytical chain from statistical modeling to forecasting to optimization—discuss the outputs from each that become the inputs to the other.

4. How is the casino problem different from the hotel problem in revenue management? What might hotels learn from the casino approach?

5. If you were asked to apply revenue management to the spa, what would the revenue per available time based inventory unit be? How would you measure success of the program?

CHAPTER 9

1. Describe a case where analytical forecasting is not as useful as expert forecasting.

2. What data would you consider when projecting the revenue potential of a possible hotel investment in Croatia? What analytical technique would you use?

3. What technique would you use to determine whether the airport hotels in the Northeast are performing better than the airport hotels in the Southeast. What data might you use to make this comparison?

4. If the development department were going to use optimization to determine their investment strategy, what might the objective function or goal of the optimization be, and what would the decision variables be?

5. What kinds of functionality would you ask for in a data visualization platform for the performance analysis function?

CHAPTER 10

1. Describe the levers that can be utilized to optimize revenue at a table game. If you were not able to start out with an optimization model, how would you decide which strategy to employ first, and how would you measure success?

2. What is the problem with looking at a static snapshot of data? How do you overcome this?

3. Describe the kind of data you would collect if you wanted to see if there was money laundering happening at your casino. What kind of analytical technique would you use to detect this activity?

4. Describe a business problem that you could use location data to address. What if you couldn't tie location data back to an individual patron? Would you still be able to use the data? If so, how; if not, what would you do?

5. Why is it crucial that casino marketing and casino revenue optimization work closely together?

CHAPTER 11

1. You are in the corporate marketing department of a mid-size hotel company, and you are trying to convince your leadership to invest in analytics. Describe a project you might take on to prove the value of analytics.

2. Describe the advantages and disadvantages of a centralized organizational model versus a center of excellence model.

3. Describe the advantages and disadvantages of building your own solution versus buying an off-the-shelf solution. When might you choose one or the other?

4. What data can operations leverage from marketing, and how? What operations data might marketing want access to and how would they use it? Would you anticipate any need to adjust the format or parameters of any of the data to make it more useable to the other department? What would that be?

5. Loyalty marketing has decided to implement a new benefit for the top-tier loyalty members. If they stay at a hotel any time in the four weeks around their birthday, they get an upgrade and a room amenity. Which departments need to be involved in this decision, and how would the organization measure the success?

References

BOOKS AND JOURNALS

Anderson, Christoper K. 2012. "The Impact of Social Media on Lodging Performance." *Cornell Center for Hospitality Research Report* 12(15): 4–11.

Burnham, K., and D. Anderson. 2002. *Model Selection and Multimodel Inference: A Practical Information Theoretic Approach,* 2nd ed. New York: Springer.

Davenport, Tom, and Jeanne Harris. 2007. *Competing on Analytics: The New Science of Winning.* Boston: Harvard Business Review Press.

Fitzsimmons, James A., and Mona J. Fitzsimmons. 1994. *Service Management for Competitive Advantage.* New York: McGraw Hill.

Grady, D. 1993. "The Vision Thing: Mainly in the Brain," *Discover Magazine.* http://discovermagazine.com/1993/jun/thevisionthingma227.

Kilby, Jim, and Jim Fox. 1998. *Casino Operations Management.* New York: John Wiley & Sons.

Kimes, S. E. 1989. "Yield Management: A Tool for Capacity-Constrained Service Firms." *Journal of Operations Management* 8(4): 348–363.

Kimes, S. E., and K. A. McGuire. 2001. "Function Space Revenue Management: A Case Study from Singapore." *Cornell Hotel and Restaurant Administration Quarterly,* 33–46.

Kimes, S. E., and L. W. Schruben. 2002. "Golf Course Revenue Management: A Study of Tee Times." *Journal of Pricing and Revenue Management* 1(2): 111–120.

Kimes, S. E., R. B. Chase, S. Choi, P. Y. Lee, and E. N. Ngonzi. 1998. "Restaurant Revenue Management: Applying Yield Management to the Restaurant Industry." *Cornell Hotel and Restaurant Administration Quarterly* 39(3): 32–39.

Kimes, S. E., and S. Singh. 2009. "Spa Revenue Management." *Cornell Hospitality Quarterly* 50(1): 82–85.

Kimes, S. E., and G. M. Thompson. 2004. "Restaurant Revenue Management at Chevy's: Determining the Best Table Mix." *Decision Sciences* 35(3): 371–392.

Laney, Doug. 2001. "3-D Data Management: Controlling Data Volume, Velocity, and Variety." Gartner, February 6. blogs.gartner.com/doug-laney/files/2012/01/ad949-3DDataManagement-Controlling-Data-Volume-Velocity-and-Variety.pdf.

Maister, David. 1985. "The Psychology of Waiting Lines." In *The Service Encounter*, edited by J. A. Czepiel, M. R. Solomon, and C. F. Surprenant, 113–128. Lexington, MA: Lexington Press.

Marieb, E. N., and K. Hoehn. 2007. *Human Anatomy & Physiology*. 7th ed. San Francisco: Pearson International Edition. See more at http://neomam .com/interactive/13reasons/#sthash.TV9co6Gc.dpuf.

McGuire, Kelly A., Sheryl E. Kimes, Michael Lynn, Madeline E. Pullman, and Russell C. Lloyd. 2010. "A Framework for Evaluating the Customer Wait Experience." *Journal of Service Management* 21 (3): 269–290.

Metters, R., C. Queenan, M. Ferguson, L. Harrison, J. Higbie, S. Ward, and A. Duggasani. 2008. "The 'Killer Application' of Revenue Management: Harrah's Cherokee Casino & Hotel." *Interfaces* 38(3): 161–175.

Noone, Breffni M., and Kelly A. McGuire. 2016. "Impact of Attitudinal Loyalty on the Frequent Unmanaged Business Traveler's Use of Price and Consumer Reviews in Hotel Choice." *Journal of Revenue and Pricing Management* 15(1): 20–36.

Noone, Breffni M., Kelly A. McGuire, and Kristin V. Rohlfs. 2011. "Social Media Meets Hotel Revenue Management: Opportunities, Issues and Unanswered Questions." *Journal of Revenue and Pricing Management* 10(4): 293–305.

Ott, R., and M. Longnecker. 2001. *An Introduction to Statistical Methods and Data Analysis*. 5th ed. Duxbury: Wadsworth.

Phillips, R. 2005. *Pricing and Revenue Optimization*. Stanford, CA: Stanford University Press.

Pullman, Madeleine, and Stephani Robson. 2006. "A Picture Is Worth a Thousand Words: Using Photo-Elicitation to Solicit Guest Feedback." Cornell Center for Hospitality Research, Research Tool. http://scholarship.sha .cornell.edu/cgi/viewcontent.cgi?article=1001&context=chrtools.

Smith, B. C., J. F. Leimkuhler, and R. M. Darrow. 1992. "Yield Management at American Airlines." *Interfaces* 22(1): 8–31.

Talluri, K. T., and G. van Ryzin. 2005. *The Theory and Practice of Revenue Management*. International Series in Operations Research & Management Science. New York: Springer.

Thomas, Gwen. n.d. "The DGI Data Governance Framework." The Data Governance Institute, www.datagovernance.com/wp-content/uploads/2014/11/dgi_framework.pdf.

OTHER RESOURCES

"Data and Analytics: The Blueprint of Service Design": www.sas.com/en_us/whitepapers/data-analytics-blueprint-service-105102.html.

"Disney's One Billion Dollar Bet on a Magical Wristband": www.wired.com/2015/03/disney-magicband.

Success story about the RCI Exchange Analytics: www.sas.com/en_us/customers/wyndham-exchange-and-rentals.html.

Suneel Grover on Digital Intelligence: http://blogs.sas.com/content/customeranalytics/2016/03/22/web-analytics-vs-digital-intelligence-whats-difference/.

Index

Page numbers followed by *f* stand for figure.

Printed and bound by CPI Group (UK) Ltd, Croydon, CR0 4YY

16/04/2025

14658516-0005